Power From On High

Power From On High

The Development of Mormon Priesthood

Gregory A. Prince

Signature Books, Salt Lake City, 1995

To JaLynn,

who appreciated before I
the necessity of writing this book

Jacket design by Brian Bean

∞ *Power From On High* was printed on acid-free paper
and was composed, printed, and bound in the United States.
© 1995 Signature Books. All rights reserved.
Signature Books is a trademark of Signature Books, Inc.
99   98   97   96   95   6   5   4   3   2   1

Library of Congress Cataloging-in-Publication Data
Prince, Gregory
Power from on high : the development of Mormon priesthood /
Gregory Prince.
p.   cm.
Includes bibliographical references and index.
ISBN 1-56085-071-X
1. Aaronic Priesthood (Mormon Church—Controversial literature.
2. Melchizedek Priesthood (Mormon Church)—
Controversial literature.   3. Priesthood—Controversial literature.
4. Authority—Religious aspects—Mormon Church.   I. Title.
BX8659.P755   1995
262'.1493—dc20   95-7802
CIP

Contents

Acknowledgements

I am indebted to several institutions and individuals associated with them for their support. Steven Sorensen and Ronald Barney, representing the archives of the Church of Jesus Christ of Latter-day Saints in Salt Lake City, Utah, and Ronald Romig, representing the Library-Archives of the Reorganized Church of Jesus Christ of Latter Day Saints in Independence, Missouri, were particularly helpful. Without their cooperation this book could not have been written. I am also grateful to David Whittaker and the Harold B. Lee Library of Brigham Young University in Provo, Utah, and to the Huntington Library in San Marino, California, for permission to use materials from their collections.

Most of the materials cited in this book are from my own library. I am indebted, in more ways than one, to Sam Weller and Joan Nay of Zion Book Store, in Salt Lake City, for assistance spanning two decades in making these resources available to me.

The sections of this book dealing with the office of patriarch and the ordinance of the patriarchal blessing reflect the insight and resources of Gary Smith and Irene Bates, who generously provided me with copies of all patriarchal blessings in their extensive collection which were given during Joseph Smith's lifetime. These blessings, both in hard copy and electronic format, are now available to researchers as the Irene Bates Collection at the Library-Archives of the Reorganized Church of Jesus Christ of Latter Day Saints.

I am grateful to Lester Bush and Val Hemming for their critical review of the manuscript and their long-standing friendship. Only my wife, JaLynn, has had to endure me more than they during the decade since I embarked on this project. For her love, endurance, and understanding I dedicate this book to her.

My professional training is in science, not history or theology, and readers familiar with the tools of science will recognize their use in the writing of this book. Whatever contribution it may make to the field of Mormon studies will rest, in large measure, on the training I received from my scientific "father," Dr. David D. Porter of the UCLA School of Medicine; my "uncles," Dr. Harold S. Ginsberg of the College of Physicians and Surgeons, Columbia University, Dr. Robert M. Chanock of the National Institutes of Health, and Dr. William H. Carnes (deceased); and my "grandfathers," Dr. Frank J. Dixon of the Scripps Clinic & Research Foundation and Dr. Albert B. Sabin (deceased).

Chapter One

Authority

A revelation to the three-year-old Church of Christ (also called Mormon) declared in 1833 that God would "give unto the faithful line upon line precept upon precept."[1] The concept of authority was not initially addressed in the Restoration movement[2] but developed gradually, or "line upon line." Now viewed as the founding Restoration event, the epiphany known as the "first vision" resulted from Joseph Smith's mourning "for my own sins and for the sins of the world."[3] In response, "the Lord opened the heavens upon me and I saw the Lord and he spake unto me saying Joseph my son thy sins are forgiven thee." Despite the importance attached to the first vision by subsequent generations of Latter-day Saints, it did not serve as Smith's call to the ministry or claim to divine authorization.

That claim began with another vision, in the autumn of 1823, when "an angel of the Lord came and stood before me." The angel

---

1. Revelation dated 8 Aug. 1833, in "Kirtland Revelations Book," 67, archives, Historical Department, Church of Jesus Christ of Latter-day Saints, Salt Lake City, Utah (hereafter LDS archives), also published by Modern Microfilm, Salt Lake City, 1979; also in *Doctrine and Covenants of The Church of the Latter Day Saints: Carefully Selected from the Revelations of God* (Kirtland, OH: F. G. Williams & Co., 1835), LXXXV:3 (hereafter cited in the text as DC, 1835).

2. The term "Restoration" applies generally to the Latter-day Saint tradition during the ministry of Joseph Smith. "LDS" refers to the Church of Jesus Christ of Latter-day Saints, headquartered in Salt Lake City, Utah; "RLDS" to the Reorganized Church of Jesus Christ of Latter Day Saints, headquartered in Independence, Missouri.

3. Joseph Smith, 1832 "History," in Dean C. Jessee, ed., *The Papers of Joseph Smith* (Salt Lake City: Deseret Book Co., 1989), 1:6.

1

called Moroni entrusted to Smith "plates of gold upon which there was engravings which was engraven by Maroni & his fathers the servants of the living God in ancient days and deposited by the commandments of God and kept by the power thereof and that I should go and get them."[4] Translating the plates into the Book of Mormon marked the beginning of Smith's ministry. It established among his followers his credentials as a prophet. Such authority, however, was implied, for Smith never claimed that Moroni bestowed formal authority by the laying on of hands, the manner sanctioned by ancient and modern Christianity.

As the Mormon restoration unfolded, the essence of divine empowerment assumed a more concrete form. Almost six years after Moroni's visit, angelic beings bestowed authority on Smith and his assistant Oliver Cowdery by the laying on of hands. Although in the Mormon church today the term "priesthood" refers to this bestowed authority, such a relationship did not develop until years after the founding of the church. Initially authority was understood to be inherent in what are now termed "offices." Three offices—elder, priest, and teacher—were present by August 1829, as were the ordinances of baptism, confirmation, and ordination, but the word "priesthood" was not used in reference to these for another three years.

In June 1831 a modern "pentecost" occurred in which supernatural powers, similar to those reported in the New Testament book of the Acts of the Apostles, chapter 2, were bestowed upon latter-day disciples through their ordination to the "high priesthood," thus coupling the concepts of "authority" and "power." Between 1831 and 1835 an organizational consolidation occurred, resulting in the 1835 designations of the "Aaronic Priesthood" and "Melchizedek Priesthood," which incorporated the elements of authority and power which had developed over the prior dozen years.

Perhaps the most important and certainly least understood development began in 1836 when Smith and Cowdery recorded a vision of Elijah, the Old Testament prophet. Although Elijah did not become associated with priesthood for another two years, he gradually became the most important figure for Latter-day Saint authority. Indeed, after 1840 Smith never associated Moroni, John the Baptist, or Peter, James,

---

4. Ibid., 8.

and John—previous angelic ministers—with the concept of priesthood, opting instead to emphasize Elijah.

The concept of bestowed authority was present prior to the organization of the church, but the structure and nomenclature developed gradually throughout the remaining years of Smith's life. Although the development occurred along a continuum, the continuity was punctuated by several key events. In attempting to understand the developmental process, it is useful to divide the continuum into several phases on the basis of those events.

Phase 1: Implied Authority, September 1823-March 1829

Visions surrounding the gold plates of the Book of Mormon provided the earliest confirmation of Joseph Smith's divine calling. Within weeks of Smith's obtaining the plates in September 1827, neighbor Martin Harris "became convinced of the visions and gave [Smith] fifty Dollars to bare my expences and because of his faith and the righteous deed the Lord appeared unto him in a vision and showed unto him his marvilous work which he was about to do."[5] A similar manifestation in 1829 converted a man whose role in Latter-day Saint priesthood would be second only to Smith's: "[The] Lord appeared unto a young man by the name of Oliver Cowdry and shewed unto him the plates in a vision and also the truth of the work and what the Lord was about to do through me his unworthy servant therefore he was desirous to come and write for me to translate."[6]

While it was apparent that Smith had a calling, the basis of his authority was implicit in his work, not the result of any "hands-on" ordination. Prior to 1829 neither Smith nor his followers claimed to have received the type of divine authorization which ultimately would become known as "priesthood."

Smith's primary concerns during this time were his own status with God and the translation of the gold plates. He expressed no intent to organize a church or to confer authority or ordinances on others. Three revelations date from this period, none of which addressed these issues. In the first, from July 1828, Smith was chastised for having lost part of the Book of Mormon manuscript and was told that he would be allowed to resume translating, but no author-

---

5. Ibid., 9.
6. Ibid., 10.

ity was mentioned.[7] In the second, dated February 1829, a ministry extending beyond publication of the Book of Mormon was implied. The qualifications for that ministry were listed: "Faith, hope, charity and love, with an eye single to the glory of God" (BC III:1). Formal authority evidently was not required. The third revelation, given to Joseph Smith one month later in behalf of Harris, described for the first time the establishment of a church, "like unto the church which was taught by my disciples in the days of old" (BC IV:5), but stipulated no prerequisites.[8]

Phase 2: Angelic Authority, April 1829-October 1830

In April 1829 itinerant schoolteacher Oliver Cowdery arrived in Harmony, Pennsylvania, to serve as Joseph Smith's new scribe. Within days their work on the Book of Mormon produced passages dealing with baptism. The first of these was from "The Book of Mosiah"[9]:

> And now it came to pass that Alma took Helam, he being one of the first, and went and stood forth in the water, and cried, saying, O Lord, pour out thy spirit upon thy servant, that he may do this work with holiness of heart. And when he had said these words, the spirit of the Lord was upon him, and he said, Helam, I baptize thee, having authority from the Almighty God, as a testimony that ye have entered

---

7. *A Book of Commandments, for the Government of the Church of Christ, Organized According to Law, on the 6th of April, 1830* (Independence, MO: W. W. Phelps & Co., 1833), II:1-6 (hereafter cited in the text as BC).

8. When this revelation was revised prior to its 1835 republication in DC, 1835, three new passages were added reflecting a subsequent consciousness regarding "ordination": "hereafter you shall be ordained and go forth and deliver my words unto the children of men" (DC, 1835 XXXII:2); "whom I shall call and ordain . . . you must wait yet a little while; for ye are not yet ordained" (v. 3).

9. Although references to baptism occur in the first two books of Nephi, which open the Book of Mormon and precede "The Book of Mosiah," they were in fact the last two books translated. After the first 116 or so pages of translation were lost, translation resumed with "The Book of Mosiah." Oliver Cowdery also mentioned that references to Christ's ministry to the Americas, found in the Book of Third Nephi, toward the end of the Book of Mormon, motivated the two men to seek baptism (*Latter Day Saints' Messenger and Advocate* [Kirtland, OH] 1 [Oct. 1834]: 15-16).

into a covenant to serve him until you are dead, as to the mortal
body; and may the spirit of the Lord be poured out upon you; and
may he grant unto you eternal life, through the redemption of Christ,
which he hath prepared from the foundation of the world. And after
Alma had said these words, both Alma and Helam was [sic] buried in
the water; and they arose and came forth out of the water rejoicing,
being filled with the spirit. And again, Alma took another, and went
forth a second time into the water, and baptized him according to the
first, only he did not bury himself again in the water.[10]

Of particular importance is the idea that before Alma baptized he
received authorization simply from "the spirit of the Lord." There is
no mention of angelic appearance, laying on of hands, or ordained
office. Alma baptized himself and Helam simultaneously.

Cowdery received the following communication from God at
about this time:

Now therefore whosoever repenteth & humbleth himself before me
& desireth to be baptized in my name shall ye baptize them. And after
this manner did he [the Lord] command me that I should baptize
them[.] Behold ye shall go down & stand in the water & in my name
shall ye baptize them. And now behold these are the words which ye
shall say calling them by name saying[,] Having authority given me of
Jesus Christ I baptize you in the name of the Father & of the Son &
of the Holy Ghost Amen. And then shall ye immerse them in the
water & come forth again out of the water & after this manner shall
ye baptize in my name.[11]

Smith's and Cowdery's baptisms in the Susquehanna River in May
1829 were thus divinely authorized, though not as a prerogative based
on the duties of any office. Later accounts described additional elements such as authority from an angel conferred by the laying on of

---

10. *The Book of Mormon: An Account Written by the Hand of Mormon,
Upon Plates Taken from the Plates of Nephi* (Palmyra, NY: E. B. Grandin,
1830), "The Book of Mosiah," Chap. IX, 192 (hereafter cited in the text
as BM, 1830). Compare the current LDS edition of the Book of
Mormon, Mosiah 18:12-13. Since the 1830 edition was not divided into
numbered verses, citations throughout this book, unless otherwise specified, refer to the current LDS edition.

11. "The Articles of the Church of Christ," written by Oliver
Cowdery in 1829, original in LDS archives; published in Robert J.
Woodford, "The Historical Development of the Doctrine and Cove-
nants," Ph.D. diss., Brigham Young University, 1974, 288.

hands and tandem rather than simultaneous baptism, in contrast to the
Book of Mormon model.

Although they possessed authority to baptize, Smith and Cowdery lacked the authority mentioned in later passages of the Book
of Mormon, which enabled recipients to confer the Holy Ghost and
to ordain priests and teachers. In these passages those holding this
"higher" authority were simultaneously called disciples and elders
and were equivalent to Christ's apostles in Palestine (BM, 1830,
574-75). Book of Mormon witness David Whitmer later said that
Smith and Cowdery obtained this authority early in June 1829, after
he took them to his father's farm in Fayette, New York, and that
following this they ordained each other elders.[12] Shortly thereafter,
Whitmer was baptized and ordained as the third elder of the Restoration.[13]

Inasmuch as a revelation dated mid-June stated that Cowdery and
Whitmer had been "called even with that same calling" as the Apostle
Paul (BC XV:11),[14] the ordinations as elders must have occurred within
the first two weeks of June 1829. The revelation reinforced the idea
that their new, higher authority was the same described in the Book
of Mormon by commissioning Cowdery and Whitmer to choose
twelve disciples who were then "to ordain priests and teachers," the
same duty given the twelve disciples/elders in "The Book of Moroni"
(BC XV:35; cf. BM, 1830, 575).

The following early Mormon and non–Mormon records support
the claim of divine restoration of authority, including (beginning in
1830) the appearance of angels, (beginning in late 1832 but not explicit
until late 1834) the receipt of priesthood from angels, and (in 1835)
the naming of angels:

---

12. "Questions asked of David Whitmer at his home in Richmond
Ray County Mo. Jan 14—1885. relating to Book of Mormon, and the
history of the Church of Jesus Christ of LDS by Elder Z. H. Gurley,"
Ms d 4681, LDS archives.

13. David Whitmer, *An Address to All Believers in Christ* (Richmond, MO: the Author, 1887), 32.

14. For the dating of this revelation, see Woodford, 263-67. The
restoration of higher authority remains a topic of considerable debate,
with disagreement over the date and circumstances. For an alternate
viewpoint, see D. Michael Quinn, *The Mormon Hierarchy: Origins of Power*
(Salt Lake City: Signature Books, 1994).

1829: Cowdery wrote that the authority "given me of Jesus Christ" was essential to performing baptisms.[15] Later accounts which mentioned the voice of Jesus in association with the visit of the angel are consistent with this earliest account.

1 June 1830: The *Palmyra Reflector* referred to Cowdery as an "apostle . . . under a command."[16]

16 November 1830: The *Painesville Telegraph*, referring to Cowdery, reported that he "pretends to have a divine mission, and to have seen and conversed with Angels."[17]

7 December 1830: The same newspaper reported claims that "Mr. Oliver Cowdry has his commission directly from the God of Heaven, and that he has his credentials, written and signed by the hand of Jesus Christ, with whom he has personally conversed, and as such, said Cowdry claims that he and his associates are the only persons on earth who are qualified to administer in his name. By this authority, they proclaim to the world, that all who do not believe *their* testimony, and [allow themselves to] be baptised by them for the remission of their sins . . . must be forever miserable."[18]

14 February 1831: The *Palmyra Reflector* published an account of Mormon missionaries, saying that "they then proclaimed that there had been no religion in the world for 1500 years,—that no one had been authorized to preach and for that period,—that Joseph Smith had now received a commission from God for that purpose . . . . Smith (they affirmed) had seen God frequently and personally—Cowdery and his friends had frequent interviews with angels . . ."[19]

19 April 1831: The *Painesville Telegraph* published a letter

15. "The Articles of the Church of Christ," in Woodford, 288.
16. *Palmyra Reflector* (New York), 1 June 1830.
17. *Painesville Telegraph* (Ohio), 16 Nov. 1830.
18. Ibid., 7 Dec. 1830.
19. *Palmyra Reflector*, 14 Feb. 1831.

from Martin Harris which included the earliest published version of "The Articles and Covenants of the Church of Christ." Greatly expanded compared to its 1829 predecessor, it stated that Smith and Cowdery were each "called of God and ordained an apostle of Jesus Christ, an elder of the church."[20]

Late 1832: Smith, when he began to write his autobiography between July and November 1832,[21] opened the account by reciting the early events of the Restoration, the third of which was "the reception of the holy Priesthood by the minist[e]ring of Aangels to admin[i]ster the letter of the Gospel[,] the Law and commandments as they were given unto him and the ordinenc[e]s."[22]

2 March 1833: A Protestant minister in Ohio, in a letter to another minister, wrote: "The following Curious occurrence occurred last week in Newburg about 6 miles from this Place [Cleveland]. Joe Smith the great Mormonosity was there and held forth, and among other things he told them he had seen Jesus Christ and the Apostles and conversed with them, and that he could perform Miracles."[23]

18 December 1833: A blessing given by Smith to Cowdery spoke of the fulfillment in Cowdery "of a prophecy of Joseph, in ancient days, which he said should come upon the Seer of the last days and the Scribe that should sit with him, and that should be ordained with him, by the hand of the angel in the bush, unto the lesser priesthood, and after receive the holy priesthood under the hands of those who had been held in reserve for a long

---

20. *Painesville Telegraph,* 19 Apr. 1831.

21. See Dean C. Jessee, ed., *The Personal Writings of Joseph Smith* (Salt Lake City: Deseret Book, 1984), 640n6.

22. Ibid., 4.

23. Rev. Richmond Taggart to Rev. Jonathon Goings, 2 Mar. 1833, American Baptist Historical Society, Rochester, New York.

season even those who received it under the hand of the Messiah."[24]

12 February 1834: In a meeting preparatory to the organization of the first High Council, Smith said: "I shall now endeavour to set forth before this council, the dignity of the office which has been conferred upon me by the ministering of the Angel of God, by his own voice and by the voice of this Church."[25]

October 1834: In a letter published in the church newspaper Cowdery described the authority to baptize and, for the first time in a published Mormon source, specifically linked the visit of an angel with this restoration: "'Twas the voice of the angel from glory . . . we received under his hand the holy priesthood, as he said, 'upon you my fellow servants, in the name of Messiah I confer this priesthood and this authority . . .'"[26]

21 February 1835: In instructing the newly chosen Quorum of Twelve Apostles, Cowdery said: "You have been ordained to the Holy Priesthood. You

---

24. Blessing given 18 Dec. 1833 by Joseph Smith, Jr., to Oliver Cowdery, original in Patriarchal Blessing Book, Vol. 1, LDS archives, photocopy in my possession; also in Irene M. Bates Collection, Library-Archives, The Auditorium, Church of Jesus Christ of Latter Day Saints (hereafter RLDS archives). Although this blessing was given in 1833, it was not recorded in the Patriarchal Blessing Book until 2 Oct. 1835. While it could be claimed that Cowdery "updated" the content when he entered it in the book, two factors argue in favor of its integrity. First, the angels were not named, even though revised revelations in the Doctrine and Covenants, published earlier in 1835, had named them. Second, the same book used the terms "Aaronic Priesthood" and "Melchizedek Priesthood," yet the 1833 blessing retained the earlier terms, "lesser priesthood" and "holy priesthood," rather than borrowing later terminology.

25. "Kirtland High Council Minutes," 12 Feb. 1834, LDS archives.

26. Latter Day Saints' Messenger and Advocate (Kirtland, OH), 1 (Oct. 1834): 15-16.

have received it from those who had their power and Authority from an Angel."[27]

Mid-1835:

1st time

Names of the

mentioned

With the publication of the Doctrine and Covenants several previously published revelations were revised, among which was one dated September 1830. Whereas the earlier 1833 Book of Commandments version made no mention of angelic visitations, this 1835 version now included the restoration of two levels of authority, identifying for the first time the restorers as "John the son of Zacharias, which Zacharias he (Elias) visited and gave promise that he should have a son, and his name should be John, and he should be filled with the spirit of Elias; which John I have sent unto you, my servants, Joseph Smith, jr. and Oliver Cowdery, to ordain you unto this first priesthood which you have received, that you might be called and ordained even as Aaron . . . And also with Peter, and James, and John, whom I have sent unto you, by whom I have ordained you and confirmed you to be apostles and especial witnesses of my name, and bear the keys of your ministry . . ." (DC, 1835 L:2, 3).

While it is not known why Smith and Cowdery delayed naming the messengers until 1835, the answer may reside in the role the Book of Mormon played during the earliest months of the Restoration. In addition to authorizing and initiating Smith's ministry, the Book of Mormon served as a blueprint for the early church. The form of the early church beginning in the summer of 1829 paralleled that described in the Book of Mormon. Its emphasis on the necessity of baptism and formal authority to baptize initiated Smith's and Cowdery's journey to the Susquehanna River. It described the mode of baptism and even specified the exact wording of the baptismal prayer. In this context one might appreciate that the actual conferral of authority to baptize (and subsequently the higher authority of the apostleship) could have been viewed by Smith and Cowdery of lesser significance. It is important to realize that Smith himself publicly associated John the Baptist and Peter, James, and

---

27. "Kirtland High Council Minutes," 21 Feb. 1835.

John with priesthood restoration only from 1835 to 1840, after which time Elijah pre-empted them in Latter-day Saint theology, even as Moroni appears to have pre-empted them prior to 1835.[28]

The status of Mormon authority in 1829 was as follows. Motivated by passages in the Book of Mormon, Smith and Cowdery had sought and received authorization to baptize. Later they encountered additional Book of Mormon passages describing a higher authority which was needed to confer the Holy Ghost and ordain to offices, which they subsequently received. Neither level of authority had yet been called "priesthood." Prior to 1831 the only use of the term was in the Book of Mormon, where it was used synonymously with the office of high priest (BM, 1830, 258-60), an office which did not exist in Mormonism until late 1831. Prior to then men acted by virtue of the office to which they had been ordained, either elder, priest, or teacher. In performing ordinances they sometimes referred to their authority explicitly, as in the baptismal prayer, though without using the term "priesthood."[29] Authority was generally implied, as in the blessing of

---

28. Two prominent Mormons, David Whitmer and William E. McLellin, a charter member of the Quorum of Twelve Apostles organized in 1835, denied angelic restoration of authority. While it is possible that neither had heard of angelic restoration of authority prior to publication of the 1835 Doctrine and Covenants, other people, both in and out of the church, were familiar with the story. The refusal of either man to acknowledge the story may have been due to the time between its occurrence (1829) and their accounts (forty-three years for McLellin, fifty-six years for Whitmer); bitterness over having been excommunicated (both in 1838); or a belief that all necessary authority came through events surrounding the Book of Mormon or, in the case of Whitmer, refusal to acknowledge as valid any visitations or visions in which he himself had not participated. Thus Whitmer defended the Book of Mormon and his own vision of Moroni yet declined to validate Smith's first vision, the restoration events of 1829, the vision of the "degrees of glory" in 1832, the vision of the Celestial Kingdom in 1836, or the 1836 appearances of Jesus Christ, Moses, Elias, and Elijah in the newly dedicated Kirtland "House of the Lord"—none of which he had participated in. (The vision of the "degrees of glory" is contained in DC, 1835 XCI; the vision of the Celestial Kingdom in the current LDS edition of the Doctrine and Covenants (Salt Lake City: Church of Jesus Christ of Latter-day Saints, 1981) [hereafter DC, LDS] 137; and the appearances of Jesus Christ, Moses, Elias, and Elijah in DC, LDS 110.)

29. "The Articles of the Church of Christ," in Woodford, 288.

the bread and wine (BM, 1830, 575-76) and in the ordination of priests and teachers (BM, 1830, 575).[30] It was not until several months after the June 1831 general conference, when the "high priesthood" was conferred, that the term "priesthood" entered Mormon usage at all.

Two offices—priest and teacher—were named in the Book of Mormon as possessing lesser authority. Neither office was specifically bestowed on Smith or Cowdery.[31] The Book of Mormon stated that both offices had authority to baptize (BM, 1830, 265), though a revised version of the "Articles and Covenants" of the church in 1831 restricted the performing of baptism to the former office.[32]

The higher authority, according to the Book of Mormon, resided in elders whose authority equaled that of Jesus' ancient apostles (BM, 1830, 574-75). Initially the term "disciple" referred to those possessing this authority (BC XV:28), but in late 1829 the term switched to "apostle."[33] In a revelation dated 6 April 1830 (the day the church was formally organized), Smith and Cowdery were called "Apostles" and "Elders" (BC XXII:1, 13, 14). Two months later the first general conference was held at which licenses to preach were given to two teachers, three priests, and five elders.[34] Two of those licenses still exist. Smith's father's states that "he is a Priest of

---

30. Prayers currently used for the Sacrament of the Lord's Supper and for baptism are essentially the same as those used in 1829 and 1830. By contrast, use of the ordination prayer for priests and teachers prescribed by the Book of Mormon was discontinued. The officiator now acts by authority of the "priesthood." See *General Handbook of Instructions* (Salt Lake City: Corporation of The President of the Church of Jesus Christ of Latter-day Saints, 1989), Sec. 5, 1-5.

31. Smith's most detailed account, published in 1842, which applied the term "priesthood" retroactively, stated that (1) the angel conferred on them the "Priesthood of Aaron," whereupon (2) they baptized each other, and (3) they subsequently ordained each other to the Aaronic Priesthood but not to the office of priest or teacher (see *Times and Seasons* 3 [1 Aug. 1842]: 865-66).

32. *Painesville Telegraph*, 19 Apr. 1831.

33. "The Articles of the Church of Christ," in Woodford, 290, refers to Cowdery as "an Apostle of the Lord Jesus Christ by the will of God the Father & the Lord Jesus Christ."

34. Donald Q. Cannon and Lyndon W. Cook, eds., *Far West Record: Minutes of the Church of Jesus Christ of Latter-day Saints, 1830-1844* (Salt Lake City: Deseret Book Co., 1983), 1.

Apostle = Elder

this Church of Christ,"[35] while John Whitmer's says "he is an Apostle of Jesus Christ, an Elder of this Church of Christ."[36] A year later the "Articles and Covenants" further clarified the dual nomenclature by stating that "an apostle is an elder."[37] William McLellin later explained that "an Apostle is not an administrative officer. When they ministered they did it as Elders."[38] That apostles existed in the church as early as 1829, and that twelve apostles may have been selected as early as 1830, is further suggested by the following sources:

> David Marks, an itinerant preacher, stayed in the home of the Whitmer family on 29 March 1830, just eight days before the church was organized. In his memoirs published in 1831 he said of his conversation with the Whitmers, "they further stated, that twelve apostles were to be appointed, who would soon confirm their mission by miracles."[39]

> An article in *The Cleveland Herald*, dated 25 November 1830, said that since the Book of Mormon "would not sell unless an excitement and curiosity could be raised in the public mind, [the leaders of the new church] have therefore sent out twelve Apostles to promulgate its doctrines, several of whom are in this vicinity expounding its mysteries and baptising converts to its principles . . ."[40]

35. Original in LDS archives, photograph in Donald Q. Cannon, "Licensing in the Early Church," *Brigham Young University Studies* 22 (Winter 1982): 97.

36. Photograph of John Whitmer license, P10, f1, Whitmer Papers, RLDS archives.

37. *Painesville Telegraph*, 19 Apr. 1831.

38. McLellin to Joseph Smith III, July 1872, RLDS archives. The term "apostle" may have carried a connotation of "witness," while "elder" was an officer with administrative responsibilities. Since the Book of Mormon spoke of twelve "disciple/elders," it appears that the total number of apostle/elders was initially limited to twelve. As growth required more administrative officers, additional elders were called without the title of apostle.

39. Mariella Marks, ed., *Memoirs of the Life of David Marks, Minister of the Gospel* (Dove, NH: Free-Will Baptist Printing Establishment, 1846), 236-37. Note that the first edition was published in 1831.

40. *The Cleveland Herald*, 25 Nov. 1830. Although no 1830 list of apostles exists, a strong case may be made for at least eight men having been called to this position. (1) Joseph Smith and (2) Oliver Cowdery

12 Apostles in 1830 [handwritten annotation]

In December 1830 letters of introduction written by Sidney Rigdon in behalf of John Whitmer called Whitmer "an Apostle of this church,"[41] and by Joseph Smith and John Whitmer called Orson Pratt (ordained an elder on 1 December 1830) "another servant and apostle."[42]

By the end of 1830 new elders were no longer also called apostles.[43]

---

were each called "an apostle of Jesus Christ, an elder of the Church" (*Painesville Telegraph*, 19 Apr. 1831). (3) David Whitmer was "called even with that same calling" as the Apostle Paul (BC XV:11). (4) John Whitmer was identified in his license, issued at the general conference on 9 June 1830, as "an Apostle of Jesus Christ, an Elder of this Church of Christ." (5) Peter Whitmer, (6) Ziba Peterson, and (7) Samuel H. Smith were ordained elders and issued licenses at the same time as John Whitmer. Although copies of their licenses do not exist, one may assume that they were identical to Whitmer's (*Far West Record*, 1). (8) Orson Pratt, in a letter of introduction, was called "another servant and apostle" (see text below). Four other men had been ordained Elders prior to the publication of *The Cleveland Herald* article (Joseph Smith, Sr., Hyrum Smith, Parley Pratt, and Thomas Marsh), however there are neither copies of licenses nor other references to them as apostles (an entry at the end of the 1830 section of the "Journal History" of the LDS church, copies of which are at the LDS archives and the Marriott Library of the University of Utah, states that these four men were ordained elders on or before 30 September 1830).

41. E. D. Howe, *Mormonism Unvailed, or, A Faithful Account of that Singular Imposition and Delusion, From its Rise to the Present Time* (Painesville, OH, 1834), 110. This book was reprinted in 1977 by AMS Press, Inc., New York, as part of its series "Communal Societies in America."

42. From the Newel Knight journal, quoted in William G. Hartley, *They Are My Friends: A History of the Joseph Knight Family, 1825-1850* (Provo, UT: Grandin Book Co., 1986), 60.

43. For example, the license of Edward Partridge, ordained an Elder on 15 December 1830, stated simply that he was "ordained as an Elder," with no mention of the word "apostle." See Orson F. Whitney, "Aaronic Priesthood," *The Contributor* 6 (Oct. 1884): 5. A letter from Ezra Booth to Rev. Eddy, 21 Nov. 1831, suggests that although no new apostles were designated, a defined group of Twelve Apostles existed as late as 1831: "And thus by commandment, poor Ziba [Peterson], one of the twelve Apostles, is thrust down; while Oliver the scribe, also an Apostle, who had been guilty of similar conduct, is set on high" (*Painesville Telegraph*, 6 Dec. 1831). Furthermore, a revelation dated 23 Sept. 1832 and addressed to "Eleven high Priests save one" who "are

14

The use of the term declined quickly. By 1835, when the Quorum of Twelve Apostles was organized, no mention was made of the earlier apostles.

Another development at the end of 1830 proved to be of even greater impact on the church and was initiated by the baptism of former Campbellite preacher and bishop Sidney Rigdon. Having been converted in Kirtland, Ohio, by four missionaries sent to the "borders of the Lamanites" (Native Americans), Rigdon was convinced that these men had authority from God but was troubled by their apparent inability to prophesy and heal. Blaming Cowdery "for attempting to work miracles" and saying that "it was not intended to be confirmed in that way,"[44] Rigdon went East to meet the prophet.

Phase 3: High Priesthood, December 1830-November 1831

Sidney Rigdon's influence on Joseph Smith was immediate and favorable. Within days of his arrival in New York, Rigdon's status in the Restoration was declared by revelation: "Behold, verily, verily, I say unto my servant Sidney, I have looked upon thee and thy works. I have heard thy prayers and prepared thee for a greater work. Thou are blessed, for thou shalt do great things. Behold thou was sent forth, even as John, to prepare the way before me, and before Elijah which should come, and thou knew it not" (BC XXXVII:3-6).

Several days later, with Rigdon as scribe, Smith received a revelation changing the qualifications for the ministry. The church was directed to move to Ohio where the elders would "be endowed with power from on high"—something Rigdon had concluded was lacking in missionaries who converted him—and thus be prepared to "go forth among all nations" (BC XL:28). Using the terminology of the Gospel of Luke, Chapter 24, the revelation likened the elders to the ancient apostles who were told that although they had been ordained, they lacked something essential to their forthcoming missions, namely "power from on high." Not until they were endowed with power on

---

present this day" stated that "you are mine Apostles even Gods high Priests" and repeatedly compared these men to the ancient Apostles ("Kirtland Revelation Book," 20-31; see also DC, 1835, Sec. IV).

44. See articles in the *Palmyra Reflector*, 14 Feb. and 9 Mar. 1831, and the *Painesville Telegraph*, 15 Feb. 1831.

the Day of Pentecost could they leave Jerusalem on their missions. The nature of the new "endowment"[45]—how and when it would be given, and of what it would consist—was not described in this revelation but emerged over the next five months.

Two February revelations gave additional insight into the endowment. The first stated the necessity of personal preparation on the part of recipients (BC XLV:16). The second reinforced the similarity between the modern and ancient elders by promising a pentecostal experience: "I will pour out my spirit upon them in the day that they assemble themselves together" (BC XLVI:2). The same revelation announced that the assembly would be held in Kirtland the first week of June.

Shortly after receiving this revelation, Smith, with Rigdon as scribe, revised the 14th chapter of Genesis which contains one of two Old Testament references to Melchizedek. They added sixteen verses defining an ancient order to which Melchizedek was ordained as a high priest and through which he possessed tangible power to break mountains, divide seas, dry up waters, and put armies at defiance.[46]

In May an unpublished revelation through Smith to Ezra Thayre stated:

> Let my servant Ezra humble himself and at the conference meeting he shall be ordained unto power from on high and he shall go from

---

45. This is not the contemporary LDS temple endowment, nor a precursor to it except in the general sense of personal empowerment.

46. For a comparison of the King James text and the "Inspired Version" produced by Joseph Smith, see *Joseph Smith's "New Translation" of the Bible* (Independence, MO: Herald Publishing House, 1970), 78. This chapter of Genesis was revised by Smith and Rigdon between 1 Feb.-8 Mar. 1831 (see Robert J. Matthews, *"A Plainer Translation:" Joseph Smith's Translation of the Bible, A History and Commentary* [Provo, UT: Brigham Young University Press, 1975], 96). While the Book of Mormon spoke of Melchizedek being a high priest and taking upon himself "the High Priesthood forever," it did not link tangible power to priesthood, nor did the King James version of Genesis 14 (see BM, 1830, 260). David Whitmer insisted that the office of high priest was Rigdon's doing. See, for example, Whitmer's letter to Joseph Smith III, in *Saints' Herald* 34 (1887): 92-93. While it is true that Rigdon, as Smith's scribe, would have had ample opportunity to discuss his views with Smith, the fact that High Priesthood was mentioned in the Book of Mormon suggests caution in accepting Whitmer's claim.

thence (if he be obedient unto my commandments) and proclaim my gospel unto the western regions with my servants that must go forth even unto the borders by the Lamanites for behold I have a great work for them to do and it shall be given unto you to know what ye shall do at the conference meeting even so amen.[47]

This revelation linked for the first time the endowment of "power from on high" to ordination,[48] though not yet specifying the "order" of priesthood which gave Melchizedek tangible power. That the elders expected to receive power and that their expectation was public knowledge was verified by an Ohio newspaper article published at the time: "In June they are all to meet, and hold a kind of jubilee in this new 'land of promise,' where they are to work divers miracles—among others that of raising the dead."[49]

The conference began on 3 June 1831 in a schoolhouse in Kirtland. On the second day a series of unusual events transpired. Of the many accounts later written, the most concise was that of John Corrill:

Previous to this there was a revelation received, requiring the prophet to call the elders together, that they might receive an endowment. This was done, and the meeting took place some time in June. About fifty elders met, which was about all the elders that then belonged to the church. The meeting was conducted by Smith. Some curious things took place. The same visionary and marvellous spirits spoken of before, got hold of some of the elders; it threw one from his seat to the floor; it bound another, so that for some time he could not use his limbs nor speak; and some other curious effects were experienced, but, by a mighty exertion, in the name of the Lord, it was exposed and shown to be from an evil source. The Melchizedek priesthood was then for the first time introduced, and conferred on several of the elders. In this chiefly consisted the endowment—it being a new order—and bestowed authority. However, some doubting took place among the elders, and considerable conversation was held on the subject. The elders not fairly understanding the nature of the endowments, it took some time to reconcile all their feelings.[50]

47. Unpublished revelation, dated May 1831, in "Kirtland Revelation Book," 91-92.

48. Note that the ordination is to be to "power" not to a specified office.

49. *Western Courier* (Ravenna, OH), 26 May 1831; reprinted in *St. Louis Times*, 9 July 1831.

50. John Corrill, *Brief History of the Church of Christ of Latter Day*

Other participants who later wrote of the experience included
Joseph Smith, Parley P. Pratt, Levi Hancock, Lyman Wight, Newel
Knight, Ezra Booth, Philo Dibble, and Zebedee Coltrin,[51] all of
whom described the event as a pentecost consisting of revelation,
prophecy, vision, healing, casting out of evil spirits, speaking in
unknown tongues, and, according to one witness, an unsuccessful
attempt to raise a dead child.[52] A new order was introduced at the

---

Saints . . . (St. Louis: Printed for the Author, 1839), chap. 10. Corrill,
writing in 1839, incorrectly used the term "Melchizedek priesthood" in
referring to the conference.

51. Joseph Smith, "History of Joseph Smith," *Times and Seasons* 5
(1 Feb. 1844): 416; Parley P. Pratt, *Autobiography of Parley Parker Pratt*
(Salt Lake City: Deseret Book, 1976), 68; Levi Hancock, "1854 Autobiography," LDS archives; Lyman Wight to Wilford Woodruff, 24 Aug.
1857, Lyman Wight Letterbook, RLDS archives (the original letter is in
LDS archives); Newel Knight, "Autobiographical Sketch," LDS archives; Ezra Booth to Rev. Ira Eddy, Sep. 1831, in Howe, 180-90; Philo
Dibble: *Juvenile Instructor* 27 (15 May 1892): 303; and Zebedee Coltrin,
"Autobiography," LDS archives.

52. Ezra Booth to Rev. Ira Eddy, 31 t., 1831, in *Painesville
Telegraph*, 15 Nov. 1831. Booth was ordained to the High Priesthood at
the conference (*Far West Record*, 6-7) but left the church a few weeks
later. His letters to Eddy are unsympathetic, and it is tempting to dismiss
his account as false. Since all other first-hand witnesses are silent on the
subject of raising the dead child, it is not possible to verify his allegation.
However, several pieces of evidence lend credence. First, newspaper
articles both prior to and following the conference described claims by
the "Mormonites" that they had power to raise the dead (see *Western
Courier*, 26 May 1831; *Niles' Weekly Register*, 16 July 1831; *Vermont Patriot
and State Gazette*, 18 Sept. 1831). Second, the death of Joseph Brackenbury, an early Mormon missionary, on 7 March 1832 was followed by a
much-publicized and similarly unsuccessful attempt by fellow elders to
raise him from the dead (see *Burlington Sentinel* [Burlington, VT], 23 Mar.
1832; and reprints of this article in the *Wayne Sentinel* [Palmyra, NY], 11
Apr. 1832, and the *Ohio Star*, 12 Apr. 1832). Two decades later LDS
Church Historian George A. Smith wrote to Brackenbury's widow
asking "the circumstances of his death, burial, and attempted resurrection" (George A. Smith to Elizabeth Brackenbury, 29 Aug. 1855, Henry
Stebbins Collection, P24/F1, RLDS archives). Third, when E. D. Howe
reprinted the Booth account in 1834, he told of an interview with the
parents who said "that they were prevented from procuring medical aid
for the child, by the representations of the elders, that it was in no

18

Order of Melchizedek = High Priesthood

conference into which about half the elders present were inducted *But* by ordination. The new order was called the Order of Melchizedek, a name derived from the Book of Mormon and Genesis, chapter *Not* 14. It was also called the High Priesthood, a term used in the Book of Mormon but not in Genesis (BM, 1830, 260). There was not *G* yet an office of high priest, even though Book of Mormon passages referred to Melchizedek as a high priest. Conference minutes from *High* 4 and 24 August; 1, 6, 12 September; 10, 11, 21 October; and 1, 8, 9, 11, and 12-13 November still listed as "elders" men who had *Priest* been ordained to the High Priesthood.[53] The term "high priest" was not used in conference minutes until 26 April 1832.[54]

Booth acknowledged that conference participants professed "to be endowed with the same power as the ancient apostles were."[55] This was chronicled most dramatically by Jared Carter. Shortly after the conference a woman belonging to the church fell from a wagon on her way to a meeting and sustained injuries feared to be fatal. Carter wrote:

> In my conversation with her, I told her that she need not have any more pain, and also mentioned my Brother Simeon who was endowed with great power from on high, and that she might be healed, if she had faith. Brother Simeon also conversed with her, and after awhile took her by the hand, saying, "I command you in the name of Jesus Christ to arise and walk." And she arose and walked from room to room.[56]

Although the new order derived its name from Melchizedek, the term "Melchizedek Priesthood" was not yet used, in spite of what Smith, Corrill, Lyman Wight, and Newel Knight later wrote. The term was first used in 1835 when it became an umbrella encompassing all prior component terms. All accounts of the 1831 conference referring to "Melchizedek Priesthood" were written after 1835, while

---

danger—that it would certainly be restored" (Howe, 190).

53. *Far West Record*, 9-31.

54. Ibid., 43.

55. Howe, 180-81.

56. Jared Carter journal, in "Journal History," 8 June 1831, LDS archives. Simeon had been ordained to the High Priesthood at the conference, Jared had not (see *Far West Record*, 7).

contemporary accounts of the conference mentioned only "High Priesthood" or "Order of Melchizedek."[57]

Enthusiasm and expectations were high following the conference, as the elders traveled from Kirtland to Independence, Missouri, to dedicate a site for a temple.[58] A national periodical commented that "some of them affect a power even to raise the dead, and perchance, (such is the weakness of human nature), really believe that they can do it!"[59] Yet their journey resulted in disappointment and lowered expectations. At another conference back in Kirtland on 25 October, Smith introduced a new dimension to the High Priesthood and simultaneously took the first step in the development of the unique Latter-day Saint theology of afterlife, by stating "that the order of the High-priesthood is that they have the power given them to seal up the Saints unto eternal life. And said it was the privilege of every Elder present to be ordained to the Highpriesthood."[60] Prior to this, authority and power, by whatever title or description, had been "here and now." With this pronouncement the priesthood was extended beyond the grave. Within two weeks, elders exercised their new power, sealing entire congregations "up unto eternal life."[61]

Shortly after the October conference, a revelation directed to four men further defined priesthood. The office of high priest was formally established. After this, High Priesthood meant the office of high priest, with no further reference to an endowment.[62] Further, the inspired

---

57. A revelation dated 16 February 1832 refers to "priests of the most high after the order of Melchisedeck" rather than "Melchizedek Priesthood" ("Kirtland Revelation Book," 5; see also *The Evening and the Morning Star* 1 [July 1832]: 10-11; and DC, 1835 XCI:5).

58. A local newspaper reported, "They still persist in their power to work miracles. They say they have often seen them done—the sick are healed—the lame walk—devils are cast out;—and these assertions are made by men heretofore considered rational men, and men of truth" (*Geauga Gazette* [Painesville, OH], 21 June 1831).

59. *Niles' Weekly Register*, 16 July 1831.

60. *Far West Record*, 20-21.

61. Between 9 and 26 November Reynolds Cahoon participated in three such "sealings." See Reynolds Cahoon diaries, LDS archives.

62. The link between endowment and missionary work, which had led to the June conference, remained intact and was the focal point of later Kirtland (Ohio) and Nauvoo (Illinois) endowments.

words of high priests were proclaimed "scripture." The revelation reaffirmed the authority of the High Priesthood to seal people to eternal life, while adding that prior divine confirmation was required.[63] Another revelation given simultaneously added a darker dimension to the sealing power, declaring that the wicked could be sealed up to condemnation (BC I:2).[64]

Phase 4: Organizational Consolidation,
November 1831-March 1836

A revelation given in November 1831 initiated a process of organizational rearrangement which continued over a period of nearly five years, culminating in the hierarchical seating at the dedication of the Kirtland House of the Lord in 1836. When the Latter-day Saint movement began in August 1829,[65] its government was democratic. Although Joseph Smith clearly occupied a favored position as translator of the Book of Mormon and as God's spokesman, administrative titles such as "President" or "First Elder" were absent during the early period.[66] At the first general conference in June 1830, Smith was called "first Elder" and Cowdery "second Elder,"[67] and church growth was forcing other changes. As a departure from Book of Mormon precedent and the early revelations which stated that only elders could ordain

---

63. This revelation probably was intended to be published in BC, but the printing press was destroyed before type was set. The first published version was in *The Evening and the Morning Star* 1 (Oct. 1832): 35. An expanded version was published in DC, 1835 XXII.

64. This revelation was dated 1 Nov. 1831.

65. David Whitmer wrote that this was the date when he, Smith, and Cowdery, the first three elders, began to preach and baptize. By the time of the "formal" establishment of the church on 6 April 1830, there were already three congregations with an aggregate membership of about seventy (*An Address to All Believers in Christ*, 32-33).

66. For example, although the 1835 version of the "Articles and Covenants of the Church" called Smith "the first elder of this Church," all earlier versions referred to him simply as "an elder of this church" (compare *Painesville Telegraph,* 19 Apr. 1831, and BC XXIV:3 to DC, 1835 II:1).

67. These terms followed the signatures of Joseph Smith and Oliver Cowdery on the licenses of John Whitmer and Joseph Smith, Sr., issued at that conference.

other officers,[68] by 1831 priests were authorized to ordain deacons, teachers, and other priests, perhaps as a concession to the overburdened elders.[69]

More significant was a revelation received that November "regulating the Presidency of the church."[70] This revelation outlined for the first time both the need for and structure of a formal presidency: "Wherefore it must needs be that one be appointed of the high Priesthood to preside over the Priesthood, and he shall be called President of the high priesthood of the Church, or in other words the presiding high Priest over the high priesthood of the Church." More than a figurehead, this president would hold the power to authorize all other officers within the church to administer "ordinances and blessings upon the church by the laying on of hands." He would serve a judicial role, as president of the court of the High Priesthood, "the highest court in the church," thus bringing the informal church judicial system under central control.[71] The revelation concluded by stating

---

68. BM, 1830, "The Book of Moroni," Chap. III; "The Articles of the Church of Christ," in Woodford, 288; BC XV:35.

69. The earliest known account of this change was "The Articles and Covenants of the Church of Christ," in the *Painesville Telegraph*, 19 Apr. 1831.

70. This revelation, although received in November 1831 (see "Kirtland Revelation Book," 84-86), was not published until 1835, when it was included in an expanded revelation dated 28 Mar. 1835 (DC, 1835 III).

71. Judicial matters were addressed informally as early as 1830 in a revelation calling upon teachers to "see that there is no iniquity in the church." (The earliest known version of this revelation was published in the *Painesville Telegraph*, 19 Apr. 1831.) The following year elders were empowered to judge church members accused of adultery or fornication (BC XLVII, dated Feb. 1831). The role of bishop was expanded by a revelation dated 1 August 1831 "to be a judge in Israel, like as it was in ancient days" (BC LIX:21). The November 1831 revelation authorized the president to call twelve counselors if he chose, and thus set the pattern for the formation of high councils two and a half years later. George A. Smith later said, "There had been several Councils of twelve High Priests called for special cases, but they organized it permanently on the 17th Feb 1834" (*Journal of Discourses,* 26 vols. [Liverpool, Eng.: Latter-day Saints' Bookseller's Depot, 1855-86), 11:7, 15 Nov. 1864).

that "the duty of the President of the office of the high Priesthood is to preside over the whole and to be like unto Moses."[72]

At a conference in Ohio on 24 January 1832, Smith was "acknowledged President of the High Priesthood" and formally ordained to that office by Sidney Rigdon. At the same time, Rigdon "ordained" Orson Pratt, who was already an elder, to "preside over the Elders," thus underscoring the recent distinction between the offices of elder and high priest.[73] Simultaneously a second conference in Independence, Missouri, moved towards centralized control of all ordinations, unanimously resolving "that there be no person ordained in the churches in the land of Zion to the office of Elder Priest Teacher or Deacon without the united voice of the Church in writing in which such individual resides."[74]

The consolidation of centralized authority was strengthened several weeks later with the selection and ordination of Rigdon and Jesse Gause as Smith's "councellors of the ministry of the presidency of the high Priesthood."[75] An unpublished revelation given to Bishop Newel K. Whitney the same month reaffirmed the primacy of the "presidency of the high Priesthood" in "all the concerns of the church."[76]

---

72. The phrase "preside over the whole" was changed to "preside over the whole church" when the revelation was published in 1835 (DC, 1835 III:42).

73. Orson Pratt journal, 25 Jan. 1832, in Elden J. Watson, ed., *The Orson Pratt Journals* (Salt Lake City: Elden J. Watson, 1975), 11. See also B. H. Roberts, ed., *History of the Church of Jesus Christ of Latter-day Saints* (Salt Lake City: Deseret Book Co., 1971), 1:243 (hereafter HC). Although this appears to have presaged the formation of "quorums" of elders, Pratt's ordination to the High Priesthood only one week later delayed for years the emergence of organized, functional groups of elders. (See Lyndon W. Cook, *The Revelations of the Prophet Joseph Smith* [Provo, UT: Seventy's Mission Bookstore, 1981], 49, for the date of Pratt's ordination.)

74. Minutes of a conference in Independence, Missouri, 23-24 Jan. 1832, contained in a letter from Oliver Cowdery to Joseph Smith, 28 Jan. 1832, photograph of original letter in RLDS archives, Miscellany, P19, f4. This was later amended to require the consent of a conference of high priests rather than of the entire church. (See *Far West Record*, 28 Aug. 1833.)

75. "Kirtland Revelation Book," 10-11.

76. Unpublished revelation, Mar. 1832, Newel K. Whitney pa-

Nearly two years passed before the next significant step occurred in the process of centralization. Having seen in vision the manner in which ancient church councils were organized, Smith convened a conference in Kirtland on 17 February 1834 and organized "the high council of the Church of Christ," consisting of twelve high priests.[77] Strictly judicial in function, the high council exercised both original and appellate jurisdiction.[78] Although delegating substantial powers to this body, Smith signalled the continuity of strong, centralized control by placing himself and his two counselors at its head. In recognition of the growth of the church beyond Kirtland and Independence, provision was also made at this conference for *ad hoc* councils to settle "the most difficult cases of church matters" abroad. These councils would be temporary and subordinate to the standing high council, which could upon appeal reverse their decisions.

One week later a revelation called Smith to lead an expedition known as Zion's Camp from Ohio to Missouri to rescue persecuted church members and "redeem Zion."[79] Although the mission failed, and several members died of cholera, Smith succeeded in organizing a high council while he was in Missouri.[80] Four days later he confidently stated "that he had lived to see the Church of Jesus Christ established on earth according to the order of heaven; and should he now be taken from this body of people, the work of the Lord would roll on."[81]

Smith's conclusion that the church organization was now com-

---

77. "Kirtland High Council Minutes," 17 Feb. 1834 (see also "Kirtland Revelation Book," 111-15, and DC, 1835 V).

78. Ibid. The draft version of the minutes placed the high council subordinate to the bishop's court, but the amended version authorized the high council to settle "important difficulties . . . which could not be settled by the Church, or the bishop's council to the satisfaction of the parties."

79. "Kirtland Revelation Book," 108-11, revelation dated 24 Feb. 1834. See also DC, LDS 103.

80. *Far West Record*, 3 July 1834.

81. Lyman Wight diary, 7 July 1834, in *The History of the Reorganized Church of Jesus Christ of Latter Day Saints* (Lamoni, IA: The Board of Publication, 1896), 1:515-16. See also *Far West Record*, 7 July 1834.

plete proved to be short-lived. After returning to Kirtland, he met with the Young brothers, Brigham and Joseph, and related a vision he had experienced while praying to know the fate of those who had died on the expedition. He said, "Brethren, I have seen those men who died of the cholera in our camp; and the Lord knows, if I get a mansion as bright as theirs, I ask no more."[82] Then, drawing from the same vision, he outlined the formation of the final two bodies of centralized authority, the twelve apostles and the seventy.[83] The following Saturday, 14 February 1835, the twelve were appointed; two weeks later, the First Quorum of Seventies was chosen. Nearly all the men in both groups had proven their dedication by serving in Zion's Camp.

Although the initial mission of the twelve was "to open the door of the gospel to foreign nations," with the seventy "under their direction to follow in their tracks,"[84] it soon became apparent that other missions awaited the twelve. Two weeks later Smith told them that they were to be a "traveling high council, who are to preside over all the churches of the Saints among the Gentiles, where there is no presidency established"[85]—that is, everywhere except Kirtland and Independence, where standing high councils presided. That the traveling high council would ultimately overshadow the standing high councils may have been indicated by a revelation given through Smith at the request of the Twelve on 28 March 1835.[86] While stating that four councils all had "authority and power" equal to that of the First Presidency, listing the twelve ahead of the seventy and high councils suggested a favored status (DC, 1835 III:12-15). Furthermore, to the twelve was given the exclusive authority "to ordain and set in order all the other officers of the church" (v. 30). By August 1835 the revelation which had established the standing high councils was

82. Joseph Young, Sen., *History of the Organization of the Seventies* (Salt Lake City: Deseret News Steam Printing Establishment, 1878), 1.

83. A revelation dated the following month stated that the seventies had been organized "according to the vision," although it gave no further information regarding the vision (DC,1835 III:43; see also HC 2:201-202).

84. Young, 2, 14.

85. "Kirtland High Council Minutes," 88, quoted in D. Michael Quinn, "The Evolution of the Presiding Quorums of the LDS Church," *Journal of Mormon History* 1 (1974): 27.

86. HC, 2:210.

changed to give further priority to the twelve: whereas decisions of the standing high councils (and of *ad hoc* councils of traveling high priests) could still be appealed, those of the twelve could not (DC, 1835 V:13).

By late 1835, then, the centralization of authority was complete. Ordinations were under central control,[87] church members in the stakes were under the control of the standing high councils and bishops, and those outside of the stakes came under the jurisdiction of the twelve apostles and the seventy. All of these bodies, in turn, answered to the president who was "to preside over the whole church, and to be like unto Moses" (DC, 1835 III:42). Although changes would yet be made in the responsibilities of these governing bodies, no new units of ecclesiastical government would be added during the remaining nine years of Smith's ministry.

In the earliest days of the Restoration only three offices existed: teachers, priests, and elders/apostles. Teachers and priests were ordained without regard to number or organization. Elders/apostles, though initially a group of twelve men, did not function as a unit. In November 1831 the revelation which appointed a president also mandated that each office be organized into well-defined groups: deacons[88] into groups of twelve; teachers, twenty-four; priests, forty-eight; and elders, 96. Each group was to be presided over by a president "to sit in council with them and to teach them their duty edifying one another as it is given according to the covenants."[89] Although the

---

87. The third historian of the church, John Corrill, wrote: "For some time after the commencement of the church, an elder might ordain an elder, priest, teacher, or deacon, when and where he thought proper, but, after Stakes were planted, and the church became organized, they established a rule that none should be ordained without consent of the church or branch that he belonged to; neither should any man be placed over a branch or take charge of it without consent of same" (Corrill, chap. 13).

88. The office of deacon did not exist either in the Book of Mormon or in the early Restoration. For example, as late as February 1831 a revelation listing the offices in the church identified only elders, priests, and teachers (BC XLIV:13). The earliest known mention of deacons was in the "Articles and Covenants of the Church," published in the *Painesville Telegraph*, 19 Apr. 1831.

89. "Kirtland Revelation Book," 84-86. Although the term "quorum" would not be applied to these groups for several years, the concept

blueprint for group function was drawn, no group was able to respond effectively at the time. When the Kirtland House of the Lord was completed in 1836 only teachers had established a significant tradition of group function.[90]

As shown earlier, the concept of dual levels of authority was present in the Book of Mormon and formed the model for the Restoration. Both levels were restored in 1829, though neither was named at that time nor were the offices within each layer specified. Through mid-1832 the only use of the word "priesthood" was in conjunction with "high priesthood" which first referred to an order of elders, then to the office of high priest. A revelation in September 1832 expanded the meaning of the word "priesthood" and for the first time made some offices subordinate to others (DC, 1835 IV). The revelation is confusing, for it deals with three terms—"holy priesthood," "high priesthood," and "lesser priesthood"—the first two having since become interchangeable. Furthermore, the revelation was given to two groups of men over a two-day period— seven elders on 22 September and "Eleven high Priests save one" the following day—and for two separate purposes—"explaining the two priesthoods" and "commissioning the Apostles to preach the gospel."[91] Without the original manuscript, it is impossible to identify with certainty the seam connecting the two parts.

The revelation describes a "holy priesthood" which Moses received from his father-in-law, Jethro, who had inherited it lineally from Adam through Melchizedek, "which priesthood continueth in the church of God, in all generations" (DC, 1835 IV:2). It then describes a second "priesthood" which the Lord confirmed "upon Aaron and his seed," which "continueth and abideth forever, with the

---

established by this revelation remains the guiding principle today.

90. The earliest known record began on Christmas Day 1834. See "Teachers Quorum Minute Book, December 25, 1834—February 12, 1845," MS 3428, LDS archives. To complete preparations for the March 1836 solemn assembly and endowment, "the quorums of the Church were organized in the presence of the Church, and commenced confessing their faults and asking forgiveness" (Oliver Cowdery diary, 17 Jan. 1836, in Leonard J. Arrington, ed., "Oliver Cowdery's Kirtland, Ohio, 'Sketch Book,'" *Brigham Young University Studies* 12 [Summer 1972]: 416).

91. "Kirtland Revelation Book," index.

priesthood which is after the holiest order of God" (v. 3). What the revelation does not clarify is how these two levels of priesthood corresponded to the three events of 1829 and 1831. Clarification comes from Smith's diary, written at the same time, in which he recounts the events of the Restoration[92]: "firstly he receiving the testamony from on high"; "seccondly the ministering of Angels"; "thirdly the reception of the holy Priesthood by the ministring of Aangels to administer the letter of the Gospel—the Law and commandments as they were given unto him—and the ordinencs"; and "forthly a confirmation and reception of the high Priesthood after the holy order of the son of the living God [and] power and ordinence from on high to preach the gospel in the administration and demonstration of the spirit."[93]

Comparison of the autobiography with the revelation shows that the term "high priesthood" (DC, 1835 IV:5) referred to the office of high priest and not to the authority of Peter, James, and John. This office, according to the revelation, is superior to its two appendages: the offices of elder and bishop. Similarly, the "lesser priesthood," that is, the office of priest, or "lesser priest" (v. 22 of the same revelation), is superior to its two appendages: the offices of teacher and deacon (ibid.).[94] While not yet using the term "Aaronic Priesthood" for authority restored by John the Baptist on 15 May 1829, the revelation moved in that direction by associating such priesthood with "Aaron and his seed." Similarly, while the term "Melchizedek Priesthood" was not yet used, the connection between this priesthood and Melchizedek was firmly established. The relationship between offices, while perhaps implied in earlier records, was explicit. Lesser priests and high priests were dominant, with teachers and deacons subordinate to the former and elders and bishops to the latter.

Prior to this revelation there had been no indication that ordination to an office or to a level of authority was a right. But by stating that

---

92. Dean Jessee dates the diary entry between 20 July and 27 Nov. 1832; the revelation is dated 22-23 Sept. 1832. See Jessee, *Personal Writings*, 640n6.

93. Ibid., 4.

94. Adding to the confusion, a later portion of this revelation, known as the "oath and covenant" of the priesthood, refers first to "these two priesthoods" (i.e., those of Moses/Peter, James, and John, and Aaron/John the Baptist) then merely to "the priesthood," apparently a generic reference to both (see v. 6).

the lesser priesthood was conferred on "Aaron and his seed throughout all their generation," a doctrine of priesthood-through-lineage emerged. Several weeks later this was formalized in a revelation stating that "ye are lawful heirs according to the flesh," and that "the Priesthood hath remained and must needs remain through you and your lineage untill the restoration of all things . . ." (DC, 1835 VI:3, 6 Dec. 1832).

The next step in defining priesthood came through a revelation in March 1835 (DC, 1835 III)[95] introducing the terms "Aaronic Priesthood" and "Melchizedek Priesthood," which have since been used by all Latter-day Saint churches to refer to formal authority. In contrast to the September 1832 revelation, this one used the word "priesthood" generically to refer to all officers in each of the two levels of authority. Thus, whereas the 1832 revelation had teachers and deacons as appendages to the "lesser priesthood"—the office of priest—the three offices of priest, teacher, and deacon were now part of the Aaronic Priesthood which in turn served an umbrella function with reference to no specific office. Similarly, the offices of elder and high priest were now part of the Melchizedek Priesthood, rather than elders being appendages to high priests, as the earlier revelation had outlined. Finally, the office of bishop, previously an appendage to the high priesthood, was part of the Aaronic Priesthood.[96]

The collected revelations were soon assembled and edited for publication as *Doctrine and Covenants of the Church of the Latter Day Saints*. Among the textual changes was an addition to a revelation dated September 1830. Whereas the earlier form was silent on angelic intervention, the new version described John the Baptist as the

---

95. The revelation as published in DC, 1835 and subsequent editions of Doctrine and Covenants does not indicate that many of the verses are from the earlier November 1831 revelation, which is in the "Kirtland Revelation Book," 84-86, but which was never published in its 1831 format. All of the material referenced here is from the 28 March 1835 portion of the revelation.

96. The office of seventy was introduced in the 1835 revelation but not specifically placed under the Melchizedek Priesthood umbrella. This suggests that the verses relating to seventies were from a third revelation. Verse 43 reads: "And it is according to the vision, showing the order of the seventy," a vision not described in this or any other known revelation.

messenger who restored the "first priesthood," while Peter, James, and John were the restorers of the apostleship, this being the first time that the ancient apostles had explicitly been linked to the June 1829 restoration (DC, 1835 L:2-3). The use of the word "apostles" rather than "Melchizedek Priesthood" was significant, for while apostleship formed a part of Melchizedek Priesthood, the latter term had come to encompass more than just the apostleship. It is unfortunate that this distinction did not remain clear. After 1835 references to earlier events, including those of June 1829 and June 1831, frequently made use of the term "Melchizedek Priesthood." The failure of later commentators to understand the anachronism led to elaborate gyrations in attempting to deal with such statements as "I was also present with Joseph when the higher or Melchizedek priesthood was restored by the holy angels of God [in 1829],"[97] and "the Melchizedek priesthood was then [June 1831] for the first time introduced."[98]

The central purpose of the Ohio gathering in 1831 and June conference that year had been the endowment of elders with "power from on high," such that they, as the ancient apostles, would be prepared to spread the message of the gospel. There had been no repeat of the pentecostal experience for elders who had not attended the June conference, nor was it mandatory thereafter that elders be ordained to the High Priesthood prior to embarking on their missionary journeys.[99]

---

97. Oliver Cowdery, 17 Oct. 1848, quoted by Reuben Miller in *Millennial Star* 21 (20 Aug. 1859): 544.

98. Corrill, chap. 10 (written in 1839). In editing Joseph Smith's history for publication, B. H. Roberts devoted a lengthy footnote to a discussion of the "apparent" problem of the Melchizedek Priesthood restoration at the June 1831 conference rather than in 1829. He concluded, incorrectly, that the accounts meant to describe the restoration of the office of high priest (HC, 1:176). In dealing with the same dilemma RLDS apostle Heman C. Smith concluded, again incorrectly, that the accounts placing the restoration of the Melchizedek Priesthood in 1831 actually "had reference to the *fullness* of the Melchisedec priesthood being bestowed for the *first time* in June, 1831" (*The History of the Reorganized Church of Jesus Christ of Latter Day Saints*, 1:193, emphasis in original).

99. For example, Samuel H. Smith and Orson Hyde were appointed on 25 January 1832 to serve a mission to the Eastern States. Smith had received the endowment at the June 1831 conference, while Hyde had not. Yet Hyde in his missionary diary never mentioned Smith's

Yet near the end of 1832, when several missionaries had returned from their travels, Smith received a revelation indicating that further preparation was required, "that ye may be prepared in all things when I shall send you again" (DC, 1835 VII:21).[100] This preparation was to be both spiritual and intellectual. In order to facilitate the preparation, Smith was commanded to establish a school for the elders (v. 36).

The opening of the "School of the Prophets" occurred on 23-24 January 1833. Although never referred to as an "endowment," the school's opening resembled the 1831 conference. Both included new ordinances: in 1831 initiation into the High Priesthood, whereas in 1833 the washing of the feet by President Smith in similitude of the gesture of Jesus to his apostles. This latter was accompanied by a pentecostal outpouring, including speaking in tongues, prophesying and "many manifestations of the holy spirit,"[101] which was not repeated with subsequent admissions of elders to the school. However, the continuing expectation existed, as underscored in a letter written by Oliver Cowdery the next year:

> God has appointed a school for his faithful Elders: In it they are to be taught *all* things necessary to qualify them for their ministry: In it they are to learn: In it they are to be endowed with power from on high: but when entrusted with the great office and authority to preach and are sent out, it is with the expectation and consideration they will do so.[102]

Coincident with the 1833 decision to build the "House of the Lord" in Kirtland was a coupling of the ideas of empowerment and sacred space. A revelation in June 1833 stated: "I gave unto you a commandment, that you should build an house, in the which house I design to endow those whom I have chosen with power from on high"

---

endowment, never mentioned that he, himself, had not received it, and nowhere indicated that his position as a missionary was subordinate to Smith's.

100. See also "Kirtland Revelation Book," 33-48.

101. Zebedee Coltrin diary, 24 Jan. 1833. The most detailed accounts are the Coltrin diary; the "Kirtland High Council Minutes," 23 Jan. 1833; and Lucy Mack Smith's manuscript history, 162-63, LDS archives, photocopy in my possession.

102. Oliver Cowdery (Kirtland, OH) to J. G. Fosdick (Pontiac, MI), 4 Feb. 1834, in Oliver Cowdery letterbook, 25-26, Huntington Library.

(DC, 1835 XCV:2, 1 June 1833). The same sentiment was stated more forcefully a year later by Oliver Cowdery: "We want you to understand that the Lord has not promised to endow his servants from on high[,] only on the condition that they build him a house; and if the house is not built the Elders will not be endowed with power, and if they are not they can never go to the nations with the everlasting gospel."[103] Several weeks later, during the return from the Zion's Camp expedition, Smith received a revelation that the redemption of Zion "cannot be brought to pass until mine elders are endowed with power from on high; for, behold, I have prepared a greater endowment and blessing to be poured out upon them."[104]

During the winter of 1835-36 the elders worked to complete the House of the Lord and prepare themselves for the anticipated endowment.[105] The dedication occurred on 27 March 1836 and involved the general membership of the church. Three days later in the same building a "solemn assembly" was conducted which involved only adult males. As in 1831 and 1833, the 1836 endowment was pentecostal: "The brethren continued exhorting, prophesying and speaking in tongues until 5 o clock in the morning—the Saviour made his appearance to some, while angels minestered unto others, and it was a penticost and enduement indeed, long to be remembered."[106] Having received the required empowerment, the elders embarked on foreign missions beginning with the British Isles in 1837.

---

103. Oliver Cowdery (Kirtland, OH) to John F. Boynton (Saco, ME), 6 May 1834, in Oliver Cowdery letterbook, 45-46, Huntington Library.

104. "Kirtland Revelation Book," 97-100, revelation dated 22 June 1834. It is significant that the phrase "greater endowment" was used, apparently a reference to the 1831 endowment whose power had been insufficient to redeem Zion. Without explanation the word "great" was substituted for "greater" in published versions of this revelation.

105. In addition to preparing oneself spiritually, it was necessary that one's body be washed and anointed and that the feet be washed in a manner similar to that used in the opening of the School of the Prophets in 1833. The best descriptions of the preparations during the winter of 1835-36 are found in the diaries of Joseph Smith (in Scott H. Faulring, ed., *An American Prophet's Record: The Diaries and Journals of Joseph Smith* [Salt Lake City: Signature Books in association with Smith Research Associates, 1987]) and Oliver Cowdery (in Arrington).

106. Joseph Smith diary, 30 Mar. 1836, in Faulring, 155.

On 18 December 1833 Smith gathered his family and gave them blessings. To his father, he said:

> He shall be called a prince over his posterity, holding the keys of the patriarchal priesthood over the kingdom of God on earth, even the Church of the Latter Day Saints; and he shall sit in the general assembly of patriarchs, even in council with the Ancient of Days when he shall sit and all the patriarchs with him—and shall enjoy his right and authority under the direction of the Ancient of Days.[107]

While the term "Patriarchal Priesthood" would be used a decade later in a markedly different context, in 1833 it referred to the office of patriarch, even as the terms "Lesser Priesthood" and "High Priesthood" used at this same time referred to the respective offices of lesser priest and high priest.[108] Although Joseph Smith, Sr., was likened by this blessing to the Old Testament patriarchs, no explanation was given of his duties in the newly created office.[109] In the first year following Joseph Sr.'s ordination, there is no evidence that he functioned in any other than honorary duties.

During the return of Zion's Camp in 1834 the subject of "patriarchal blessings" was raised by Joseph Young. His brother Brigham later reminisced:

> My brother, Joseph Young, and myself were in this camp. When we

---

107. Patriarchal Blessings Book, Vol. 1, copy in Irene Bates Collection, RLDS archives. For a comprehensive treatment of the office of Presiding Patriarch, see Irene M. Bates, "Transformation of Charisma in the Mormon Church: A History of the Office of Presiding Patriarch, 1833-1979," Ph.D. diss., 1991, University of California, Los Angeles.

108. The Irene Bates Collection contains seventy blessings given by Joseph Smith, Sr. Those which specify the authority by which Smith gave the blessings cite only the "Holy Priesthood." In no instance does the phrase "Patriarchal Priesthood" appear, thus strengthening the assertion that the 1833 use of "Patriarchal Priesthood" referred merely to the office of patriarch.

109. That the office was intended to be passed to the oldest son was indicated in a blessing which Joseph Smith, Jr., gave to his brother Hyrum at the same time: "He shall stand in the tracts of his father and be numbered among those who hold the right of patriarchal priesthood" (ibid.). Blessings given by Joseph Smith, Jr., to his other brothers (Samuel, William, and Don Carlos) at the same time made no reference to "Patriarchal Priesthood."

were on our return home my brother Joseph spoke very frequently with regard to patriarchs and patriarchal blessings, and finally said he, "When we get to Kirtland I am going to ask Brother Joseph Smith if we can have the privilege of calling our father's family together and receiving a patriarchal blessing under the hands of our father." Brother Joseph Young saw the Prophet Joseph Smith, and said he, "I do not see any inconsistency in this at all, and I think it would be a good thing." A day was appointed for the family to gather together, and Brother Joseph Smith was asked to attend this meeting. He came, and while we sat chatting together on the things of the kingdom, the Prophet said, "I believe it will be necessary for Father Young to receive his patriarchal blessing and be ordained a patriarch, so that he can bless his family;" and after our little meeting was opened Brother Joseph Smith laid his hands upon Father Young and blessed him and gave him an ordination to bless his family—his own posterity. When this was done Father Young laid his hands upon the children that were there, commencing at the eldest and continuing until he had blessed all that were in the house. We were not all there, some of the brothers and sisters were absent. After that, Brother Joseph Smith said, "I think I will get my father's family together and we will have a patriarchal blessing from Father Smith." He did so. In a few days he called his father's house together and gave him the authority to bless his children, and Father Smith blessed his children. In the course of a few weeks, I think, Brother Joseph Smith received a revelation to ordain patriarchs, and he called his father's family together again, and gave his father the full ordination of patriarch for the church; and in this revelation the Lord instructed him to have a record kept, in which should be written all the blessings of the patriarch of the church, and from these circumstances were ordained a few, but only a very few, patriarchs.[110]

The first recorded blessings given by Joseph Smith, Sr., were on 9 December 1834 to Smith family members and their wives.[111] Beginning in 1835 he gave blessings to other church members. By the time the Kirtland House of the Lord was dedicated in 1836 the patriarchal blessing had become an important rite of passage for Latter-day Saints.

In addressing the elders at the solemn assembly in the Kirtland House of the Lord on 30 March 1836, Joseph Smith said "that I had

---

110. Brigham Young discourse, 30 June 1873, in *Deseret News Weekly*, 23 July 1873, 388.

111. Patriarchal Blessings Book, Vol. 1. Copies of the blessings of Hyrum and Jerusha Smith, Joseph and Emma Smith, Samuel and Mary Smith, and William Smith are in the Irene Bates Collection.

now completed the organization of the Church and we had passed through all the necessary ceremonies."[112] Four days later the vision of Elijah may have given him second thoughts.

Phase 5. Elijah and the Fullness of Priesthood, April 1836-April 1844

On Sunday morning, 3 April 1836, Joseph Smith and Oliver Cowdery sequestered themselves behind curtains in the House of the Lord. As they prayed they experienced a series of visions, first of Jesus, then Moses, Elias, and finally Elijah:

> After this vision had closed, another great and glorious vision burst upon us; for Elijah the prophet, who was taken to heaven without tasting death, stood before us, and said:
>
> Behold, the time has fully come, which was spoken of by the mouth of Malachi—testifying that he (Elijah) should be sent, before the great and dreadful day of the Lord come—
>
> To turn the hearts of the fathers to the children, and the children to the fathers, lest the whole earth be smitten with a curse—
>
> Therefore the keys of this dispensation are committed into your hands; and by this ye may know that the great and dreadful day of the Lord is near, even at the doors (DC, LDS 110:13-16).

From an obscure figure in the early years of the Restoration, Elijah emerged as the dominant figure both in priesthood and in afterlife theology. At the time of Smith's death in 1844, Elijah's importance was second only to that of Jesus Christ. In order to understand this important doctrinal development, it is necessary to examine the references to Elijah according to the time at which they were written. For example, the account of Moroni's 1823 visit to Joseph Smith, which included a promise of Elijah's return, was not written until 1838[113] and reflects the theology of the later date.

That the expectation of Elijah's return dates to the early Restoration is indicated by a revelation dated December 1830 in which Sidney Rigdon was told that he had unknowingly been a forerunner both of

---

112. Joseph Smith diary, 30 Mar. 1836, in Faulring, 155.

113. This account, written as part of Joseph Smith's history of the church, was first published in *Times and Seasons* 3 (15 Apr. 1842): 753 but was not published in LDS editions of the Doctrine and Covenants until 1876; subsequent LDS editions have included it as Sec. 2. RLDS editions have never included this account.

Jesus (whose return to initiate the Restoration had already occurred) and of Elijah (whose return was still anticipated).[114] However, Elijah's role in the Restoration was not described, nor does any other record exist from the period between 1830 and 1835 to further clarify his role. But in preparing revelations for publication in the 1835 Doctrine and Covenants, Smith added several verses to the Rigdon revelation. Whereas the 1830 text stated merely that Elijah would come, the new verses added that Elijah held "the keys of the power of turning the hearts of the fathers to the children and the hearts of the children to the fathers, that the whole earth may not be smitten with a curse," repeating the essence of Malachi's prophecy (DC, 1835 XXIX:2).[115]

One year later, when Smith and Cowdery experienced the vision of Elijah, the essence of Malachi's prophecy was unchanged. The hearts of fathers and children would be turned to each other. But whereas the redacted revelation of 1835 only spoke of Elijah's keys, the vision of 1836 committed them to Smith and Cowdery (DC, LDS 110:16). No explanation was given regarding what this may have meant.[116] Two years later, in 1838, when Smith began to dictate the history of the church, he returned to the prophecy of Malachi. The history described the initial visit of Moroni in 1823 and Moroni's quotation of Malachi with a significant change from the biblical text. While earlier references spoke of fathers and children, Moroni focused on children's adherence to tradition and said the earth would otherwise be "utterly wasted": "And he [Elijah] shall plant in the hearts of the

---

114. The earliest publication of this revelation was BC XXXVII (1833). An earlier reference to Elijah was published in the Book of Mormon, p. 505, wherein the resurrected Jesus Christ quotes the Old Testament prophecy of Malachi. There is no inference in this passage of Elijah's return in the context of the Restoration.

115. In revising the King James Bible, a project completed in July 1833 (see Matthews, *"A Plainer Translation,"* 96), Smith made no changes to Malachi's prophecy (Mal. 4:5-6). In editing the above revelation, Smith clearly drew from the King James text without changing its meaning. As will be seen, however, subsequent references added new meaning to the biblical text.

116. The turning of hearts of fathers and children to each other is now associated by the LDS church with the temple-based ordinance of "sealing" children to parents. At the time of this vision (1836) neither the word "seal," nor the concept, nor the formal ordinance had been introduced.

children the promises made to the fathers, and the hearts of the children shall turn to their fathers, if it were not so the whole earth would be utterly wasted at his coming."[117] In addition, the 1838 account quoted Moroni linking for the first time Elijah and priesthood: "Behold, I will reveal unto you the Priesthood by the hand of Elijah the prophet before the coming of the great and dreadful day of the Lord."[118]

In the summer of 1839 Smith gave a discourse on priesthood in which he again referred to Elijah, this time making explicit a necessary relationship between living and dead: "The hearts of the children will have to be turned to the fathers, & the fathers to the children living or dead to prepare them for the coming of the Son of Man. If Elijah did not come the whole earth would be smitten."[119] The following summer Smith gave form to the relationship between living and dead when he announced that it was the privilege of Latter-day Saints to be baptized in behalf of their deceased kin who had died without baptism.[120]

On 5 October 1840 Smith returned to the relationship of Elijah

---

117. Jessee, *Personal Writings*, 204. Although not explicitly referring to deceased fathers, this account represents an incremental step towards a doctrine of salvation of the dead through intervention by the living.

118. Ibid. Several lines of evidence suggest that this account, though cast in a setting of 1823, reflects the understanding of 1838 and is thus anachronistic. As has been shown, the term "priesthood" was not used until 1832—three years after the Restoration events and nine years after Moroni's visit. Earlier accounts of Moroni's visit failed to mention either Elijah or priesthood. Also, no Restoration reference to Elijah prior to the 1838 account mentions or infers a relationship between Elijah and priesthood. The sequential redactions of Malachi 4:6, which formed the basis of a developing theology of afterlife, demonstrate a continuum.

119. Although some writers have dated this sermon 2 July 1839, it appears more appropriate to leave the date uncertain but prior to 8 Aug. 1839. For a detailed explanation of the dating, see Andrew F. Ehat and Lyndon W. Cook, eds., *The Words of Joseph Smith: The Contemporary Accounts of the Nauvoo Discourses of the Prophet Joseph Smith* (Provo, UT: Religious Studies Center, Brigham Young University, 1980), 22.

120. The announcement was made during a sermon at the funeral of Seymour Brunson on 15 August 1840. Eyewitness accounts, written by Jane Neymon and Simon Baker, are in the Journal History of the LDS church under that date, LDS archives.

and priesthood. In what was apparently the only discourse for which he ever prepared a text, he acknowledged that in spite of the Restoration events of 1829, 1831, and 1836, there was more to "priesthood" than had yet been revealed:

> As it is generally supposed that Sacrifice was entirely done away when the great sacrif[ic]e was offered up—and that there will be no necessity for the ordinance of Sacrifice in the future, but those who assert this, are certainly not acquainted with the duties, privileges and authority of the priesthood. or with the prophets[.] The offering of Sacrifice has ever been connected and forms a part of the duties of the priesthood. It began with the pries[t]hood and will be continued untill after the coming of Christ from generation to generation—We freequently have mention made of the offering of Sacrifice by the servants of the most high in antient days prior to the law of moses, [and will] See which ordinances will be continued *when the priesthood is restored with all its authority power and blessings*. Elijah was the last prophet that held the keys of this priesthood, and who will, before the last dispensation, restore the authority and delive[r] the Keys of this priesthood in order that all the ordinances may be attended to in righteousness.
>
> It is true the Saviour had authority and power to bestow this blessing but the Sons of Levi were too prejudi[ced]. And I will send Elijah the Prophet before the great and terrible day of the Lord &c., &c.
>
> Why send Elijah[?] [B]ecause he holds the Keys of the Authority to administer in all the ordinances of the priesthood and without the authority is given the ordinances could not be administered in righteousness.[121]

This discourse stated explicitly that the concept of priesthood was fluid, that one could not point to a single date when "the priesthood was restored." The events of 1829, 1831, and 1836 were all part of the gradual restoration of priesthood, a restoration best understood as a process rather than an event. Smith not only linked Elijah with priesthood but placed Elijah at its forefront. Perhaps it is not surprising that only once after this discourse did Smith ever refer to the Restoration events of 1829 and 1831 and then mentioned only an unnamed

---

121. Joseph Smith discourse, 5 Oct. 1840 (emphasis added). The original manuscript, in the hand of Robert B. Thompson, is in LDS archives. The discourse was published in its entirety in Ehat and Cook, 38-44.

angel who restored authority to baptize. This reference was part of an 1844 discourse highlighting the priority of Elijah's authority.[122]

One year after the initiation of baptisms for the dead Smith delivered a discourse which specifically linked Elijah to the restoration of that ordinance.[123] Two epistles in September 1842 further reinforced the relationship among Elijah, priesthood, and salvation of the dead. The first, written on 1 September, stated "for I am about to restore many things to the earth, saith the Lord of Hosts" (DC, LDS 127:8).[124] The second, written five days later, connected St. Paul's reference to being "baptized for the dead" (1 Cor. 15:29) to the mission of Elijah. Quoting Malachi's prophecy of Elijah, Smith continued:

> The earth will be smitten with a curse unless there is a welding link of some kind between the fathers and the children, upon some subject or other—and behold what is that subject? It is the baptism for the dead. For we without them cannot be made perfect; neither can they without us be made perfect. . . . It is necessary . . . that a whole and complete and perfect union, and welding together of dispensations, and keys, and powers, and glories should take place (DC, LDS 128:18).[125]

A year later, in August 1843, Smith applied for the first time the term "sealing" to the relationship between parents and children, invoking in the process the name of Elijah: "A measure of this sealing is to confirm upon their head in common with Elijah the doctrine of election or the covenant with Abraham—which when a Father & mother of a family have entered into[,] their children who have not transgressed are secured by the seal where with the Parents have been sealed."[126]

---

122. This was a discourse in the Nauvoo temple, 10 March 1844, published in Ehat and Cook, 327-36.

123. Joseph Smith discourse, 3 Oct. 1841, in Ehat and Cook, 76-79.

124. This was first published in *Times and Seasons* 3 (15 Sept. 1842): 919-20.

125. *Times and Seasons* 3 (1 Oct. 1842): 934-36. Although the similarity between "welding" and "sealing" is obvious, the latter term had not yet been used in the context of binding one person to another, although in 1831 it had been used in a related context wherein "sealing up to eternal life" indicated binding an individual to God.

126. Joseph Smith discourse, funeral of Judge Elias Higbee, 13

Two weeks later Smith preached a sermon on priesthood, deriving his remarks from Hebrews, Chapter 7, and stated that the author of the epistle was referring to three priesthoods: Melchizedek, Patriarchal, and Aaronic (or Levitical). The account of Franklin D. Richards reported: "There are 3 grand principles or orders of Priesthood portrayed in this chapter[:] 1st Levitical which was never able to administer a Blessing but only to bind heavy burdens which neither they nor their father [was] able to bear[;] 2 Abrahams Patriarchal power which is the greatest yet experienced in this church[;] [and] That of Melchisedec who had still greater power." James Burgess wrote: "Hebrewes 7 chap. Paul is here treating of three priesthoods, namely the preisthood of Aron, Abraham, and Melchizedek, Abraham's preisthood was of greater power than Levi's and Melchizedeck's was of greater power than that of Abraham." Levi Richards wrote: "J. Smith . . . afterwards preached from Hebrews 7 upon the priesthood Aaronic, Patriarchal, & Melchisedec."[127] Of these, only the Aaronic and Patriarchal had yet been fully experienced in the church. While it sounds inconsistent to say that the highest of the three, Melchizedek, was not yet fully developed, Smith was about to embark on the ultimate step in its restoration. Only one month after this discourse he bestowed on members of his inner circle the "second anointing," also termed the "fullness of the Priesthood."[128] Wishing to place this in a separate category, Smith used the text of Hebrews, Chapter 7, to validate the concept of three priesthoods rather than the two which previously had been formulated. Abraham (a patriarch) paid tithes to Melchizedek and was thus portrayed as subordinate to him. Having previously associated Abraham (and other Old Testament patriarchs) with Melchizedek Priesthood, Smith merely kept the essence of what had been called

---

Aug. 1843. Accounts of this discourse by Willard Richards, Howard and Martha Coray, Franklin D. Richards, William Clayton, and Levi Richards are in Ehat and Cook, 238-42. The passage quoted here is from the Coray account.

127. Ibid., 243-48.

128. For discussions of this subject, see Andrew F. Ehat, "Joseph Smith's Introduction of Temple Ordinances and the 1844 Mormon Succession Question," M.A. thesis, Brigham Young University, 1982; and David J. Buerger, "'The Fullness of the Priesthood': The Second Anointing in Latter-day Saint Theology and Practice," *Dialogue: A Journal of Mormon Thought* 16 (Spring 1983): 10-44.

Melchizedek Priesthood, renamed it after the patriarchs, and applied the former term to the new order. Since the second anointing had not been introduced at the time of this sermon, Smith was correct in saying that the newly renamed Patriarchal Priesthood was the greatest yet experienced in the church.[129] In discussing the highest of the three priesthoods (now to be called Melchizedek), Smith again invoked the name of Elijah, stating: "how shall god come to the rescue of this generation. he shall send Elijah."[130]

On 21 January 1844, Joseph Smith delivered a sermon in which he summarized the mission of Elijah as he then understood it:

> What is the object of this important mission [of Elijah] or how is it to be fulfilled[?] The keys are to be deliverd[,] the spirit of Elijah is to Come, The gospel to be esstablished[,] the Saints of God gatherd Zion built up, & the Saints to Come up as Saviors on mount Zion[.] [B]ut how are they to become Saviors on Mount Zion[?] [B]y building their temples[,] erecting their Baptismal fonts & going forth & receiving all the ordinances, Baptisms, confirmations, washings anointings ordinations & sealing powers upon our heads in behalf of all our Progenitors who are dead & redeem them that they may come forth in the first resurrection & be exalted to thrones of glory with us, & herein is the chain that binds the hearts of the fathers to the children & the children to the Fathers *which fulfills the mission of Elijah.*[131]

Not only had Elijah become the paramount figure in priesthood theology, he now was seen as primarily responsible for all salvific ordinances for the living and the dead. Three months prior to his own death, Smith reinforced Elijah's position at the pinnacle of the priesthood hierarchy and indeed the entire Kingdom of God on earth:

> The spirit power & calling of Elijah is that ye have power to hold the keys of the revelations, ordinances, oracles, powers & endowments of

---

129. Brigham Young, knowing of the forthcoming anointing, had said three weeks earlier that if any in the church had the Melchizedek Priesthood, he did not know it. "For any person to have the fullness of that priesthood he must be a king & a Priest" (Wilford Woodruff diary, 6 Aug. 1843, in Scott G. Kenney, ed., *Wilford Woodruff's Journal* [Salt Lake City: Signature Books, 1983], 2:271).

130. Ehat and Cook, 244.

131. Joseph Smith discourse, 21 Jan. 1844 (emphasis added), *Wilford Woodruff's Journal*, 2:341-43, 21 Jan. 1844; also in Ehat and Cook, 318.

the fullness of the Melchizedek Priesthood & of the Kingdom of God on the Earth & to receive, obtain & perform all the ordinances belonging to the Kingdom of God even unto the sealing of the hearts of the fathers unto the children & the hearts of the children unto the fathers even those who are in heaven. . . .
This is the spirit of Elijah that we redeem our dead & connect ourselves with our fathers which are in heaven & seal up our dead to come forth in the first resurrection & here we want the power of Elijah to seal those who dwell on earth to those who dwell in heaven. This is the power of Elijah & the keys of the Kingdom of Jehovah.[132]

In the same discourse Smith returned to a bipartite model of priesthood. Patriarchal Priesthood was now folded into Melchizedek Priesthood, which continued to include the "fullness of the Priesthood," or second anointing.[133] Smith's final reference to Elijah came in the famous King Follett Sermon on 7 April 1844 when he stated that "the greatest responsibility in this world is to seek after our dead." He equated that responsibility with the mission of Elijah.[134]

Summary

In reviewing the development of Latter-day Saint priesthood during Joseph Smith's ministry, one might be reminded of the work of Harvard biologist Stephen Jay Gould who described biological evolution as "punctuated equilibrium"—that is, a gradual process of development accented at irregular intervals by major changes over brief periods of time. In the case of priesthood the "punctuation marks" are readily identifiable in 1823, 1829, 1831, and 1836. Between the punctuation marks came periods of incremental change, as Smith gradually came to understand the implications of his visionary experiences and changed policy and doctrine to reflect his own under-

---

132. Joseph Smith discourse, 10 Mar. 1844, in *Wilford Woodruff's Journal*, 2:359-66, 10 Mar. 1844. The account of Woodruff, plus those of James Burgess, Franklin D. Richards, Willard Richards, Thomas Bullock, and John Solomon Fullmer are in Ehat and Cook, 327-36.

133. The Lesser Priesthood had undergone little change since 1835, although a variety of synonyms—Aaronic, Levitical, Lesser, and Priesthood of Elias—had been used at various times. It was not changed by Smith's reversion to the bipartite model.

134. Joseph Smith discourse, 7 Apr. 1844, William Clayton account, in Ehat and Cook, 340-62.

standing. Nevertheless, these "quiet periods" were of enormous significance, seen most clearly in the case of the theology surrounding Elijah. Whereas the vision of Elijah was important, he was but one of four figures appearing to Smith and Cowdery that day. It was not the vision alone but the added process of reflection, prayer, and gradual enlightenment over the following eight years that moved Elijah from obscurity to virtually unparalleled importance.

The development of priesthood is evident in contemporary accounts of the early years of the Mormon restoration. Five relatively distinct phases have been identified. In the earliest years no explicit notion of authority was mentioned in any records relating to the Restoration. Smith acted in his unique position by virtue of his relationship with Moroni rather than by formal ordination. The dictation of the Book of Mormon was accompanied by a May 1829 bestowal on Smith and Oliver Cowdery of "authority" to baptize each other, followed in early June 1829 by "authority" to confer the Holy Ghost and ordain other officers. The term "priesthood" was not used; rather, men acted by virtue of the office to which they had been ordained. The terms "elder" and "disciple" were interchangeable and implied authority equal to that of the twelve apostles of Jerusalem. By the latter part of 1829 preference was given to the term "apostle." It was later explained that "elder" was an administrative title, while "apostle" referred to witnesses of Jesus Christ.

In 1831, as Smith revised the book of Genesis, he added several verses describing an ancient order to which Melchizedek belonged as a high priest which entitled him to immense this-worldly powers. At a conference in June 1831 ordinations were performed to a new order called both the Order of Melchizedek and the High Priesthood. This was accompanied by a pentecostal outpouring of miracles. A revelation in November formally established the office of high priest which then became synonymous with High Priesthood.

During this important period a number of parallel yet interrelated developments took place. Church government was centralized, and Smith was designated "President of the High Priesthood." Four governing bodies were formed to assist him, but Smith's primacy over all these was explicit. The offices of elder, priest, teacher, and deacon were organized into formal groups, each with a president chosen from among its members.

Amidst these organizational developments a new understanding of priesthood emerged, while a hierarchy of offices—with bishops and elders being appendages to high priests, and teachers and deacons as appendages to priests—was formulated. In March 1835 priests, teachers, and deacons became offices in an "Aaronic Priesthood," while elders and high priests were in a "Melchizedek Priesthood."

Shortly after this 1835 revelation Smith first identified the angels who years before had bestowed on him the authority to baptize and ordain: John the Baptist and Peter, James, and John, respectively. Just a year later, however, their roles began to be eclipsed by the Old Testament prophet Elijah. It gradually became apparent that through Elijah's instrumentality all salvific ordinances for the living and the dead were made both possible and essential.

Oliver Cowdery had participated with Smith in each of the angelic ministrations associated with priesthood: John the Baptist and Peter, James, and John in 1829, and Elijah in 1836. However, at the time of Cowdery's dissociation and subsequent excommunication in 1838, Smith had not begun to make the association among Elijah, priesthood, and salvation theology. Shortly after Smith's death, Cowdery began to show renewed interest in the church, eventually rejoining in 1848. In 1846, writing to Phineas Young, he spoke only of the events of 1829: "I have been sensitive on this subject, I admit; but I ought to be so—you would be, under the circumstances, had you stood in the presence of John, with our departed Joseph, to receive the Lesser Priesthood—and in the presence of Peter, to receive the Greater, and look down through time, and witness the effects these two must produce."[135] Similarly, when he reentered the church in 1848 Cowdery recounted the events of 1829 but was silent concerning Elijah.[136] Since Cowdery was the only living witness to the events he described, it is likely that his audience, both immediate and extended, focused on what he described, not on what he did not describe. Alternatively, church members did not yet understand Elijah theology in the same light as Smith. Since Smith was sole exponent of the theology, his death, and the abrupt halt it brought to the developing theology, was

---

135. Oliver Cowdery to Phineas Young, 23 Mar. 1846, Ms 3408 fd 3, LDS archives. This letter was quoted in an LDS general conference address by Alonzo A. Hinckley on 8 April 1934 and published in *One Hundred Fourth Annual Conference of The Church of Jesus Christ of Latter-day Saints* (Salt Lake City: LDS Church, 1934), 129.

136. Reuben Miller journal, 21 Oct. 1848, Ms 1392, LDS archives.

probably sufficient to effect the subsequent silence on the subject. This would explain the otherwise baffling silence of both churches on a matter so important to Joseph Smith.

Chapter Two

Offices

When Joseph Smith and Oliver Cowdery were given authority to baptize, they were not ordained to a specific office. The earliest first-hand account of the event is in Smith's 1832 history which describes "the reception of the holy Priesthood by the ministring of Aangels to administer the letter of the Gospel."[1] Later accounts by both Smith and Cowdery, while reflecting the developing nomenclature, made no mention of a specific office. Cowdery wrote: "we received under his hand the holy priesthood, as he said, 'upon you my fellow servants, in the name of Messiah I confer this priesthood and this authority.'"[2] He added that "He [Smith] was ordained by the Angel John, unto the lesser or Aaronic priesthood, in company with myself . . ."[3] Smith elaborated:

> While we were thus employed, praying, and calling upon the Lord, a messenger from heaven descended in a cloud of light, and having laid his hands upon us, he ordained us, saying unto us, "Upon you my fellow servants, in the name of Messiah, I confer the priesthood of Aaron, which holds the keys of the ministering of angels, and of the

---

1. Dean C. Jessee, ed., *The Personal Writings of Joseph Smith* (Salt Lake City: Deseret Book Co., 1984), 4. Although the Book of Mormon made it clear that priests were authorized to baptize, it implies that teachers could perform the same ordinance (Alma 15:13, in The Book of Mormon [Salt Lake City: Church of Jesus Christ of Latter-day Saints, 1981], hereafter cited in the text as BM, LDS).

2. Cowdery, in *Messenger and Advocate* 1 (Oct. 1834): 15-16.

3. Cowdery in, "Patriarchal Blessing Book," Vol. 1, Sept. 1835, archives, Historical Department, Church of Jesus Christ of Latter-day Saints, Salt Lake City, Utah (hereafter LDS archives).

gospel of repentance, and of baptism by immersion, for the remission of sins" . . . and he commanded us to go and be baptized . . .

Accordingly we went and were baptized, I baptized him first, and afterwards he baptized me, after which I laid my hands upon his head and ordained him to the Aaronic priesthood, and afterwards he laid his hands on me and ordained me to the same priesthood, for so we were commanded.[4]

By August 1829, as Mormons began proselyting, adult male converts were ordained to one of the three offices described in the Book of Mormon: teacher, priest, and elder/disciple.[5] The offices of bishop and deacon, neither of which was mentioned in the Book of Mormon, were introduced early in 1831, followed by high priest in late 1831, patriarch in 1833, and seventy and apostle in 1835. Thus all nine ordained offices currently recognized in the Latter-day Saint churches were in place by 1835, whereas the larger concept of "priesthood," of which they were part, continued to evolve through 1844, the year of Smith's death.

The manner in which these offices were introduced, occurring over six years and with no indication of a prior blueprint, raises the question of why these and not other offices of a similar nature became attached to priesthood through ordination. For instance, a case may be made that the office of high councilor functioned much like that of apostle. Indeed, two types of high councils were formed in the mid-1830s: the "Standing High Council," with responsibility over stakes (dioceses), and the "Traveling High Council," with responsibility outside of stakes. Yet the latter body was composed of apostles, an ordained office, while the former consisted of high councilors, which were never considered officers, even though some men were "ordained" to the calling.[6]

A related case is that of "pastor." Although included in Smith's

---

4. Smith, in *Times and Seasons* 3 (1 Aug. 1842): 865-66.

5. David Whitmer, *An Address to All Believers in Christ* (Richmond, MO: the Author, 1887), 32.

6. For example, in 1836 Thomas Grover, Noah Packard, Joseph Kingsbury, and Samuel James were all "ordained" high councilors in Kirtland ("Kirtland Council Minutes," 13 Jan. 1836, LDS archives). Similarly, in 1841 James Allred and Leonard Soby were "ordained . . . to the office of High Councellors of Nauvoo" ("Nauvoo High Council Minutes," 6 Apr. 1841, LDS archives).

1842 "Articles of Faith" as part of the primitive church organization mirrored by the Mormon restoration,[7] pastor did not become an ordained office during Smith's lifetime. In 1856 Apostle Franklin D. Richards created the ordained office of pastor in the British Mission "to take charge of three or four Conferences, to preside over the Presidents, and to teach and counsel them by the light of the spirit of Zion."[8] The following year Apostle Orson Pratt endorsed the concept and further outlined its duties.[9] The office apparently did not extend beyond the British Isles, and by 1861 its name was changed to district president.[10]

In attempting to define the rationale behind the nine offices now recognized by the Utah church, one is thus constrained by historical irregularities, complicated by the fact that no comprehensive list of offices was ever contained in canonical writings. While it may seem appropriate to define "office" as something to which one is "ordained," use of the word "ordain" during Smith's ministry carried a broader connotation, with men and women often "ordained" to callings and responsibilities never associated with priesthood offices. An alternative definition might assume that offices named in Latter-day Saint revelations would all be included in the priesthood umbrella. However, high councilors were the subject of an entire revelation.[11] Another definition might rest upon biblical precedent. All nine offices are mentioned in the Bible, although the assigned functions were often without biblical precedent. As with pastors, inclusion in the Bible did not guarantee a place in the Restoration. Therefore, one is left with a circular and not entirely satisfactory definition of "office" as a calling with a biblical precedent to which men were ordained and which

---

7. "We believe in the same organization that existed in the Primitive Church, viz., apostles, prophets, pastors, teachers, evangelists, etc."

8. "Minutes of a Special Conference of the Authorities of the European Missions," 21 July 1856, in *Millennial Star* 18 (30 Aug. 1856): 545-46.

9. "Duties of Pastors and Presidents," *Millennial Star* 19 (8 Aug. 1857): 504-505.

10. George Q. Cannon, in *Millennial Star* 23 (12 Jan. 1861): 24-25.

11. See *Doctrine and Covenants of The Church of the Latter Day Saints: Carefully Selected from the Revelations of God* (Kirtland, OH: F. G. Williams & Co., 1835): V; hereafter cited in the text as DC, 1835.

gradually became accepted in the church as an office. In other words, offices became such by convention.

Teacher

The distinction between the offices of teacher and priest is ambiguous in the Book of Mormon. Nephi "consecrate[d] Jacob and Joseph, that they should be priests and teachers over the land of my people" (BM, LDS, 2 Ne. 5:26). A later passage confirms this dual consecration: "For I, Jacob, and my brother Joseph had been consecrated priests and teachers of this people, by the hand of Nephi" (BM, LDS, Jacob 1:18). Responsibilities were common to the two offices. Both were commissioned to baptize (BM, LDS, Alma 15:13) and preach (BM, LDS, Moro. 3:3), although priests, not teachers, were authorized to administer "the flesh and blood of Christ unto the church" (BM, LDS, Moro. 4:1).

An 1829 revelation to Oliver Cowdery[12] repeated verbatim the job description of Moroni 3:3 but mentioned only priests. By April 1831 the duties of teachers had been expanded and further differentiated:

> The teacher's duty is to watch over the church always, and be with them and strengthen them, and see that there is no iniquity in the church, nor no hardness with each other, nor no lying nor backbiting nor no evil speaking; and see that the church meets together oft, and also see that every member does his duty, and he is to take the lead of the meetings in the absence of the elder or the priest, and is to be assisted always and in all his duties in the church by the deacons. But neither the teacher nor the deacon has the authority to baptize nor administer the sacrament; but are to warn, exhort, expound and teach and invite all to come to Christ.[13]

This statement is significant both for what it says and for what it does not say. The first phrase, "to watch over the church always," became the primary role for teachers for the rest of the nineteenth century until a decision was made to encourage the ordination of boys

---

12. "The Articles of the Church," in Robert J. Woodford, "The Historical Development of the Doctrine and Covenants," Ph.D. diss., Brigham Young University, 1974, 288.

13. "The Articles and Covenants of the Church of Christ," *Painesville Telegraph*, 19 Apr. 1831.

rather than men to this office. Also of significance is its silence regarding any ordinances which teachers could perform.[14] At no time during Joseph Smith's ministry did teachers receive specific authorization to perform ordinances.

The same revelation which outlined the duties of teachers specified those of priests. Ironically, the injunction to priests to "visit the house of each member"[15] became the main function of teachers. Lucy Mack Smith, mother of Joseph Smith, wrote: "I will now return to Waterloo after Joseph and his father left [1831]. William being one of the teachers visited the Church calling on every family (as our custom is) [and] he prayed with them and did not leave the house untill every member of the family prayed vocally that was over eight years old."[16] The pastoral role of teachers was strengthened by an 1832 revelation which mandated that high priests, elders, and priests were to travel and preach, while "the deacons and teachers should be appointed to watch over the church, to be standing ministers unto the church" (DC, 1835 IV:22, 22 and 23 Sept. 1832). For the remainder of Smith's ministry they functioned both in watching over church members and as standing ministers—or presiding officers—over church congregations.

When teachers were organized into a quorum in December 1834 a more systematic oversight became possible.[17] Beginning with the entry for 25 December 1834, the quorum minutebook frequently detailed the teachers' concern for errant members. Assignments were given to labor with specific individuals. An 1835 church newspaper article commented on the teachers' activities: "They must strengthen the members' faith; persuade such as are out of the way to repent, and turn to God and live; meekly persuade and urge every one to forgive one another all their trespasses, offences and sins, that they may work out their own salvation with fear and trembling."[18] Teachers mediated disputes to avoid the necessity of formal church or civil judicial proceedings. Church historian John Corrill wrote: "If two members

---

14. The 1835 revision of this revelation further restricted teachers and deacons by forbidding them to "lay on hands" (DC, 1835 II:11).

15. "The Articles of the Church," in Woodford.

16. Lucy Mack Smith Manuscript, 131, LDS archives.

17. The activities of teachers are chronicled in "Teacher's Quorum Minutebook, Dec., 1834-Dec., 1845," LDS archives.

18. *Messenger and Advocate* 1 (June 1835): 138.

had a difficulty, they were to settle it between themselves, or by the assistance of another, according to the scriptures; but if they could not do this, then it went before the bishop's court for trial."[19]

That the teachers' function was crucial to the welfare of the Saints was stated most eloquently by First Presidency member Sidney Rigdon in 1838:

> [President Rigdon said] that the foundation of the happiness of the Church rests upon the heads of the Teachers and Deacons, whose duty it is to go from house to house and see that each family in the Church is kept in order, and that the children are taught the principles of righteousness . . .
>
> He compared the Elders to quarriers of stone, who merely quarried the stones and brought them to the building, where the Priests, Teachers, and Deacons, are polishers, whose duty it is to prepare them for the building.[20]

A second function of teachers was to preside over congregations.[21] Corrill wrote: "The high priests, elders, and priests, were to travel and preach, but the teachers and deacons were to be standing ministers to the church. Hence, in the last organizing of the church, each branch of the church chose a teacher to preside over them, whose duty it was to take particular charge of that branch, and report from time to time to the general conference of elders."[22] A meeting of the high council at Far West, Missouri, in 1838 formally acknowledged the presiding authority of the teacher:

> Resolved, by the High Council that it be considered that no High Priest, Elder or Priest (except the Presidency, High Council and Bishoprick) has any right or authority to preside over or take the charge of any Branch, Society or neighbourhood within the bounds of this Stake: but that the teachers, assisted by the deacons, be consid-

---

19. John Corrill, *Brief History of the Church of Christ of Latter Day Saints . . .* (St. Louis: Printed for the Author, 1839), chap. 13.

20. Donald Q. Cannon and Lyndon W. Cook, eds., *Far West Record: Minutes of the Church of Jesus Christ of Latter-day Saints, 1830-1844* (Salt Lake City: Deseret Book Co., 1983), 199, 6 July 1838.

21. Although this role is foreign to Latter-day Saints today, it must be recalled that bishops did not preside over congregations until the Utah period of LDS history.

22. Corrill, chap. 13.

ered the standing ministry to preside each over his respective branch of the Stake agreeable to the covenants.

3rd Resolved that we recommend to all High Priests, Elders and Priests who are in good standing & friends to Joseph Smith jr, the Prophet that they do not take the lead of nor appoint meetings in any branch or neighbourhood of Saints within the bounds of this Stake without the invitation or consent of the Presiding officer of that branch. We also, consider that the teacher, who is the presiding officer, has a right to object to any official character, who may come among them to officiate, who is not in good standing or a friend to the true cause of Christ. And also, that the teacher report, to the High Council, such as are unruly or teach corrupt doctrine among them.

4th Resolved that the High Council recommend to each neighbourhood or settlement of Saints, within the bounds of this Stake, to choose for themselves a teacher, who is skilled in the word of God, faithful in his ministry, full of the Holy Ghost, and a friend to Joseph Smith jr, the Prophet of God, to take the watchcare over them, and preside agreeably to the covenants, who shall be assisted by the other teachers and deacons in the Branch.[23]

Of the nine priesthood offices, eight were organized for group function during Smith's ministry, the exception being the office of patriarch. Of those eight, it appears that teachers had the greatest impact in terms of ministering to lay members.

Priest

As seen in the previous section, the one duty which priests in the Book of Mormon could perform that teachers could not was administering the sacrament of the Lord's Supper. By 1831 the role of priests as baptists was clarified.[24] Priests were also allowed to ordain certain other officers: "The priests' duty is to preach, teach, expound, exhort, and baptize and administer the sacrament, and to visit the house of each member, and exhort them to pray vocally and in secret, and also to attend to all family duties, to ordain priests, teachers and deacons, and to take the lead in meetings."[25]

---

23. *Far West Record*, 142-43, 24 Feb. 1838.

24. "The Articles and Covenants of the Church of Christ," *Painesville Telegraph*, 19 Apr. 1831.

25. Ibid. Prior to this, only elders/apostles could ordain other officers. While no explanation was given for the change, the expansion of the early church likely made it advisable to decentralize this function.

Although an 1832 revelation established a hierarchy of offices with deacon and teacher subservient to priest (DC, 1835 IV:5, 22 and 23 Sept. 1832), this distinction was not significant. There is no record of priests supervising the other officers. The relative sovereignty of teachers was later indicated by a question asked of Apostle Wilford Woodruff: "Is it right for a Priest to be appointed to accompany a Teacher to visit the houses of each member?"[26]

Although priests could act as proselyting missionaries (DC, 1835 IV:22),[27] their inability to confer upon converts the gift of the Holy Ghost limited their utility. As a result most missionaries held higher offices. Thus, priests appear to have served primarily as officiators in the ordinances of baptism, administering the sacrament, and ordaining some officers. The organization of priests into quorums did not result in a significant record of group function during Smith's lifetime.

Elder

After baptism, David Whitmer took Joseph Smith and Oliver Cowdery from Pennsylvania to his father's farm in New York where, in early June 1829, Smith and Cowdery ordained each other to the office of elder.[28] The Book of Mormon described the office as superior to both teacher and priest since only elders could confer the gift of the Holy Ghost (BM, LDS, Moro. 2:1-3) and ordain other officers (3:1-4).

Initially, the responsibilities of elders paralleled those described in the Book of Mormon:

> It is his calling to baptize and to ordain other elders, priests, teachers, and deacons, and to administer the flesh and blood of Christ according to the scriptures, and to teach, expound, and exhort, and to baptize and to watch over the church, and to confirm the church by the laying on of hands and the giving of the Holy Ghost, and to take the lead of all meetings.[29]

---

26. Scott G. Kenney, ed., *Wilford Woodruff's Journal* (Midvale, UT: Signature Books, 1983), 2:278-80, 26 Aug. 1843.

27. Wilford Woodruff, for example, served his first mission as a priest.

28. "Questions asked of David Whitmer at his home in Richmond Ray County Mo. Jan 14—1885. relating to Book of Mormon, and the history of the Church of Jesus Christ of LDS by Elder Z H. Gurley," LDS archives.

29. *Painesville Telegraph*, 19 Apr. 1831.

For the first year after the formal organizing of the church in 1830, elder remained the highest ordained office. During this year four additional ordinances were introduced—blessing babies, cursing, healing the sick, and casting out evil spirits—and all were performed by elders. With the introduction of the High Priesthood in June 1831, a subdivision in the office of elder occurred, and a new ordinance was introduced. Thereafter only elders who also had been ordained to the High Priesthood could seal people to eternal life. By the end of 1831 the High Priesthood had evolved into the office of high priest. With the introduction of the offices of bishop (1831), patriarch (1833), seventy (1835), and apostle (1835),[30] each of which was associated with special responsibilities, the office of elder gradually diminished in importance. In some instances, duties previously performed by elders were reassigned to higher offices. For example, an 1831 revelation outlined a judicial role for Elders, stating that "if any man shall commit adultery, he shall be tried before two elders of the church or more."[31] The subsequent introduction of the office of bishop, and the formation of high councils composed of high priests, removed elders from judicial and regulatory responsibilities: "The Elders in Zion or in her immediate region, have no authority nor right to meddle with her affairs, to regulate or *even hold any courts*. The high council has been organized expressly to minister in all her spiritual affairs; and the Bishop and his council are set over her temporal matters; so thus the Elders acts are null and void."[32] The term "elder" continued to be used in a generic sense referring to any officer holding the higher authority later known as Melchizedek Priesthood.[33]

---

30. Although there were "apostles" in the Restoration by 1830, the separate office of apostle was not introduced until 1835.

31. *A Book of Commandments, for the Government of the Church of Christ, Organized According to Law, on the 6th of April, 1830* (Independence, MO: W. W. Phelps & Co., 1833), XLVII:5, Feb. 1831; hereafter cited in the text as BC.

32. W. W. Phelps to John M. Burk, 1 June 1835, in Journal History, 1 June 1835, LDS archives (emphasis in original). See also Whitmer, chap. 16.

33. One early example involved the 1834 designation of the "first elders" to receive an endowment in the Kirtland House of the Lord, all of whom had previously been ordained high priests (*Far West Record*, 68-69, 23 June 1834).

Apostle

Understanding the office of apostle is complicated by the fact that apostles existed since 1830, five years before the Quorum of Twelve Apostles was organized in February 1835. A group of twelve apostles functioned as early as 1830, and the primary mission of both groups was the same: declaration of the gospel to gentile and Jew.

The model for the early apostles came from the Book of Mormon, in which the Nephite twelve (BM, LDS, Moro. 3:1) held unique authority to confer the gift of the Holy Ghost (2:1-3) and to ordain other officers (3:1-4). In deference to the twelve apostles in Jerusalem, the twelve Nephites were called "disciples," a term also used in the earliest reference to the twelve of the Restoration (BC XV:27-43, June 1829). By the time the church was organized a year later the biblical term "apostle" was used.[34]

One week prior to the church's formal organization David Marks, an itinerant preacher, stayed at the Whitmer home and later wrote of his visit, "They further stated, that twelve apostles were to be appointed, who would soon confirm their mission by miracles."[35] A revelation dated the following week confirmed that two apostles had already been chosen: "There shall be a record kept among you, and in it thou [Joseph Smith] shalt be called a seer, a translator, a prophet, an apostle of Jesus Christ, an elder of the church . . . Wherefore, it behooveth me, that he [Smith] should be ordained by you, Oliver, mine apostle" (BC XXII:1, 13, 6 Apr. 1830).

On 9 June 1830 ten officers of the new church received licenses for the ministry. The license of John Whitmer, an elder, confirmed the relationship between elder and disciple/apostle: "A License Liberty Power & Authority Given to John Whitmer signifying & proveing that he is an Apostle of Jesus Christ an Elder of this Church of Christ."[36] A revelation similarly stated that "an apostle

---

34. The same revelation implied that Oliver Cowdery was already (1829) an apostle: "I speak unto you, even as unto Paul mine apostle, for you are called even with that same calling with which he was called" (BC XV:11).

35. Mariella Marks, ed., *Memoirs of the Life of David Marks, Minister of the Gospel* (Dove, NH: Free-Will Baptist Printing Establishment, 1846), 236-37. The first edition was published in 1831.

36. A photograph of the license is in Library-Archives, The Auditorium, Reorganized Church of Jesus Christ of Latter Day Saints,

is an elder,"[37] William McLellin, a member of the 1835 Quorum of Twelve Apostles, explained that "an Apostle is not an administrative officer. When they ministered they did it as Elders."[38] Although some were called apostles as late as 1832, they continued to function as elders, and it was not until 1835 that apostles were ordained as a separate office.

Direct evidence of a group of twelve apostles as early as 1830 comes from two contemporary sources. Describing attempts to sell the Book of Mormon, an 1830 newspaper article stated: "[They] have therefore sent out twelve Apostles to promulgate its doctrines . . . "[39] A letter written by Ezra Booth in 1831, just weeks after he left the movement, described his journey from Kirtland to Independence, Missouri. He wrote: "While descending the Missouri river, Peter [Whitmer] and Frederick [G. Williams], two of my company, divulged a secret respecting Oliver [Cowdery], which placed his conduct on a parallel with Ziba's; for which Ziba [Peterson] was deprived of his Elder and Apostleship. . . . And thus by commandment, poor Ziba, one of the twelve Apostles, is thrust down; while Oliver the scribe, also an Apostle, who had been guilty of similar conduct, is set on high."[40]

There is not a complete listing of the apostles chosen in 1830, though indirect evidence suggests that the number did not exceed twelve. The "Elder's license" of Edward Partridge, issued on 15 December 1830, stated that he was "ordained as an Elder under my hand" but made no mention of apostleship.[41] That twelve apostles continued to function after 1830 is suggested by Booth's letter, as well as an 1832 revelation stating "for you are mine Apostles even Gods high Priests."[42]

Independence, Missouri (hereafter RLDS Library-Archives).

37. *Painesville Telegraph*, 19 Apr. 1831.

38. William E. McLellin to Joseph Smith III, July 1872, RLDS Library-Archives.

39. *The Cleveland Herald*, 25 Nov. 1830. This article was reprinted in at least two other Ohio newspapers, the *Ashtabula Journal* (4 Dec. 1830) and the *Western Reserve Chronicle* (9 Dec. 1830).

40. Ezra Booth to Rev. I. Eddy, 21 Nov. 1831, in *Painesville Telegraph*, 6 Dec. 1831.

41. Orson F. Whitney, "Aaronic Priesthood," *The Contributor* 6 (Oct. 1884): 5.

42. "Kirtland Revelation Book," 25, revelation dated 22/23 Sept.

Between 1832 and the formation of the Quorum of Twelve Apostles in 1835, no other records describe further activities of the 1830 apostles or the ordination of additional members. However, two sources written in 1833 anticipate that additional apostles would eventually be called. Following a vision associated with the opening of the School of the Prophets in 1833, Smith said, "Brethren now you are prepared to be Apostles of Jesus Christ, for you have seen both the Father and the Son."[43] This statement is particularly significant for it represents the first time that the Latter-day Saint office of apostle reached back to its New Testament precedent which required an apostle to be an actual eyewitness to Jesus (Acts 1:21-26). Several months later a revelation gave directions "concerning the building of mine house for the preparation wherewith I design to prepare mine Apostles to prune my vineyard for the last time."[44]

For nearly two years after this revelation no further reference was made to apostles. The catalyst for the formation of the quorum in 1835 appears to have been a vision as Smith prayed to know the fate of his brethren who died during the Zion's Camp expedition. Joseph Young described Smith's account of the vision:

> When he had relieved himself of his feelings, in describing the vision, he resumed the conversation, and addressed himself to Brother Brigham Young. Said he to him, "I wish to notify all the brethren living in the branches, within a reasonable distance from this place, to meet at a General Conference on Saturday next. I shall then and there appoint twelve special witnesses, to open the door of the gospel to foreign nations, and you," said he (speaking to Brother Brigham), "will be one of them."[45]

On 14 February 1835 a meeting was held to choose "twelve men from the Church, as Apostles, to go to all nations, kindreds, tongues, and people."[46] Smith delegated to Cowdery, David Whitmer, and

---

1832, LDS archives; also DC, 1835 IV:10.

43. Zebedee Coltrin diary, Jan. 1833, LDS archives.

44. "Kirtland Revelation Book," 59, revelation dated 1 June 1833; also DC, 1835 XCV:1.

45. Joseph Young, Sr., *History of the Organization of the Seventies* (Salt Lake City: Deseret News Steam Printing Establishment, 1878), 1.

46. B. H. Roberts, ed., *History of the Church of Jesus Christ of Latter-day Saints* (Salt Lake City: Deseret Book Co., 1971), 2:186 (hereafter cited as HC).

Martin Harris, the three witnesses of the Book of Mormon, the task of selecting twelve men, one of whom described the event:

> These brethren ordained us to the apostleship, and predicted many things which should come to pass, that we should have power to heal the sick, cast out devils, raise the dead, give sight to the blind, have power to remove mountains, and all things should be subject to us through the name of Jesus Christ, and angels should minister unto us, and many more things too numerous to mention.[47]

Mastery of the elements and spirits promised a continuity with the Jerusalem twelve (Mark 16:15-18) and the Nephite twelve (BM, LDS, 4 Ne. 1:5). Another thread of continuity was related in the charge given the twelve by Cowdery:

> You have been indebted to other men in the first instance for evidence [of God's existence, and] on that you have acted. But it is necessary that you receive a testimony from Heaven for yourselves, so that you can bear testimony to the truth of the Book of Mormon. And that you have seen the face of God; that is more than the testimony of an Angel. When the proper time arrives you shall be able to bear this testimony to the world. When you bear testimony that you have seen God. This testimony God will never suffer to fall, but will bear you out. Although many will not give heed, yet others will. You will, therefore see the necessity of getting this testimony from heaven. Never cease striving until you have seen God, face to face. Strengthen your faith, cast off your doubts, your sins and all your unbelief and nothing can prevent you from coming to God. Your ordination is not full and complete till God has laid his hand upon you. We require as much to qualify us as did those who have gone before us. God is the same. If the Saviour in former days laid his hands upon his deciples. Why not in the latter Days.[48]

A letter written several decades later by another of the original twelve apostles (who had since defected) underscored both the seriousness with which this charge was taken and the contingency of its fulfilment: "[Smith's] calling and ordination of Apostles in Feb. 1835, instead of having Christ personally to call, and appoint, and ordain

---

47. Heber C. Kimball diary, in Stanley B. Kimball, ed., *On the Potter's Wheel: The Diaries of Heber C. Kimball* (Salt Lake City: Signature Books in association with Smith Research Associates, 1987), 207.

48. "Kirtland Council Minutes," 21 Feb. 1835. Compare Smith's admonition at the opening of the School of the Prophets in 1833.

them was wrong in the extreme. They could not be Apostles of Jesus, but they were only Apostles of Joseph Smith. An Apostle is witness, and he (as Paul) must see Jesus in order to be his witness."[49]

The apostles' primary responsibility during Smith's lifetime was missionary activity "to all nations, kindreds, tongues and people."[50] This was re-emphasized one week after their calling by Cowdery who said, "You are to preach the gospel to every nation,"[51] and one week thereafter by Smith who stated: "[The apostles] are to travel and preach among the Gentiles, until the Lord shall command them to go to the Jews. They are to hold the keys of this ministry to unlock the door of the kingdom of heaven unto all nations and to preach the gospel to every creature. This is the power, authority and virtue of their Apostleship."[52] The following month the same responsibility was further emphasized by revelation: "The twelve travelling counsellors are called to be the twelve apostles, or special witnesses of the name of Christ, in all the world: thus differing from other officers in the church in the duties of their calling" (DC, 1835 III:11, 28 Mar. 1835). Their role in foreign proselyting efforts is beyond question,[53] with initial activities in 1837 followed by considerable success in the British Isles beginning in 1839. At that time, the majority of apostles was serving overseas missions, something which would never recur following Smith's death.

The secondary role of the apostles was regulation of the church. Their regulatory duties were defined two weeks after their ordination when, in response to the question, "What importance is there attached to the calling of these twelve Apostles different from the other callings or offices of the Church?" Smith answered: "They are the Twelve Apostles, who are called to the office of traveling high council, who are to preside over all the churches of the Saints among the Gentiles, where there is no presidency established."[54]

---

49. William E. McLellin to Joseph Smith III, July 1872, RLDS Library-Archives.

50. HC, 2:186.

51. "Kirtland Council Minutes," 21 Feb. 1835.

52. Ibid., 27 Feb. 1835.

53. See James B. Allen, Ronald K. Esplin, and David J. Whittaker, *Men With a Mission: The Quorum of the Twelve Apostles in the British Isles, 1837-1841* (Salt Lake City: Deseret Book Co., 1992).

54. "Kirtland Council Minutes," 27 Feb. 1835.

In other words, the presiding authority of the twelve apostles was unquestioned in all areas of the world except the organized stakes in Ohio and Missouri. Although this response suggested that they would have no regulatory role in the stakes, a revelation one month later described one duty whose fulfillment clearly extended into the stakes, another which might be interpreted as involving stakes, and verification that the authority of the twelve was unsurpassed by any other ruling body. The revelation stated that "it is the duty of the twelve, also, to ordain and set in order all the other officers of the church" (DC, 1835 III:30, 28 Mar. 1835). Although Smith, as church president, retained the right to ordain men to any office, only the twelve apostles, among all other individuals or groups in the church, were given this authority. Further suggesting authority that might not end at stake boundaries, the revelation continued: "The twelve are a travelling, presiding high council, to officiate in the name of the Lord, under the direction of the presidency of the church, agreeably to the institution of heaven; to build up the church, and *regulate all the affairs of the same, in all nations*: first unto the Gentiles, and secondly unto the Jews" (ibid., v. 12, emphasis added). The apostles were said to "form a quorum equal in authority and power to the three presidents" (ibid., v. 11), possibly foreshadowing their ascendancy to lead the church following Smith's death.

This revelation caused confusion concerning the relative authority of high councils in the stakes. In a meeting one month later Smith attempted to clarify the relationship: "The Twelve will have no right to go into Zion or any of its stakes and there undertake to regulate the affairs thereof where there is a standing High Council. But it is their duty to go abroad and regulate all matters relative to the different branches of the church."[55] But a revelation later the same year again emphasized the priority of the apostles: "There is a distinction between the high council of travelling high priests abroad, and the travelling high council composed of the twelve apostles, in their decisions: From the decision of the former there can be an appeal, but from the decision of the latter there cannot" (DC, 1835 V:13). Several months later Smith returned to the subject, this time stating that the twelve had "authority which is next

---

55. Ibid., 2 May 1835.

to the present Presidency," and that they were "not subject to any other than the First Presidency."[56]

After the 1836 endowment in the Kirtland House of the Lord, the primary focus of the twelve apostles was missionary work. Yet a statement by Smith on 16 August 1841, following their return from their second mission to the British Isles, signalled a shift in their role away from proselyting and towards governing: "[Joseph Smith stated] that the time had come when the Twelve should be called upon to stand in their place next to the First Presidency, and attend to the settling of emigrants and the business of the Church at the stakes, and assist to bear off the kingdom victoriously to the nations."[57]

Although this statement clearly cemented the standing of the apostles, neither it nor any other public statement or document prior to Smith's death stated explicitly that the twelve would succeed Smith if he died. That he probably intended to have the twelve succeed him is best evidenced by the fact that all of the twelve apostles received their second anointing prior to Smith's death, whereas the other major aspirant, Sidney Rigdon, did not. This was the primary argument used by the twelve in successfully rebuffing Rigdon's claim. On 25 August 1844, two months after Smith's death, Apostle Wilford Woodruff wrote: "Elders O. Hyde and P. P. Pratt testifyed that Joseph Smith the Prophet and Seer had ordained, anointed, and appointed the Twelve to lead the Church."[58] Two weeks later, when Rigdon was tried for his membership and excommunicated, Apostle John Taylor wrote: "He [Rigdon] has been holding secret meetings; he has ordained men illegally, and contrary to the order of the priesthood; he has been ordaining men to the offices of prophets, priests and kings; whereas he does not hold that office himself; who does not know that this is wrong?"[59]

Bishop

The office of bishop had no precedent in the Book of Mormon,

56. Scott H. Faulring, ed., *An American Prophet's Record: The Diaries and Journals of Joseph Smith* (Salt Lake City: Signature Books in association with Smith Research Associates, 1987), 110, 16 Jan. 1836.

57. HC, 4:403.

58. *Wilford Woodruff's Journal*, 2:455, 25 Aug. 1844.

59. John Taylor, "Trial of Sidney Rigdon," 8 Sept. 1844, in *Times and Seasons* 5 (1 Oct. 1844): 661.

although it was named in the New Testament (see 1 Tim. 3:1-7). While it is not clear how the office came to be introduced to the Restoration, evidence suggests that Sidney Rigdon, a convert from Campbellism, played the pivotal role in bringing the matter to Joseph Smith's attention.

The central feature of Campbellism was a return to "primitive" Christianity, that is, to an organization and belief system felt by its adherents to reflect more accurately the church of the New Testament than contemporaneous Catholic and Protestant traditions. The founder of the movement, Alexander Campbell, argued strongly that there were only two legitimate offices in the ancient church, bishop and deacon, and that only these two should be present in the modern church: "Instead of the divinely established order of bishops and deacons . . . we have popes, cardinals, archbishops, metropolitan bishops, diocesan bishops, rectors, prebendaries, deans, priests, arch deacons, presiding elders, ruling elders, circuit preachers, local preachers, licentiates, class leaders, abbots, monks, friars, etc., etc."[60]

Campbell's assistant, Walter Scott, echoed this sentiment the following year when he wrote, "To manage the business of the church in all ages, it pleased the Head of the church to appoint bishops and deacons."[61] By 1828 Rigdon had joined the Campbellite movement and risen to the office of bishop.[62] Eventually he and Campbell parted ways over gifts of the spirit, which Campbell, despite his attraction to primitivism, refused to accept as part of a modern church. Shortly thereafter, Oliver Cowdery, Ziba Peterson, Parley P. Pratt, and Peter Whitmer preached in Kirtland and converted Rigdon. Within weeks Rigdon and fellow Campbellite Edward Partridge journeyed to New York to meet Joseph Smith, arriving there in December 1830. Although direct evidence is lacking to prove that Rigdon presented the concept of bishops to Smith, it is significant that the first bishop of the

---

60. Alexander Campbell, "The Christian Religion," *Christian Baptist*, 3 Aug. 1823.

61. Walter Scott, "Primitive and Modern Christianity," *Christian Baptist*, 6 Sept. 1824.

62. See *Christian Baptist*, 2 June 1828; and "Minutes of the Mahoning Baptist Convention" for 1828 and 1829, The Disciples of Christ Historical Society, Nashville, Tennessee.

Restoration was Partridge and that he was ordained by Rigdon[63] in Smith's presence.

Partridge was called to his office by a revelation given the same day he was ordained:

> A commandment given February 4th 1831 to choose a Bishop &c. And again I have called my servant Edward and give a commandment that he should be appointed by the voice of the church and ordained a Bishop unto the church to leave his merchandise and to spend all his time in the labours of the church to see to all things as it shall be appointed in my law in the day that I shall give them and this because his heart is pure before me for he is like unto Nathaniel of Old in whom there is no guile.[64]

Although this revelation did not describe the bishop's duties, it indicated that such would be forthcoming. A revelation five days later outlined what would remain the primary function of bishops during the remainder of Smith's ministry, the redistribution of personal wealth for the dual purposes of assisting the poor and financing the operations of the church (BC XLIV, 9 Feb. 1831). Subsequent revelations added secondary and tertiary functions. Bishops were to sit in judgment of transgressors (BC XLVII, 23 Feb. 1831) and preside over the Lesser Priesthood (DC, 1835 III:40, 28 Mar. 1835).

In the June 1831 general conference Isaac Morley and John Corrill were selected as counselors or assistants to Partridge.[65] Shortly afterwards Smith and several other elders, including Partridge, traveled to Independence, Missouri, to dedicate a temple site and proclaim that area "Zion," with Partridge as bishop. Although Missouri was designated the eventual gathering place of the Saints, most of the church remained in Kirtland. A revelation in November 1831 acknowledged the necessity of calling other bishops for Kirtland and other locales: "There remaineth hereafter in the due time of the Lord, other bishops to be set apart unto the church, to minister even according to the first; wherefore it shall be an high priest who is worthy; and he shall be appointed by a conference of high priests."[66]

---

63. This occurred on 4 February 1831. A copy of Partridge's license was published in *The Contributor* 6 (Oct. 1884): 5-6.

64. "Kirtland Revelation Book," 93-94; also BC XLIII:11-12.

65. *Far West Record*, 7, 3 June 1831.

66. *Evening and Morning Star*, Oct. 1832; revelation dated Nov. 1831. A revised version of this revelation, containing substantial addi-

In spite of the instruction, the calling of the second bishop the following month was not accomplished by a conference of high priests but rather by a revelation: "Verily saith the Lord it is expedient in me for a bishop to be appointed u[n]to you or of you unto the Church in this part of the Lords viniard . . . and verily I say unto you my servant Knewel Whitney is the man which shall be appointed and ordained unto this power."[67] Thereafter, Partridge served as bishop in Zion, while Newel K. Whitney served as bishop in the other center of the Saints, Kirtland. In June 1833 two additional bishops were called to assist Partridge with the growing body in Missouri: "Concerning Bishops, we recommend the following: Let Brother Isaac Morley be ordained second Bishop in Zion, and let Brother John Corrill be ordained third."[68]

With the disintegration of both centers of the church in the late 1830s and the subsequent regrouping of the Saints in Illinois, reorganization of the bishops became necessary. On 5 October 1840, Commerce (later renamed Nauvoo) was divided into three wards[69] with the two original bishops, Partridge and Whitney, serving the Upper and Middle Wards and newly called Vinson Knight over the Lower Ward. In addition, Alanson Ripley was called to serve as bishop on the Iowa side of the Mississippi River.[70] One year later the Lima, Quincy, Mt. Hope, Freedom, Geneva, and Springfield stakes were organized, each with one bishop. In addition, William Allred and William Whiteman were called as bishops in Pleasant Vale and Ramus, both outside of organized stakes. Similarly, John M. Bernhisel was chosen bishop in New York City on 15 April 1841, although no stake existed there.[71] Thus jurisdiction was quite different from that of

tions regarding the office of bishop, was published in DC, 1835 XXII.

67. "Kirtland Revelation Book," 13; revelation dated 4 Dec. 1831. Also DC, 1835 LXXXIX:1-2.

68. Joseph Smith, Sidney Rigdon, and Frederick G. Williams (Kirtland) to W. W. Phelps "and others in Zion," 2 July 1833, in *Times and Seasons* 6 (15 Feb. 1845): 801.

69. Wards initially served as political units, as in eastern cities. It was not until the migration to Utah that the ward became an ecclesiastical unit whose leader was the bishop.

70. Orson F. Whitney, "The Aaronic Priesthood," *The Contributor* 6 (Aug. 1885): 404.

71. Ibid. Other subdivisions of Nauvoo wards occurred on 1

current Latter-day Saint bishops, for while their primary function is to preside over ecclesiastical wards, early bishops never presided over congregations.

When Partridge was called as the first bishop, no other office was specified as prerequisite to his calling. Shortly thereafter, the High Priesthood was introduced, and by the end of 1831 the office of high priest emerged. By the time Whitney was called to be the second bishop, it was necessary that he and all bishops be ordained high priests.[72]

An interesting theoretical exception to this rule was introduced by Smith in 1835. In preparing the collection of revelations for publication that year, he made significant additions to two previous texts regarding the office of bishop. A man could serve as bishop without being a high priest and without counselors if he could demonstrate that he was a literal descendant of Aaron (DC, 1835 III:8, 31-34; XXII:2). These passages remain enigmatic because they occurred without precedent, there was no indication of how one would document that he was a literal descendant of Aaron, and the provision was never implemented. An 1837 church newspaper article explained: "The Bishop was a high priest, and necessarily so, because he is to preside over that particular branch of church affairs that are denominated the lesser priesthood, and because we have no direct lineal descendant of Aaron to whom it would of right belong."[73]

On 9 February 1831, only five days after Partridge was called as the first bishop, a revelation instructed the Saints to "consecrate all thy properties . . . and they shall be laid before the bishop of my church" (BC XLIV:26). The bishop, in turn, was to determine what each donor family needed and appoint back to them that amount. It was assumed that there would be a residue after these transactions, which the bishop would then use to support the poor, himself and his assistants, and "for the purpose of purchasing land and building up the New Jerusalem" (vv. 27-29, 54). The scope of activities to be financed in this manner

---

March 1842 and 20 August 1842. In each case, one bishop was called to serve in each new ward (HC, 5:119-20).

72. *Evening and Morning Star*, Oct. 1832; revelation of Nov. 1831. See also DC, 1835 XXII:2.

73. Warren Cowdery (ed.), *Messenger and Advocate* 3 (Apr. 1837): 486-87.

was broadened by a revelation that December which authorized use of these assets for subsidizing "the literary concerns of my church."[74]

Because of the broad authority initially given the bishop, dissatisfaction occurred. In an attempt to develop a more equitable system, Smith wrote to Partridge in 1833:

> The matter of consecration must be done by the mutual consent of both parties; for, to give the bishop power to say how much every man shall have, and he be obliged to comply with the bishop's judgment, is giving to the bishop more power than a king has; and, upon the other hand, to let every man say how much he needs, and the bishop be obliged to comply with his judgment, is to throw Zion into confusion, and make a slave of the bishops. The fact is, there must be a balance or equilibrium of power, between the bishop and the people; and thus harmony and good will, be preserved among you.[75]

In spite of this attempt at reformation, the system of progressive redistribution soon failed and was replaced in 1838 by the regressive system of tithing, wherein all members paid a tenth of their "increase."[76] In spite of the change, the bishop continued to administer the assets.

Three weeks after Partridge was ordained, a revelation indicated the advisability of the bishop assisting elders in judging transgressors: "If any man shall commit adultery, he shall be tried before two elders of the church or more . . . And if it can be, it is necessary that the bishop is present also" (BC XLVII:5, 8, 23 Feb. 1831). Although this revelation made the role of the bishop secondary to that of the elders, a revelation the following month, which spoke of judging spiritual gifts, reversed the order of priority, placing bishop first: "And unto the bishop of the church, and unto such as God shall appoint and ordain to watch over the church, and to be elders unto the church, are to have it given unto them to discern all those gifts" (BC XLIX:23, Mar. 1831).

---

74. "Kirtland Revelation Book," 15, revelation of 4 Dec. 1831; also DC, 1835 LXXXIX:4.

75. Letter of 2 July 1833, in *Times and Seasons* 6 (15 Feb. 1845): 801.

76. Doctrine and Covenants of the Church of Jesus Christ of Latter-day Saints (Salt Lake City: Church of Jesus Christ of Latter-day Saints, 1981), 119:1-3 (hereafter cited in the text as DC, LDS).

A revelation five months later extended the judicial role, giving the bishop sole responsibility for judging church members:

> And whoso standeth in this mission [the office of bishop], is appointed to be a judge in Israel, like as it was in ancient days, to divide the lands of the heritage of God unto his children; and to judge his people by the testimony of the just, and by the assistance of his counsellors, according to the laws of the kingdom which are given by the prophets of God (BC LIX:21, 1 Aug. 1831).

Although a revelation one month later added another layer of judicial authority in the form of "the court of the church before the President of the high Priesthood" to judge "the most difficult cases of the church,"[77] the bishop remained a key judicial figure.

Much later, in 1835, a revelation stated: "The duty of the president over the priesthood of Aaron, is to preside over forty-eight priests, and sit in council with them, to teach them the duties of their office, as is given in the covenants. This president is to be a bishop; for this is one of the duties of this priesthood" (DC, 1835 III:40, 28 Mar. 1835).[78] In spite of the apparent clarity of these instructions, this role was not consistently followed during Smith's ministry. For example, Smith himself recorded in his diary the following year: "Bishop Whitney and his counselors then proceded to ordain Wm. Cowdery to the office whereunto he had been called, viz. to preside over the priests of the Aaronic priesthood in Kirtland."[79]

A conference in Missouri the following year revisited the issue and "resolved unanimously that . . . the Bishop shall take charge of the Lesser Priesthood."[80] Nonetheless, the organization of the Lesser Priesthood in Nauvoo in 1841 failed to include a bishop in the prescribed presiding role: "The Lesser Priesthood was organized in the City of Nauvoo, March 21, 1841, by Bishops Whitney, Miller, Higbee, and Knight. Samuel Rolf was chosen president of the Priests' quorum."[81]

---

77. "Kirtland Revelation Book," 85, revelation dated Nov. 1831. This revelation later became part of DC, 1835 III.

78. The first part of this verse dates to 1831, but that describing the role of the bishop was added in 1835.

79. *Joseph Smith Diary*, 106, 15 Jan. 1836.

80. *Far West Record*, 117, 1 Aug. 1837.

81. HC, 4:312.

Deacon

As with bishop, the office of deacon likely was introduced into the Restoration at the suggestion of Sidney Rigdon. It was not mentioned in the Book of Mormon or in any document prior to April 1831 but drew upon New Testament precedent (1 Tim. 3:8-13). Although it is mentioned in Section 20 of the current LDS Doctrine and Covenants, which carries a date of April 1830, several lines of evidence show that it was a later addition whose retroactive insertion was never commented on by the redactor. The earliest version of this revelation, addressed to Oliver Cowdery in 1829, mentions teachers, priests, and elders but not deacons.[82] In the later versions, the mention of deacons is awkward and not parallel with the other offices. For instance, the offices of teacher, priest, and elder are juxtaposed to a detailed job description, while that of a deacon appears to be an afterthought with no mention of unique duties: "[The teacher] is to be assisted always in all his duties by the deacons."[83] Furthermore, a phrase in the 1835 version of this revelation, "Each priest, teacher, or deacon, who is ordained by a priest" (DC, 1835 II:15), did not contain the word "deacon" in earlier versions,[84] although the word is used in other verses, suggesting carelessness on the part of the redactor in inserting it retroactively in all appropriate verses. A revelation given in January 1831, which mentions in descending order the offices of the church, makes no mention of deacons: "I give unto you a commandment, that every man both elder, priest, teacher and also member, go to with his might . . . " (BC XL:35, 2 Jan. 1831). The first record of deacons having been ordained was a general conference on 25 October 1831.[85]

The office of deacon remained enigmatic for the rest of Smith's ministry, for it was never given unique functions, serving instead to help teachers. There were numerous instances in which the role of "teachers and deacons" was mentioned, but not a single reference to the role of deacons in the absence of teachers. That the office could have had significant (though not unique) function was indicated by the policy that "the Teachers and Deacons are the standing ministers

---

82. "Articles of the Church," in Woodford.

83. *Painesville Telegraph*, 19 Apr. 1831; also BC XXIV:40.

84. *Painesville Telegraph*, 19 Apr. 1831; *Evening and Morning Star* 1 (June 1832): 1-2; BC XXIV:44.

85. *Far West Record*, 19, 25 Oct. 1831.

of the Church,"[86] yet there is only one known reference of a deacon, rather than a teacher, presiding over a branch of the church,[87] and no record of significant group activity by deacons' quorums. The function generally associated today with Latter-day Saint deacons, distributing the bread and water of the sacrament of the Lord's Supper, was never mentioned during Smith's lifetime.

High Priest

The office of high priest is unique, for it is the only office mentioned in the Book of Mormon not incorporated in the church at its inception. Within the "pre-Christian" portion of the Book of Mormon high priest was an important and benevolent figure: "And now, Alma was their high priest, he being the founder of their church. And it came to pass that none received authority to preach or to teach except it were by him, from God. Therefore he consecrated all their priests and all their teachers; and none were consecrated except they were just men" (BM, LDS, Mosiah 23:16-17).

In the Christian portion of the Book of Mormon the office of high priest had degenerated to the point where its holders became antagonists of those who spoke of Christ: "Now there were many of the people who were exceeding angry because of those who testified of these things; and those who were angry were chiefly the chief judges, and they who had been high priests and lawyers" (BM, LDS, 3 Ne. 6:21).

Whether Joseph Smith's initial failure to ordain high priests was due to this passage, or to a desire to emulate the organization described in the Christian portion of the book, is not clear. What is clear, however, is that one of Smith's closest associates credited Sidney Rigdon with successfully proposing to Smith that high priests be added in 1831:

> As you know, the teachings of Christ are the same at Jerusalem and upon this land; but on account of the plain and precious things being taken from the Bible, there is room therein for disputation on

---

86. Joseph Smith, Oliver Cowdery, W. W. Phelps, and John Whitmer (Kirtland) to John M. Burk (Liberty, Missouri), 1 June 1835, in Journal History, 1 June 1835.

87. "[B]rother Caswell Medlock was ordained A Deacon over the Egle Creek branch" (*Wilford Woodruff's Journal,* 1:33, 28 June 1835).

some points; but the teachings of Christ in the Book of Mormon are *pure*, plain, simple, and full. Christ chose "twelve" and called them *disciples*, or Elders,—not apostles, and the "twelve" ordained elders, priests, and teachers. These are *all* the spiritual offices in the Church of Christ, and their duties are plainly given. . . .

But they did not rely upon the Book of Mormon in building up the church; but Joseph "went on in the persuasion of men," as he did while translating, and heeded Rigdon who expounded the old scriptures to him and showed him that *high priests* and *other offices* should be added to "elders, priests and teachers."[88]

While Smith's and Rigdon's silence on the subject disallows verification of David Whitmer's assertions, they are consistent with the historical record, for there was no known mention of high priests prior to Rigdon's arrival in New York, and the first Restoration document mentioning the office was Smith's revision of Genesis written late in the winter of 1830-31, for which Rigdon served as scribe. That document, based on Genesis, Chapter 14, placed the office of high priest in a positive light, one consistent with the developing theology of endowment:

Now Melchizedek was a man of faith, who wrought righteousness; . . .

And thus, having been approved of God, he was ordained an high priest after the order of the covenant which God made with Enoch . . .

For God having sworn unto Enoch and unto his seed, with an oath by himself; [said] that every one being ordained after this order and calling should have power, by faith, to break mountains, to divide the sea, to dry up waters, to turn them out of their course;

To put at defiance the armies of nations, to divide the earth, to break every band, to stand in the presence of God; to do all things according to his will . . .

And now, Melchizedek was a priest of this order (Joseph Smith Translation, Gen. 14:26-33).

Ordination to the High Priesthood was a prerequisite to the promised endowment of "power from on high," which first occurred in June 1831. Those ordained to the High Priesthood were still considered elders.[89] However, by October these men began to use the

<hr>

88. David Whitmer to Joseph Smith III, *Saints' Herald* 34 (1887): 92-93, emphasis in original.

89. Similarly, Roman Catholic priests who are of a religious order

title High Priest.[90] A revelation the following month established the priority of the office of high priest over all other offices:

> Then cometh the High Priesthood which is the greatest of all wherefore it must needs be that one be appointed of the high Priesthood to preside over the Priesthood, and he shall be called President of the high priesthood of the Church, or in other words the presiding high Priest over the high priesthood of the Church [and] from the same cometh the administering of ordinances and blessings upon the church by the laying on of the hands wherefore the office of a Bishop is not equal unto it.[91]

Whereas prior to this time bishop was the highest judicial officer in the church, high priest now filled that role:

> And again verily I say unto you the most important business of the church and the most difficult cases of the church inasmuch as there is not satisfaction upon the decision of the judges [i.e., bishops] it shall be handed over and carried up unto the court of the church before the President of the high Priesthood and the President of the court of the high priesthood shall have power to call other high priests even twelve to assist as councellors and thus the president of the high priesthood and his councellors shall have power to decide upon testimony according to the laws of the church.[92]

The priority of the office of high priest was given further emphasis in an unpublished revelation in March 1832. Although addressed to Bishop Newel K. Whitney regarding the office of bishop, the revelation also affirmed the presiding function of the High Priesthood: "Unto the office of the presidency of the high Priesthood I have given authority to preside with the assistence of his councellors over all the concerns of the church."[93]

The same month, in commenting on a passage from the Book of Revelation, Smith reemphasized the superiority of high priests:

---

such as the Society of Jesus are still priests.

90. Luke S. Johnson diary, in Journal History, 25 Oct. 1831.

91. "Kirtland Revelation Book," 84-85; revelation dated Nov. 1831. This revelation was later incorporated into DC, 1835 III.

92. Ibid., 85.

93. Unpublished revelation dated Mar. 1832, Newel K. Whitney papers, Special Collections, Harold B. Lee Library, Brigham Young University, Provo, Utah.

Q. What are we to understand by sealing the one hundred and forty-four thousand, out of all the tribes of Israel—twelve thousand out of every tribe?

A. We are to understand that those who are sealed are high priests, ordained unto the holy order of God, to administer the everlasting gospel (DC, LDS 77:11).

A revelation later the same year stated that "the office of elder and bishop are necessary appendages belonging unto the high priesthood" (DC, 1835 IV:5, 22/23 Sept. 1832). Similarly, when the first high council was organized in February 1834, it consisted solely of high priests (DC, 1835 V:1).

The most detailed statement came in a revelation in March 1835:

High priests, after the order of the Melchizedek priesthood, have a right to officiate in their own standing, under the direction of the presidency, in administering spiritual things, and also in the office of an elder, priest, (of the Levitical order,) teacher, deacon and member.
. . .

As a high priest, of the Melchizedek priesthood, has authority to officiate in all the lesser offices, he may officiate in the office of bishop when no literal descendant of Aaron can be found . . .

And again, I give unto you Don C. Smith to be a president over a quorum of high priests;

Which ordinance is instituted for the purpose of qualifying those who shall be appointed standing presidents or servants over different stakes scattered abroad;

And they may travel also if they choose, but rather be ordained for standing presidents; this is the office of their calling, saith the Lord (DC, 1835 III:5, 8, 133-35).

No significant changes in the office of high priest occurred during the remainder of Joseph Smith's ministry.

Patriarch

While the Book of Mormon and the New Testament served as models for previous offices, that of patriarch reached back to an Old Testament model wherein Jacob blessed his sons and grandsons shortly before his death (Gen. 49:1-28). In blessing his parents and siblings in December 1833, John Smith blessed his father to hold the same title as Jacob and the other ancient patriarchs:

He shall be called a prince over his posterity; holding the keys of the patriarchal priesthood over the kingdom of God on earth, even of

the Latter Day Saints, and he shall sit in the general assembly of patriarchs, even in council with the Ancient of Days, when he shall sit and
all the patriarchs with him, and shall enjoy his right and authority under the direction of the Ancient of Days. And blessed also is my
mother, for she is a mother in Israel, and shall be a partaker with my
father in all his patriarchal blessings.[94]

Although Joseph Smith, Sr., was ordained to the office of patriarch
the same day, there is no evidence that he gave any patriarchal blessings
for a full year thereafter. When he blessed his family in December 1834,
he appeared to acknowledge this when he said, "I desire, and for a long
time have, to bless my children before I go hence."[95] John Young,
father of Brigham Young, who was ordained a patriarch several months
after Joseph Smith, Sr., blessed his own family prior to Smith.[96]

Although a revelation in March 1835 stated that the office was
intended to pass from father to son (DC, 1835 III:17-18), only in the
case of the Smith family did this occur. Other patriarchs, starting with
Isaac Morley in 1837,[97] served without regard to lineage and did not
automatically pass the office to a son. Instead, as noted by the Church
Historian at the time, the office generally went to an old man: "It also
was a rule in the church to have one in each stake (most generally the
oldest, if suitable) appointed and ordained a patriarch, whose duty it
was to be a sort of father to the church, and bless such children as had
no natural father to bless them."[98]

For all patriarchs except Joseph Smith, Sr., and his lineal successors,
the sole duty of the office was to give blessings to church members. In
addition, the Smiths served as "Presiding Patriarchs," and as such bore
other responsibilities. For instance, an account of the regular meetings
being held in the Kirtland House of the Lord stated: "On Thursday
P.M. a prayer meeting is held in the lower part of the house where

---

94. "Patriarchal Blessings Book," Vol. 1, 18 Dec. 1833, LDS
archives.

95. Oliver Cowdery minutes of the Smith family patriarchal
blessing meeting, 9 Dec. 1834, typescript, Irene Bates Collection, RLDS
Library-Archives.

96. Brigham Young discourse, 30 June 1873, *Deseret Weekly News*
22 (23 July 1873), 25:388. There is no evidence that Father Young gave
blessings to anyone other than his own family.

97. *Elders' Journal* 1 (Nov. 1837): 30.

98. Corrill, chap. 27.

any and all persons may assemble and pray and praise the Lord. This meeting, though free for all, is conducted more particularly by J. Smith senior, the patriarch of the church."[99]

By the time Hyrum Smith succeeded his father as Presiding Patriarch, the theology of sealing had undergone significant development, part of which was assigned by revelation to that office:

> And again, verily I say unto you, let my servant William be appointed, ordained, and anointed, as counselor unto my servant Joseph, in the room of my servant Hyrum, that my servant Hyrum may take the office of Priesthood and Patriarch, which was appointed unto him by his father, by blessing and also by right;
>
> That from henceforth he shall hold the keys of the patriarchal blessings upon the heads of all my people,
>
> That whoever he blesses shall be blessed, and whoever he curses shall be cursed; that whatsoever he shall bind on earth shall be bound in heaven; and whatsoever he shall loose on earth shall be loosed in heaven.
>
> And from this time forth I appoint unto him that he may be a prophet, and a seer, and a revelator unto my church, as well as my servant Joseph;
>
> That he may act in concert also with my servant Joseph; and that he shall receive counsel from my servant Joseph, who shall show unto him the keys whereby he may ask and receive, and be crowned with the same blessing, and glory, and honor, and priesthood, and gifts of the priesthood, that once were put upon him that was my servant Oliver Cowdery; . . .
>
> First, I give unto you Hyrum Smith to be a patriarch unto you, to hold the sealing blessings of my church, even the Holy Spirit of promise, whereby ye are sealed up unto the day of redemption, that ye may not fall notwithstanding the hour of temptation that may come upon you (DC, LDS 124:91-95, 124).

At Hyrum's death this function ceased to be part of the office.

Seventy

On 8 February 1835 Joseph Smith related to Brigham and Joseph Young a vision he had experienced regarding the fate of the men who had died during the Zion's Camp expedition. It appears that the vision included details regarding the final two governing bodies of the Restoration, the Quorum of Twelve Apostles and the First Quorum

---

99. *Messenger and Advocate* 3 (Jan. 1837): 444.

of Seventies. Joseph Young later described the manner in which the latter group was introduced: "He [Smith] then turned to Elder Joseph Young with quite an earnestness, as though the vision of his mind was extended still further, and addressing him, said: 'Brother Joseph, the Lord has made you President of the Seventies.'"[100]

Three weeks later the First Quorum of Seventy was organized, and Smith gave this explanation of the role Zion's Camp had played:

> Brethren, some of you are angry with me, because you did not fight in Missouri; but let me tell you, God did not want you to fight. He could not organize his kingdom with twelve men to open the gospel door to the nations of the earth, and with seventy men under their direction to follow in their tracks, unless he took them from a body of men who had offered their lives, and who had made as great a sacrifice as did Abraham.
>
> Now, the Lord has got his Twelve and his Seventy, and there will be other quorums of Seventies called, who will make the sacrifice, and those who have not made their sacrifices and their offerings now, will make them hereafter.[101]

Although the primary function assigned to the seventies, "to constitute traveling quorums, to go into all the earth,"[102] appeared straightforward, both the nature of the office and its actual functions remained enigmatic not only during Smith's ministry but for over a century thereafter. From the outset the nature of the office of seventy was ambiguous, as indicated by an account of the ordination of Joseph Young on 28 February 1835: "Prior to his [Young's] ordination the Prophet instructed his counselor, Sidney Rigdon, to confer upon him all the Priesthood, powers, blessings, keys and authority that they themselves possessed, which was strictly observed."[103]

Since Smith was an apostle, president of the High Priesthood, and president of the church, and Rigdon was a high priest and member of the First Presidency, one cannot infer exactly what Smith had in mind in instructing Rigdon. Indeed, discussions in the decades following Smith's death which debated whether a seventy was also an apostle are consistent with this initial ambiguity.

---

100. Joseph Young, Sr., *History of the Organization of the Seventies* (Salt Lake City: Deseret News Steam Printing Establishment, 1878), 1-2.

101. Ibid., 14.

102. HC, 2:201-202.

103. "Seventies Minute Book #1," 281, LDS archives.

Adding to the uncertainty was a revelation one month later which simultaneously placed the seventy "under the direction of the twelve," yet stated that "they form a quorum equal in authority to that of the twelve especial witnesses or apostles" (DC, 1835 III:11, 13, 28 Mar. 1835). Similarly confusing was the contrast between a statement by Smith in May 1835 that more seventies could be called, "even until there shall be one hundred & forty and four thousand,"[104] an apparent reference to the 144,000 spoken of in the Book of Revelation which an 1832 revelation had proclaimed to be high priests (DC, LDS 77:11), and an 1837 statement by Smith that "the seventies are to be taken from the quorum of elders and are not to be high priests."[105] In fact, a second account of the same meeting recorded that "it was decided by Joseph Smith that the Seventies were not High Priests, as they had been previously taught."[106]

Although the latter statement would appear to have clarified the issue, the same dispute arose again in a general conference in 1840:

> A letter was read from presidents of the seventies, wishing for an explanation of the steps, which the high council had taken, in removing Elder F. G. Bishop, from the quorum of the sev[en]ties, to that of the High Priest, without any other ordination than he had when in the seventies, and wished to know, whither, those ordained into the seventies at the same time F. G. Bishop was, had a right to the High Priesthood, or not. After observations on the case by different individuals, the president gave a statement of the authority of the seventies, and stated that they were Elders and not High Priests, and consequently brother F. G. Bishop had no claim to that office. It was then unanimously resolved that Elder F. G. Bishop be placed back again into the Quorum of the seventies.[107]

Given the persistent controversy over the nature of the office, and the fact that no more definitive guidance was given by Smith prior to his

---

104. "Kirtland Council Minutes," 2 May 1835.

105. *Messenger and Advocate* 3 (Apr. 1837): 486-87.

106. "Seventies Record," A 17, in Journal History, 6 Apr. 1837. Attempting to resolve the issue, Smith thereupon released six of the seven presidents of the First Quorum of Seventy who were found to have been high priests prior to their calling to the seventies.

107. Conference minutes of the general conference in Nauvoo, 6 Apr. 1840, in *Times and Seasons* 1 (Apr. 1840): 92.

death, it is perhaps not surprising that the office of seventy remained problematic for more than a century thereafter.

In establishing the office, Smith stated what would remain the ideal of their function: "to go into all the earth, whithersoever the Twelve Apostles shall call them."[108] This was endorsed by revelation the following month: "The seventy are also called to preach the gospel, and to be especial witnesses unto the Gentiles and in all the world. Thus differing from all other officers in the church in the duties of their calling" (DC, 1835 III:11).

By the end of 1838, however, the expectation had not been fulfilled, leading several apostles to stress "the necessity of their going immediately into the vineyard of the Lord to labor therein in righteousness for him."[109] The same apostles again called on the seventies the following week "to go on their mission as soon as their circumstances would admit,"[110] yet despite the pleas, and even the added impetus of an 1841 revelation mandating that the seventies were "to travel continually" (DC, LDS 124:140, 19 Jan. 1841), no consistent record of missionary labor was established by the seventies during Smith's lifetime. In fact, the most significant example of group activity by the seventies, the successful organizing and moving of the Saints from Ohio to Missouri in 1838,[111] had nothing to do with their scriptural mandate.

---

108. HC, 2:201-202.
109. "Seventies Record," A 53, in Journal History, 28 Dec. 1838.
110. "Seventies Record," A 57, in Journal History, 5 Jan. 1839.
111. HC, 3:87.

Chapter Three

Ordinances
1829-30

In a Latter-day Saint context whatever tradition has defined as a ordinance is one. Otherwise what Latter-day Saints accept as ordinances defies simple definition. For instance, an ordinance may be any act which, by scriptural mandate, is assigned to a priesthood office. Or it may be any act performed by a priesthood officer which involves the laying on of hands in one form or another—that is, one which involves physical contact between the officiator and recipient. Or it may be any act performed exclusively by a priesthood officer. Or it may be any act performed by a priesthood officer which derives from a biblical precedent.

The revelation outlining the function of early LDS priesthood offices[1] lists as duties of elder and priest: baptism, ordination, and administration of the sacrament, all of which are recognized as ordinances. The other duties of these offices, including preaching, teaching, expounding, exhorting, visiting the houses of members, and taking the lead of meetings, are not so recognized. Conversely, several ordinances were never scripturally assigned to any priesthood office. And although many common ordinances such as baptism, confirmation, ordination, patriarchal, and other blessings involve physical

---

1. See *A Book of Commandments, for the Government of the Church of Christ, Organized According to Law, on the 6th of April, 1830* (Independence, MO: W. W. Phelps & Co., 1833), XXIV; hereafter cited in the text as BC; *Doctrine and Covenants of The Church of the Latter Day Saints: Carefully Selected from the Revelations of God* (Kirtland, OH: F. G. Williams & Co., 1835), II; hereafter cited in the text as DC, 1835.

contact, this is not the case for administration of the Lord's Supper, some forms of administering to the sick (particularly prior to 1836), casting out evil spirits, cursing, marriage, raising the dead, and some forms of sealing (such as the early practice of "sealing" entire congregations up to eternal life). Frequently women, who do not hold priesthood office, have administered to the sick, and they regularly perform washings and anointings in the temple. Similarly, marriage performed by a minister of another faith or by a civil officer is recognized as valid. And biblical precedents such as preaching, which was considered an "ordinance" by other 1830s American churches[2] and which in the Latter-day Saint tradition were initially restricted to priesthood officers, have never been considered to be ordinances.

Therefore one returns to the initial definition of an ordinance as being something which church members recognize as such. While no comprehensive list was made during Joseph Smith's lifetime, the following fits this popular definition of ordinances:

Ordinance	Year First Practiced[3]
Ordination	1829
Baptism	1829
Confirmation	1829
The Sacrament of the Lord's Supper	1829
Blessing Children	1830
Administering to the Sick	1830
Cursing	1830
Casting out Evil Spirits	1830
Endowment	1831
Raising the Dead	1831
Blessing	1831
Sealing	1831
Washing Feet	1833
Patriarchal Blessing	1834
Marriage	1835
Washing and Anointing	1836
Second Anointing	1843

---

2. Charles Buck, *A Theological Dictionary Containing Definitions of All Religious Terms . . .* (Philadelphia: Joseph J. Woodward, 1830), 418.

3. Some dates are estimates.

Ordination

The first ordinance identified in the Restoration was the ordination of Joseph Smith and Oliver Cowdery by the angel. Cowdery later reported: "[Smith] was ordained by the angel John, unto the lesser or Aaronic priesthood, in company with myself, in the town of Harmony, Susquehannah county, Pennsylvania, on Friday the 15th day of May, 1829: after which we repaired to the water, even to the Susquehannah river, and were baptized: he first ministering unto me, and after, I to him."[4]

Shortly thereafter Smith dictated the text of the Book of Moroni with the prescribed prayer for ordination of priests and teachers: "After they had prayed unto the Father in the name of Christ, they laid their hands upon them, and said: In the name of Jesus Christ I ordain you to be a priest, (or, if he be a teacher) I ordain you to be a teacher, to preach repentance and remission of sins through Jesus Christ, by the endurance of faith on his name to the end. Amen."[5] This simple ordination prayer was repeated without change in an unpublished 1829 revelation[6] and served as an acceptable, though not mandatory, form through the remainder of the nineteenth century.[7]

The only significant change in ordination protocol during Smith's ministry occurred in January 1832 when a conference ruled that no officers were to be ordained without the consent of the congregation.[8] Church Historian John Corrill later explained: "For

---

4. Oliver Cowdery, in "Patriarchal Blessing Book," vol. 1, dated Sept., 1835, archives, Historical Department, Church of Jesus Christ of Latter-day Saints, Salt Lake City, Utah (hereafter LDS archives). Cowdery's use of the name of the angel and of the term Aaronic Priesthood are anachronisms, as is explained in chap. 1 of this book.

5. Moro. 3:2-3, in The Book of Mormon (Salt Lake City: Church of Jesus Christ of Latter-day Saints, 1981) (hereafter cited in the text as BM, LDS). Since this pre-dated the concept of priesthood, it is not surprising that there is no reference to Aaronic Priesthood.

6. "Articles of the Church of Christ," in Robert J. Woodford, "The Historical Development of the Doctrine and Covenants," Ph.D. diss., Brigham Young University, 1974, 288.

7. For example, First Presidency member George Q. Cannon endorsed its use as late as 1896. See Juvenile Instructor 31 (1 Mar. 1896): 139.

8. Minutes of a conference in Independence, Missouri, 23-24 Jan.

some time after the commencement of the church an elder might ordain an elder, priest, teacher, or deacon, when and where he thought proper, but, after Stakes were planted, and the Church became organized, they established a rule that none should be ordained without consent of the church or branch that he belonged to."[9]

A source of confusion is the frequency with which the word "ordination" was used to refer to actions other than designation of a priesthood office. For example, a revelation to Emma Smith, dated July 1830, promised her a form of authority and specified that the authority was to be conferred to her by Joseph Smith in the same manner used to ordain church officers, that is, by the laying on of hands: "And thou shalt be ordained under his hand to expound scriptures, and to exhort the church, according as it shall be given thee by my Spirit" (BC XXVI:4).

Numerous other examples exist which employ the verb "ordain" in a manner foreign to today's usage. For example, an 1830 revelation proclaimed that men who had been ordained to the office of elder and who desired to serve on proselyting missions "shall be ordained and sent forth to preach" (BC XXXVIII:3, Dec. 1830). A June 1831 revelation mandated that William W. Phelps "be ordained to assist my servant Oliver [Cowdery] to do the work of printing, and of selecting, and writing books for schools, in this church" (BC LVII:5). In March 1833 Ezra Thayre and Joseph Coe "were ordained under the hands of Sidney Rigdon" to purchase farms for the church.[10] An 1834 revelation directed the establishment of a treasury and stated "ye shall appoint one among you to keep the treasure, and he shall be ordained unto this blessing" (DC, 1835 XCVIII:11, 23 Apr. 1834). As late as 1842, with the formation of the Female Relief Society of Nauvoo, Emma

---

1832, Oliver Cowdery, clerk, Library-Archives, The Auditorium, Church of Jesus Christ of Latter Day Saints, Independence, Missouri; also in Donald Q. Cannon and Lyndon W. Cook, eds., *Far West Record: Minutes of the Church of Jesus Christ of Latter-day Saints, 1830-1841* (Salt Lake City: Deseret Book Co., 1983).

9. John Corrill, *Brief History of the Church of Christ of Latter Day Saints* . . . (St. Louis: Printed for the Author, 1839), chap. 13.

10. B. H. Roberts, ed., *History of the Church of Jesus Christ of Latter-day Saints* (Salt Lake City: Deseret Book Co., 1971), 1:335 (hereafter cited as HC).

Smith was "ordained" president of the society by Joseph Smith, with Sarah M. Cleveland and Elizabeth Ann Whitney "ordained" as her counselors by Apostle John Taylor.[11]

The problem was not one of understanding but of syntax. There is no evidence that church members had trouble distinguishing between ordination to offices and to duties outside the priesthood umbrella. It was the nature of the calling rather than the terminology and procedure employed in commissioning the recipient which distinguished the two. After Smith's death there was a gradual move towards more definitive terminology, and today Latter-day Saints restrict use of the verb "ordain" to the nine recognized priesthood offices, while using the related term "set apart" to refer to commissions to all other callings and responsibilities. During Smith's lifetime such a distinction was not made.

Baptism

The first ordinance performed by Joseph Smith was baptism. Although the foundational document of the Restoration, the Book of Mormon, speaks only of baptism for remission of sins upon entry into the church, Smith eventually introduced three other types. In 1840, after several years of doctrinal development, he declared that salvation for those who died without baptism could be effected by the ordinance of baptism performed in their behalf by a living descendant. One year later rebaptism for a renewed remission of sins and baptism for physical healing were introduced.

Coincident with the arrival of Oliver Cowdery in April 1829 and the resumption of dictation, Smith's attention was directed to several Book of Mormon passages regarding baptism, the most intriguing of which described events at the "waters of Mormon" (BM, LDS, Mosiah 18:10-17). Alma took Helam into the water but before baptizing him acknowledged his lack of proper authority by saying, "O Lord, pour out thy Spirit upon thy servant, that he may do this work with holiness of heart" (v. 12). Thereupon "the Spirit of the Lord was upon him" (v. 13), and after pronouncing a prayer different from that used later in the Book of Mormon, he baptized

---

11. "A Record of the Organization, and Proceedings of The Female Relief Society of Nauvoo," 17 Mar. 1842, LDS archives.

both Helam and himself (v. 14) by submerging themselves simultaneously in the water.[12]

This incident provided two parallels with the manner of baptism practiced by Smith, the requirement of divine authorization and the mode of baptism by immersion. By contrast, Alma's authorization came by the Spirit of the Lord, while Smith and Cowdery recorded that an angel had laid hands on them.[13] Similarly, Alma baptized himself, whereas Smith and Cowdery baptized each other. There is no record of Smith or any other contemporary church member commenting on the differences.

The second key passage from the Book of Mormon describes the interaction of the resurrected Christ with his twelve disciples (BM, LDS, 3 Ne. 11:21-28). In this, as in the case of Alma, hands-on ordination is not described. Rather the Lord gave Nephi verbal authorization to baptize (v. 21). The baptismal prayer given in this passage (v. 25) was used in the church from 1829[14] until at least 1833 (BC XXIV:53), after which the first phrase was changed from "Having authority given me of Jesus Christ . . ." to "Having been commissioned of Jesus Christ . . . " (DC, 1835 II:22). In October 1834 Oliver Cowdery wrote of his baptism, "the voice of the Redeemer spake peace to us, while the vail was parted and the angel of God came down clothed with glory. . . . We heard the voice of Jesus."[15] It thus appears reasonable that the baptismal prayer would invoke the name of the Savior rather than that of the angel.

The final book in the Book of Mormon contains Mormon's epistle to his son, Moroni, on the subject of infant baptism (BM, LDS, Moro. 8:4-24). Because of this passage, baptism of infants was never an issue in the Restoration.[16] Its very presence in the Book of Mormon,

---

12. A second reference to self-baptism, though not as explicit, is found in BM, LDS, 3 Ne. 19:10-14. There is no known instance of self-baptism in the Restoration.

13. Apostle Joseph Fielding Smith wrote: "While it is the practice to lay on hands, there are many incidents recorded in the scriptures where divine authority has been bestowed by the divine edict to the prophets" ("Your Question," *Improvement Era* 65 [June 1962]: 390-91).

14. "The Articles of the Church of Christ," in Woodford.

15. *Messenger and Advocate* 1 (Oct. 1834): 15-16.

16. A revelation "on priesthood," dated September 1832, contained a reference to John the Baptist suggesting a form of infant baptism.

however, is puzzling, because it appears in isolation, with no other references in the rest of the book. One may only ponder the possible relationship between this passage and the death, at birth, of Joseph and Emma Smith's firstborn child in 1828, one year before this passage was translated.

On the same day Smith and Cowdery baptized each other they also baptized Smith's younger brother, Samuel.[17] The following month David Whitmer was baptized.[18] By August these men began to preach and baptized about 80 members prior to the formal organization of the church the following April.[19] They taught that they were "the only persons on earth who are qualified to administer in his name" and that those refusing their baptism "must be forever miserable."[20]

With the exception of the minor word change, the mode of baptism has not changed since the beginning of the Restoration. Minor procedural questions were answered in 1831 when it was declared by revelation that baptism was not required until the age of eight years,[21] and in 1840 when it was decided that, although immersion was the only acceptable form of baptism, a good faith effort on the part of the baptist, which inadvertently resulted in part of the body not being totally immersed, was nonetheless acceptable in the eyes of God.[22]

Two examples of "baptism in extremis" bear note, the first

The earliest known manuscript of the revelation, found in the Kirtland Revelations Book, says, "he was baptized while he was yet in the womb, and was ordained by the Angel of God at the time he was eight days old" (23). Later the words "the womb" were crossed out, and the words "his childhood" were written above. There is no known commentary explaining the change, and while it corrects an otherwise awkward reference to infant baptism in an ancient context, it creates an anachronism by having John ordained prior to his baptism.

17. Lucy Mack Smith, "Manuscript History," 101, LDS archives.

18. David Whitmer, *An Address to All Believers in Christ* (Richmond, MO: the Author, 1887), 32; also "A Visit to David Whitmer," *Juvenile Instructor* 22 (15 Feb. 1887): 55.

19. Whitmer, 33.

20. *Painesville Telegraph*, 7 Dec. 1830.

21. Revelation of Nov. 1831, in *Evening and Morning Star*, Oct. 1832; also DC, 1835 XXII:4.

22. "Questions and Answers," *Millennial Star* 1 (Aug. 1840): 94. The questions were submitted by Joseph Fielding to the editor, Apostle Parley P. Pratt.

intentional, the second accidental. In May 1841, while Andrew Henry and a "Brother Holden" were preaching in southern Illinois, a young man was sharply rebuked for his continual outbursts. The following morning the matter was resolved by water:

> They said as he was under conviction he must be baptised but as the morning was rather cold he was unwilling to go into the water, but as they were going to compel him he thought it best to submit quietly so they went off and plunged him into the mill pond which was near at hand and kept him under longer than is customary with those that baptise for the remission of sin but as it was for bad be-haviur they thought he must stay under a little longer, and to use the administrators own words he kept him under until the bubles began to rise, but as they had no authority to lay on hands they would not administer that ordinance so they let him go with the admonition to behave better next time he came to meeting.[23]

A more serious incident occurred three years later in the British Isles. In January 1844 elders Jonathan Pugmire and Thomas Cartwright were arrested and charged with manslaughter because of the accidental drowning of a convert in baptism. Because the prosecution failed to produce witnesses at the trial, the two elders were acquitted on technical grounds. An editorial in the church newspaper, while rejoicing at their acquittal, added a somber note of caution:

> It is with feelings of no ordinary kind, that we address you on the present occasion, relative to the administration of the ordinance of baptism. Whereas, two fatal accidents have lately occurred, in connexion with this ordinance, one at Crewe, in Cheshire, and the other near to Sheffield, whereby two individuals have been drowned. We, therefore, strenuously urge upon the attention of the elders and priests of the church of Jesus Christ of Latter-day Saints, that they use every precaution in attending to the all-important ordinance of baptism for the remission of sins, and not be over anxious, so as to endanger themselves or the candidate.[24]

The 1832 revelation which first delineated the Latter-day Saint belief in a multi-tiered heaven made it clear that only those who had been baptized could inherit the highest tier, the Celestial Kingdom. Otherwise righteous people "who died without Law" could rise no

---

23. Andrew Henry diary, May 1841, Huntington Library, San Marino, California.

24. *Millennial Star* 4 (Jan. 1844): 142-44.

higher than the Terrestrial Kingdom.[25] That this doctrine remained fixed in the minds of the Saints was shown dramatically in Smith's vision of the Celestial Kingdom four years later.[26] In that vision he saw his deceased brother, Alvin, in the Celestial Kingdom, in spite of his having died prior to the Restoration and hence, without baptism. According to Smith's previous understanding, Alvin should have been in the Terrestrial Kingdom. He recorded that he

> marvled how it was that he [Alvin] had obtained an inheritance in that Kingdom, seeing that he had departed this life, before the Lord had set his hand to gather Israel the second time and had not been baptised for the remission of sins—Thus came the voice of the Lord unto me saying all who have died with[out] a knowledge of this gospel, who would have received it, if they had been permited to tarry, shall be heirs of the celestial Kingdom of God—also all that shall die henseforth, without a knowledge of it, who would have received it, with all their hearts, shall be heirs of that Kingdom.[27]

Although Latter-day Saints today would offer this vision as the beginning of the doctrine of baptism for the dead, such was not the case. For example, a lengthy article the following year in the church periodical stated that the salvation of the dead would be effected by their acceptance of the gospel which would be preached to them in the afterlife, citing 1 Peter 4:6 as justification for this doctrine: "For, for this cause was the gospel preached to them that are dead, that they might be judged according to men in the flesh, but live according to God in the spirit."[28] That their salvation was contingent upon belief and not baptism was further clarified in 1840 by Apostle Parley P. Pratt. Writing in the church newspaper in England, he stated:

> Q.—Was not the thief on the cross saved without baptism?
> A.—If he was, it was because he had no opportunity to obey; and, therefore, was not saved through a Gospel ministration, but was

---

25. Revelation of 16 Feb. 1832, in Kirtland Revelation Book, 1-10; also DC, 1835 XCI.

26. Scott H. Faulring, ed., *An American Prophet's Record: The Diaries and Journals of Joseph Smith* (Salt Lake City: Signature Books in association with Smith Research Associates, 1987), 118-20, 21 Jan. 1836. This vision was canonized by the Latter-day Saint church in 1978 and now comprises sec. 137 of the Doctrine and Covenants.

27. Ibid.

28. *Messenger and Advocate* 3 (Apr. 1837): 470-71.

included in the same mercy as the heathens, who have never had the offer of the Gospel, and therefore, are under no condemnation for not obeying it.[29]

Two months later, in the course of delivering a funeral sermon in Nauvoo, Smith introduced a new doctrine to the church. Citing Paul's isolated reference to those who were "baptized for the dead," a scripture with which Smith had long been familiar but never previously cited,[30] he went on to say that church members could now perform this ordinance in behalf of their deceased kin.[31]

The following month, as Joseph Smith, Sr., lay on his deathbed, Joseph Jr. informed his father that "it was then the privilege of the Saints to be baptized for the dead." His father requested that Joseph Jr. immediately be baptized for Alvin. He died later that same day.[32]

Initially, the rules governing baptism for the dead were liberal. Proxies could be baptized for deceased kin of either sex[33] provided they believed that the deceased "would have embraced the gospel if they had been priviledged with hearing it."[34] Although most baptisms

---

29. Parley P. Pratt, "The Gospel Illustrated in Questions and Answers," *Millennial Star* 1 (June 1840): 27.

30. Prior to the vision of 1832 defining the degrees of glory in the afterlife, Smith had revised 1 Corinthians 15 in the course of "retranslating" the Bible, making changes in verses 26, 27, and 31 but none in verse 29 which speaks of baptism for the dead.

31. Journal History, 15 Aug. 1840, LDS archives.

32. Lucy Mack Smith, *Biographical Sketches of Joseph Smith the Prophet, and His Progenitors for Many Generations* (Liverpool: Orson Pratt, 1853), 265-66.

33. For example, in 11 October 1840 William Huntington was baptized for his deceased mother (William Huntington diary, Huntington Library). This practice continued past Smith's death, as Heber C. Kimball recorded that on 3 September 1844 his wife was baptized for "Samwell Ellis and wife Ellen Fitch" (Stanley B. Kimball, ed., *On the Potter's Wheel: The Diaries of Heber C. Kimball* [Salt Lake City: Signature Books in association with Smith Research Associates, 1987], 84, 3 Sept. 1844). Only later was the requirement imposed that the proxy be of the same sex as the recipient. See Susa Young Gates, "Temples in Modern Times," *Young Woman's Journal* 19 (1908): 617.

34. Joseph Smith to the Twelve Apostles, 15 Dec. 1840, in Dean C. Jessee, ed., *The Personal Writings of Joseph Smith* (Salt Lake City: Deseret Book Co., 1984), 486.

were initially performed in the Mississippi River adjacent to Nauvoo, some were conducted in Ohio[35] and Iowa.[36] Having received baptism and confirmation through proxies, and accepting Jesus' gospel in the spirit world, the dead could "be blessed with a part in the first resurrection, and be a partaker and an inheritor of a celestial glory," with no other ordinances necessarily being performed in their behalf.[37]

As time went on the rules changed. Coincident with the construction of the Nauvoo temple came a requirement that subsequent baptisms for the dead be performed in the temple font.[38] The necessity of a recorder was stated in 1842,[39] for "whatsoever you do not record on earth shall not be recorded in heaven."[40] Though initially only baptism and confirmation were required, in January 1844 Smith declared that "all the ordinances, Baptisms, confirmations, washings anointings ordinations & sealing"—that is, all ordinances required for the living—were now required for the dead.[41]

While the mode of baptism described in the Bible and the Book of Mormon enabled entry into the church as well as the cleansing of one's sins, a new form of the ordinance served only the latter purpose: "April 11th 1841. Joseph and Sidney baptized each other for the remission of their sins as this order was then instituted in the church. According on the 27th of April I was baptized for the remission of my sins."[42] Although it is not known what precipitated their action, Smith

35. Some were performed at a conference in Kirtland on 22 May 1841 and reported in *Times and Seasons* 2 (1 July 1841): 458-60.

36. HC, 4:382-83.

37. *Times and Seasons* 2 (1 May 1841): 397-99.

38. Joseph Smith discourse, 3 Oct. 1841, in *Times and Seasons* 2 (15 Oct. 1841): 577-78. An exception occurred in 1842 while the font was being renovated (HC, 5:350).

39. Joseph Smith discourse, 31 Aug. 1842, in Andrew F. Ehat and Lyndon W. Cook, eds., *The Words of Joseph Smith* (Provo, UT: Religious Studies Center, Brigham Young University, 1980), 131.

40. Joseph Smith epistle, "To the Church of Jesus Christ of Latter Day Saints," 6 Sept. 1842, in *Times and Seasons* 3 (1 Oct. 1842): 934-36.

41. Joseph Smith discourse, 21 Jan. 1844, in Scott G. Kenney, ed., *Wilford Woodruff's Journal* (Midvale, UT: Signature Books, 1983), 2:341-43, 21 Jan. 1844. Smith reiterated this new requirement on at least two other occasions, 8 April 1844 (Ehat and Cook, 362-65) and 12 May 1844 (ibid., 368-72).

42. William Huntington diary. Although there is evidence of at

and Rigdon thereby began a practice which lasted throughout the remainder of the nineteenth century and periodically included most of the church membership. Participation in rebaptism was not considered negatively, as an admission of grievous sin. Rather, it was seen in a positive sense, as a sign of faithfulness and recommitment, as indicated by Apostle Wilford Woodruff:

> After the meeting closed the congregation again assembled upon the bank of the river & Joseph the seer went into the river & Baptized all that Came unto him & I considered it my privilege to be Baptized for the remission of my sins for I had not been since I first Joined the Church in 1833. I was then Baptized under the hands of Elder Zerah Pulsipher. Therefore I went forth into the river & was Baptized under the hands of JOSEPH THE SEER.[43]

Although rebaptism generally was practiced as a stand-alone ordinance, it was occasionally combined with baptism for the dead: "Brothers [Wilford] Woodruff and [Charles C.] Rich baptized about 100 for the remission of sins and for their dead."[44] The popularity of the ordinance is described in an 1843 letter written from Nauvoo: "Nearly *All* the Church have been *Baptised again*, for the Remission of their *sins*, since they joined the Church; I have also, by the hands of *Br. Joseph*, (as he himself has been.) & I would advise Jane[,] and you[,] Mary, to attend to it as soon as you can have the opportunity of an Elder or Priest of the Church to Administer."[45]

The final development in baptism theology and practice, baptism for the restoration of health, appears to have relied on both Old and New Testament precedents. In the former case, Naaman, a leper, was instructed by Elisha to "go and wash in Jordan seven times, and thy flesh shall come again to thee, and thou shalt be clean" (2 Kgs. 5:10-14). Although refusing the directive at first, Naaman eventually complied,

---

least one "rebaptism" as early as 1832 (D. Michael Quinn, "The Practice of Rebaptism at Nauvoo," *Brigham Young University Studies* 18 [Winter 1978]: 227, quoting from the Journal of Jared Carter, 1831-33, 7 May 1832), that case appears to have derived from the excommunication of the man who performed the original baptism.

43. *Wilford Woodruff's Journal*, 2:165, 27 Mar. 1842.

44. Manuscript History of Brigham Young, 15 May 1842, LDS archives.

45. Jacob Scott to Mary Warnock, 13 May 1843, LDS archives (emphasis in original).

"and his flesh came again like unto the flesh of a little child, and he was clean."[46] In the New Testament case, the waters of Bethesda were famed for their curative powers: "For an angel went down at a certain season into the pool, and troubled the water: whosoever then first after the troubling of the water stepped in was made whole of whatsoever disease he had" (John 5:1-4).

While formal introduction of this new ordinance followed completion of the baptismal font in the basement of the Nauvoo temple, two earlier unexpected instances may have been instructive to Smith. The first, in 1832, involved the baptism of his uncle, John Smith:

> My father had been for several years very feeble in health, and, for about six months previous to his baptism, had not been able to visit his barn, and was pronounced by physicians in the last stage of consumption. His neighbors all believed that baptism would kill him. I [George A. Smith] cut the ice in the creek, and broke a road for forty rods through the crust on two feet of snow; the day was very cold; the neighbors looked on with astonishment, expecting to see him die in the water, but his health continued improving from that moment.[47]

A similar episode occurred seven years later, when Hyrum Smith baptized John Rigdon, son of Sidney Rigdon.[48]

The baptismal font was dedicated in November 1841. One month earlier, in anticipation of the event, the Quorum of the Twelve published an epistle stating that the font would serve not only for baptisms for the dead but also as "a place, over which the heavenly messengers may watch and trouble the waters as in days of old, so that when the sick are put therein they shall be made whole."[49] Two weeks later, when the font was first used for baptisms, Wilford Woodruff delineated the types of baptism to be performed therein: "I then met the Twelve at B. Youngs untill 4 o-clock at which time we repaired to the *Baptismal Font* in the Temple for the purpose of Baptizing for the dead, for the remission

---

46. The parallel is inescapable in the case of Horace Eldredge who in 1842 was baptized seven days in a row in a freezing river for restoration of his health (Horace S. Eldredge diary, Dec. 1842, LDS archives).

47. George A. Smith, in Journal History, 9 Jan. 1832.

48. *Improvement Era* 3 (July 1900): 697.

49. "An Epistle of the Twelve, to the brethren scattered abroad on the Continent of America," 12 Oct. 1841, in *Times and Seasons* 2 (15 Oct. 1841): 567-69.

of Sins & for healing."[50] Another epistle by the Twelve, published the following month, spoke not only of the practice but also of its efficacy, stating that "several have already attended to this ordinance by which the sick have been made whole."[51] Although Smith stated that baptism "for the healing of the body must be in the font," there were occasional exceptions, as when his wife, Emma, was baptized in the river[52] and when baptisms for health were performed in Philadelphia.[53] Although one baptism for health was generally considered sufficient, occasionally the ordinance was performed repeatedly.

By the end of 1841 four types of baptism were being practiced in the church. Smith stated in April 1842 that "baptism for the dead, and for the healing of the body must be in the font, those coming into the church and those rebaptized may be done in the river."[54] Of these, three had scriptural precedent, while rebaptism for sins was strictly a Latter-day Saint innovation. Although the latter continued throughout the nineteenth century, and baptism for health lasted into the 1920s, only baptism for entry into the church and for the dead are today sanctioned by the Utah church.

Confirmation

The gift of the Holy Ghost is described in the New Testament and the Book of Mormon, and in both cases two forms of bestowal are described. During Jesus' ministry he promised his disciples the gift but stated that they would not receive it until he was gone. On the Day of Pentecost the promise was fulfilled—not through hands-on conferral but by "cloven tongues like as of fire" (Acts 2:3). Later the disciples conferred the gift by the laying on of hands.

In the Book of Mormon there is only one reference to the laying on of hands: "The words of Christ, which he spake unto his disciples, the twelve whom he had chosen, as he laid his hands upon

---

50. *Wilford Woodruff's Journal*, 2:138, 21 Nov. 1841.

51. *Times and Seasons* 3 (15 Dec. 1841): 625-27.

52. HC, 5:167-68.

53. Philadelphia Branch Record, Oct. 1843, Library-Archives, The Auditorium, Reorganized Church of Jesus Christ of Latter Day Saints, Independence, Missouri (hereafter RLDS Library-Archives).

54. *Times and Seasons* 3 (15 Apr. 1842): 763.

them— . . . [and said] ye shall have power that to him upon whom ye shall lay your hands, ye shall give the Holy Ghost. . . . and on as many as they laid their hands, fell the Holy Ghost" (BM, LDS, Moro. 2:1-3). In other Book of Mormon instances the Holy Ghost was conferred without a human intermediary, similar to the Day of Pentecost. The Lamanites, for example, "were baptized with fire and with the Holy Ghost, and they knew it not" (BM, LDS, 3 Ne. 9:20). On another occasion, "when they were all baptized and had come up out of the water, the Holy Ghost did fall upon them" (19:13).

It appears that Joseph Smith and Oliver Cowdery received the gift of the Holy Ghost in the same way. Smith recorded that "no sooner had I baptized Oliver Cowdery than the Holy Ghost fell upon him."[55] Once the church was organized, confirmation was by the laying on of hands, and, aside from the special case of Smith and Cowdery,[56] there

---

55. *Times and Seasons* 3 (1 Aug. 1842): 865-66. In addressing concerns about confirmation without the laying on of hands, Apostle Joseph Fielding Smith wrote: "We may correctly believe that the Lord may bestow the gift of the Holy Ghost by other means than by the laying on of hands if occasion requires it" ("Your Question," 390-91).

56. In 1900 First Presidency member Joseph F. Smith wrote: "As to the means through which the Holy Ghost confirms the ordinance of baptism, this is by the laying on of hands. If it be asked why this is so, the answer is, simply because God has so ordained. There are two instances on record when the Spirit confirmed baptism without the laying on of hands, (so far as we know). The one was that of Christ, the other that of Joseph Smith and Oliver Cowdery. In the case of the Savior, the Holy Ghost manifested itself in the sign of a dove, and a voice from heaven said, 'This is my beloved Son in whom I am well pleased.' In the case of Joseph and Oliver, 'the ordinance of baptism by water was immediately followed by a most glorious baptism of the Holy Ghost.' Divine joy and inspiration fell upon the two brethren and each in turn exercised to a remarkable degree the spirit of prophecy. (See *Millennial Star*, vol. 3, p. 148.)

"It will be noticed, however, that these two exceptions mark the beginning of dispensations. There was at hand no one with authority to confer the Holy Ghost by laying on of hands. But even if we had not these good reasons, the simple fact that God ordained that confirmation is to be by laying on of hands must forever dispose of the question" ("Editor's Table," *Improvement Era* 4 [Nov. 1900]: 52-53).

is no record of members receiving the gift of the Holy Ghost by other means.[57]

No confirmation prayer is contained in the Book of Mormon or in Latter-day Saint revelations. Two early sources suggest that the prayer was generally brief and that, like the baptismal and sacramental prayers which were prescribed by revelation, the authority of the officiator was inferred. Ezra Booth, an elder and participant in the June 1831 general conference, quoted a form of the prayer, "In the name of Jesus Christ, receive ye the the Holy Ghost."[58] A year later Heber C. Kimball wrote:

> Brother Ezra Landon preached in Avon and Genesee, baptized eighteen or twenty, and being afraid to confirm them and promise them the Holy Ghost, he requested me to confirm them, which I did according to the best of my knowledge, pronouncing only a few words on the head of each one, and invariably saying, "recieve ye the Holy Ghost in the name of Jesus Christ." Immediately the Holy Ghost fell upon them and several commenced speaking in tongues before they arose from their knees.[59]

There is evidence that all four types of baptism were accompanied by confirmation, although the forms of the prayers are not recorded. In the case of baptism for the dead, confirmation was performed concomitantly with baptism, as shown by the record of the first baptisms performed in the temple font: "At 4 p.m., brothers [Heber C.] Kimball, [John] Taylor and I baptized about forty persons in the font, for the dead; brothers [Willard] Richards, [Wilford] Woodruff and George A. Smith confirming."[60] After being rebaptized for the remission of sins in 1842, Wilford Woodruff wrote that "we then again repaired to the place of meeting near the Temple & Elder [John] Taylor & meself was confirmed by the laying on of hands."[61] Confirmation following baptism for health was much less common.[62]

---

57. The June 1831 general conference was likened to a Pentecost by participants, but the Latter-day Saint elders had already been confirmed prior to the conference.

58. Ezra Booth to Rev. Ira Eddy, Sept. 1831, in E. D. Howe, *Mormonism Unvailed . . .* (Painesville, OH: Published by the Author, 1834), 180-81.

59. Journal History, Apr. 1832.

60. Manuscript History of Brigham Young, 21 Nov. 1840.

61. *Wilford Woodruff's Journal*, 2:165, 27 Mar. 1842.

62. One example was Elijah Newman who had been unable to

The Sacrament of the Lord's Supper

The Book of Mormon provided the model for Latter-day Saint observance of the Eucharist.[63] In introducing the ordinance to the Nephites, the resurrected Christ blessed bread and wine, gave it to his disciples, who ate and drank until they "were filled," and said that one of them would be ordained to perpetuate the ordinance "unto all those who shall believe and be baptized in my name" (BM, LDS, 3 Ne. 18:1-5). The prophet Moroni later echoed the admonition of Paul by warning "that ye partake not of the sacrament of Christ unworthily" (BM, LDS, Morm. 9:29; cf. 1 Cor. 11:27-29) and prescribed the prayers for blessing the bread and wine which are still used within the Latter-day Saint tradition (BM, LDS, Moro. 4:3, 5:2). Moroni stipulated that the officiator and the church members kneel together for the blessings (4:2) and recorded that "they did meet together oft to partake of bread and wine" (6:6).

In one of the earliest known revelations, Oliver Cowdery was given similar instructions, including the texts of the prayers over the bread and wine (identical to those in the Book of Mormon), instructions that the officiator (a priest or elder) was to "kneel with the Church," and an admonition that "the Church shall oft partake of bread & wine."[64] Although no major changes occurred in this ordinance during Joseph Smith's lifetime, several aspects of the ordinance were discussed, clarified, and in some cases changed.

The earliest change concerned the substances to be consumed. While the Book of Mormon and the 1829 "Articles of the Church" specified bread and wine, an 1830 revelation stated that "it matters not what ye shall eat or what ye shall drink, when ye shall partake of the sacrament."[65] The same revelation, reflecting suspicions about those

---

walk without crutches. "After the baptism and confirmation, he returned without any help" (William Clayton diary, 25 Apr. 1847, in *Juvenile Instructor* 21 [15 Oct. 1886]: 310).

63. Within the Christian community the term "sacrament" generally refers to many observances, of which the eucharist is but one. In the Latter-day Saint tradition "sacrament" is synonymous with eucharist and carries no other connotation. Therefore, its use throughout this section will always be in reference to the Lord's Supper.

64. "The Articles of the Church of Christ," in Woodford, 288.

65. Revelation dated Aug. 1830, in *Painesville Telegraph*, 19 Apr. 1831; also BC XXIX:2.

not sympathetic to their cause, warned: "ye shall not purchase wine, neither strong drink, of your enemies." While this revelation justifies current Latter-day Saint use of water instead of wine, it is important to note that the proscription was against "your enemies," not wine. Furthermore, the Word of Wisdom, given three years later, which stated that "wine or strong drink" were "not good," specifically endorsed the use of sacramental wine (DC, 1835 LXXX:1). Indeed, there is no known reference to a liquid other than wine being used for the sacrament during Smith's lifetime. Later references demonstrate that wine remained the preferred substance, even after water began to be used:

> Q. Are bread and wine always used in the Sacrament?
> A. No, water is occasionally used, when wine made by the Church cannot be obtained.[66]

As late as 1884 the president of the St. George, Utah, Stake "advised such of the wards of the Stake as do not use wine in administering the sacrament to make arrangements to do so."[67] The counsel that "it matters not what ye shall . . . drink" led one missionary in the Society Islands to opt for a local product: "On the 5th of August [1844], I administered the sacrament. For wine I substituted cocoanut milk, that was a pure beverage, which never had come to the open air till we broke the nut for that purpose."[68]

Another concern was who should officiate. The 1829 "Articles of the Church" had named elders and priests as officiators, only implying that teachers and deacons were not authorized. An 1831 revision of the same revelation clarified the matter, stating that "neither the teacher nor the deacon has the authority to . . . administer the sacrament."[69] The same revision emphasized the seriousness with which the ordinance was to be administered by stating: "The elders or priests are to have a sufficient time to expound all things concerning

---

66. John Jaques, "Catechism for Children," in *Millennial Star* 16 (28 Jan. 1854): 59.

67. St. George Stake Conference minutes, 16 Mar. 1884, in *Deseret News Weekly*, 2 Apr. 1884, 175.

68. Addison Pratt letter, published in *Millennial Star* 6 (1 Aug. 1845): 58.

69. *Painesville Telegraph*, 19 Apr. 1831.

this church of Christ to their understanding previous to their partaking of the sacrament."[70]

Worthiness of the recipient, mandated both by the New Testament and the Book of Mormon, was taken seriously. An 1831 revelation, while forbidding the exclusion of transgressors from meetings, required that "if any have trespassed, let him not partake until he makes reconciliation" (BC XLIX:4-5). The worthiness of officiators also became a matter of concern. Some members refused to take the sacrament "because the Elders administering it did not observe the words of wisdom to obey them."[71]

It is not clear how often the sacrament was administered. Although the Book of Mormon records that "they did meet together oft to partake of bread and wine" (BM, LDS, Moro. 6:6), and the 1829 "Articles of the Church" instructed that "the Church shall oft partake of bread & wine," there is no record of the frequency with which the ordinance was observed. That it probably was not weekly is suggested by the records of one branch of the church, which resolved "to partake of the sacrament every second sabbath."[72]

Blessing Children

One of the most touching moments in Jesus' New World ministry was when he blessed the children. The Book of Mormon records:

And it came to pass that he commanded that their little children should be brought.

So they brought their little children and set them down upon the ground round about him, and Jesus stood in the midst; and the multitude gave way till they had all been brought unto him.

. . . and he took their little children, one by one, and blessed them, and prayed unto the Father for them (BM, LDS, 3 Ne. 11:11, 12, 21).

An early revelation (and the only revelation to Joseph Smith which mentioned the subject) instructed: "Every member of this church of Christ having children are to bring them to the elders before the church

70. Ibid.
71. "Kirtland Council Minutes," 20 Feb. 1834.
72. "Record of the New Trenton Branch," 16 Nov. 1844, RLDS Library-Archives.

who are to lay hands upon them in the name of the Lord, and bless them in the name of Christ."[73] Aside from the requirement that the children be blessed "in the name of Christ," no form of blessing was recorded. Inasmuch as "every member" was to have his or her children blessed, one may assume that this ordinance was commonly performed, although few records refer to it.

Reynolds Cahoon noted that one "Satuerday Evening [we] held a Met[ing] with the Br[e]th[ren] at Mr Reevs & Blest the Children in the name of the lord & sealed the Church unto eternal life."[74] On the other hand, Orson Pratt indicated that children could be blessed as part of a normal Sunday service: "Being the Sabbath we held a meeting in the forenoon also one in the afternoon, and Brother Lyman [Johnson] ordained Brother Horace Cowen, an elder, and laid hands upon the little children and blessed them in the name of the Lord, and administered the sacrament, and sealed up the Church unto eternal life."[75] And the minutes of a Missouri conference read, "The meeting adjourned for one hour—and again opened by David W. Patten—After which the bread and wine was administered, and 95 infants were brought forward and blessed."[76]

Although parents were instructed to have their children blessed, this was not considered an ordinance necessary for one's salvation. There was no requirement that those joining the church receive it.

Healing

Of all the miracles of Jesus, healing the sick was the most prominent. Similarly, the Book of Mormon records that the resurrected Christ "did heal them every one as they were brought forth unto him" (BM, LDS, 3 Ne. 17:9). From the early days of the Restoration, healing was an important ordinance for church members, as well as a source of considerable commentary by the non-Mormon press.

A revelation in July 1830 warned Joseph Smith and Oliver Cowdery against seeking after miracles yet allowed some exceptions, among them "healing the sick" (BC XXV:23). A revelation later the

---

73. *Painesville Telegraph*, 19 Apr. 1831.

74. Reynolds Cahoon diary, 26 Nov. 1831, LDS archives.

75. Orson Pratt diary, 8 Sept. 1833, LDS archives.

76. Minutes of a Conference in Far West, Missouri, 6 Apr. 1838, in *Elder's Journal* 1 (July 1838): 47.

same year went a step further, promising the elders the ability to heal: "I will show miracles, signs and wonders, unto all those who believe on my name. And whoso shall ask it in my name, in faith, they shall cast out devils; they shall heal the sick; they shall cause the blind to receive their sight, and the deaf to hear, and the dumb to speak, and the lame to walk" (BC XXXVII:9-10, Dec. 1830).

From 1830 through Joseph Smith's life numerous attempts were made at healing. John Corrill, the Church Historian, wrote in 1839: "The Mormons believe in, and constantly practice the laying on of hands and praying for the healing of the sick; sometimes they have been healed, sometimes partly healed, and sometimes not benefitted at all."[77] In the early years, when expectations were high, newspapers in New York and Ohio reported that Mormons "pretend to heal the sick and work miracles" and "say much about working miracles, and pretend to have that power."[78] Shortly before the June 1831 general conference, an Ohio newspaper reported that "in June they are all to meet, and hold a kind of jubilee in this new 'land of promise,' where they are to work divers miracles,"[79] and shortly after the conference several Ohio papers stated that "they still persist in their power to work miracles. They say they have often seen them done—the sick are healed—the lame walk."[80] This wave of publicity soon subsided but was followed four years later by similar reports in anticipation of the endowment in the Kirtland House of the Lord: "They assure you, with the utmost confidence, that they shall soon be able to raise the dead, to heal the sick, the deaf, the dumb, and the blind, &c. Indeed, more than one assured me, that they had, themselves, by the laying on of their hands, restored the sick to health."[81]

That many attempts were successful was attested to by a variety of people who either performed, received, or witnessed the healing ordinance. Church Historian John Whitmer wrote of a time in 1831

77. Corrill, chap. 27.

78. *Palmyra Reflector*, 14 Feb. 1831; *Painesville Telegraph*, 15 Feb. 1831.

79. *Western Courier*, 26 May 1831.

80. *Geauga Gazette* (Painesville), 21 June 1831; *Western Reserve Chronicle* (Warren), 30 June 1831; *Ohio Repository* (Canton), 8 July 1831; *Republican Advocate* (Wooster), 16 July 1831.

81. *Ohio Atlas*, 16 Mar. 1836; also *Painesville Telegraph*, 20 May 1836.

when "some were sick of various diseases, and were healed by the power which was in them through Jesus Christ."[82] A particularly dramatic case occurred just after the June 1831 general conference. Simeon Carter, who by virtue of ordination to the High Priesthood at that conference had been "endowed with great power from on high," visited a woman who had fallen from a wagon on her way to church. "She was so badly bruised that she could not even move a toe, and her pain was intense. . . . [Carter] took her by the hand, saying, 'I command you in the name of Jesus Christ to arise and walk.' And she arose and walked from room to room."[83]

The following month Jared Carter recorded that he and his missionary companion healed a woman who for six years had suffered from tuberculosis, stating that she "was healed, suddenly, and continued well, being freed from all afflictions."[84] Carter was particularly gifted and recorded other successful administrations during 1831-32.[85] Other gifted healers were David Patten[86] and Orson Pratt,[87] both of whom later became apostles. Patten recorded healing a man with a three-year infirmity, a woman who had been ill for six months, another whose illness for eight years had caused her not to be able to "walk fifty steps at one tyme," and other less dramatic instances. Pratt healed a woman who "had been sick about 12 weeks & vomited much blood" and another who "lay sicke of a disease with which she had been afflicted 5 or 6 years & she covenanted to obey the gospel if the Lord would heal her & I prayed for & laid my hands upon her in the name of Jesus & she began to recover & a few days after was baptized."[88]

More such accounts could be cited. However, not all attempts to heal were successful. A report in late 1830 stated that "these newly

---

82. "The Book of John Whitmer, Kept by Commandment," chap. 3, in F. Mark McKiernan and Roger D. Launius, eds., *An Early Latter Day Saint History* (Independence, MO: Herald Publishing House, 1980), 45.

83. Jared Carter journal, in Journal History, 8 June 1831.

84. Jared Carter journal, in Journal History, July 1831.

85. For example, see Journal History excerpts from Carter's journal for July, 27 Sept. 1831, and 19 Oct. 1832.

86. David Wyman Patten journal, LDS archives.

87. Orson Pratt diary, LDS archives.

88. Ibid., 13 and 23 June 1833.

commissioned disciples [Oliver Cowdrey, Peter Whitmer, Parley P. Pratt and Ziba Peterson] have totally failed thus far in their attempts to heal."[89] Two months later a New York newspaper said that "they pretend to heal the sick and work miracles, and had made a number of unsuccessful attempts to do so."[90] At the same time the *Painesville Telegraph* reported that Sidney Rigdon, a new convert, was critical of the missionaries' inability to heal. "Mr. R. now blames Cowdery for *attempting* to work miracles, and says it was not intended to be confirmed in that way."[91]

A particularly embarrassing attempt to heal involved Smith and a young man, Warner Doty, who died in spite of all efforts and promises to the contrary. A local newspaper reported: "The Mormonites will probably contradict many of these statements, as they have many positive facts heretofore; but we have our information from a relative of the deceased, who was present during the last 18 hours of his life."[92] The incident caused enough of a stir that at least one eastern newspaper reported it.[93]

A revelation in December 1830 stated that it was necessary to act "in faith" to effect healing, implying that lack of faith would negate the attempt (BC XXXVII:10). Another revelation two months later acknowledged that in some cases even faith was not enough: "The elders of the church, two or more shall be called, and shall pray for, and lay their hands upon them in my name, and if they die, they shall die unto me . . . And again, it shall come to pass, that he that has faith in me to be healed, and is not appointed unto death, shall be healed."[94] A revelation the following month implied that some would be more successful than others, for "to others it is given to have faith to heal" (BC XLIX:18). Smith had told the Quorum of Twelve Apostles prior to the 1836 endowment, "that you will not have power, after the endowment to heal those that have not faith."[95] One month later, when Smith's attempt to

---

89. *Painesville Telegraph*, 7 Dec. 1830.

90. *Palmyra Reflector*, 14 Feb. 1831.

91. *Painesville Telegraph*, 15 Feb. 1831, emphasis in original.

92. Ibid., 5 Apr. 1831.

93. *Independent Chronicle & Boston Patriot*, 7 May 1831.

94. *Painesville Telegraph*, 13 Sept. 1831; also BC XLIV:35, 38.

95. *Joseph Smith Diary*, 58, 12 Nov. 1835. Compare *Burlington*

heal a man was unsuccessful, he stated that the recipient's "faith was not sufficient to effect a cure."[96] "Whenever any miracle fails," wrote an outside observer, "they have a convenient salve at hand to account for the failure; that is the want of faith: a most impudent and efficious intruder, always ready at hand to nullify all their pious efforts, and to render them weak and feeble as other men."[97]

A crisis occurred when the Saints first moved to Illinois and many fell prey to malaria, including Smith. When reports reached him that the elders, in spite of blessing the sick, were not getting results, he rose from his bed and began to circulate among the Saints, apparently healing all whom he blessed. According to Joseph B. Noble, who was healed that day, "Joseph [Smith], at this time, rebuked the Elders for administering the form without the power. Said he, 'Let the Elders either obtain the power of God to heal the sick, or let them cease to administer the form without the power.'"[98] Several months later Smith told the Saints how to get the requisite power: "If the Saints are sick or have sickness in their families, and the Elders do not prevail[,] every family should get power by fasting & prayer & anointing with oil & continue so to do [and] their sick shall be healed[;] this also is the voice of the Spirit."[99] The ordinance continued to be performed throughout Smith's ministry and beyond, and although there were notable instances of miraculous healings, the observation of a non-Mormon in 1832 continued to hold true: "The people eat and drink, and some get drunk, suffer pain and disease, live and die like other people."[100]

The most common form of the healing ordinance consisted of the officiator (and often one or more assistants) laying hands on the head of the afflicted and uttering a prayer. This form had ample New Testament precedent and was advocated in the Book of Mormon, which stated "they shall lay hands on the sick and they shall recover" (BM,

---

Sentinel, 23 Mar. 1832.

96. Ibid., 14 Dec. 1835.

97. Rev. Truman Coe, in *The Ohio Observer,* 11 Aug. 1836.

98. *Juvenile Instructor* 15 (15 May 1880): 112.

99. Joseph Smith discourse of 30 July 1840, in John Smith diary, LDS archives; in Ehat and Cook, *Words of Joseph Smith,* 37.

100. B. Pixley, letter of 12 Oct. 1834, in *Journal and Telegraph* (Albany, NY), 12 Nov. 1832.

LDS, Morm. 9:24). An early Latter-day Saint revelation directed the elders to "lay their hands upon them in my name."[101] Dozens, perhaps hundreds, of accounts exist of healings via the laying on of hands between the years of 1830 and 1836. However, prior to November 1835 there is only one known account in which the recipient was anointed with oil.[102] Neither the Book of Mormon nor any known Latter-day Saint revelation prescribes anointing the sick with oil.[103]

While it is not certain what led to anointing with oil, it is possible that the idea was reinforced in Smith's mind during three days' discussion with Robert Matthews, who stayed with Smith in Kirtland from 9-11 November 1835 disguised as "Joshua, the Jewish Minister." Although Smith ultimately decided he was an imposter and expelled him from his home,[104] it is likely that Matthews's advocacy of anointing the sick with oil was appealing.[105] Although the Epistle of James admonished the elders to pray over the sick, "anointing him with oil in the name of the Lord" (James 5:14), Smith had not referred to this passage prior to the visit of Matthews, and the fact that Smith began regularly anointing the sick with oil only two weeks after Matthews's visit[106] suggests the likelihood of his influence.

---

101. *Painesville Telegraph*, 13 Sept. 1831; also BC XLIV:35.

102. This occurred on 8 September 1834 when Smith and Cowdery "united in anointing with oil and laying hands upon a sick sister who said she was healed" (Kirtland Council Minutes, 8 Sept. 1834).

103. In 1955 Apostle Joseph Fielding Smith addressed this issue by writing, "It is true there is no mention in the Doctrine and Covenants to the use of oil in administering to the sick, but there are references to the anointing with oil in the conferring of authority and sacred blessings. This practice has come down to us from the time of the organization of the Church, according to the pattern anciently given" ("Your Question," *Improvement Era* 58 [Sept. 1955]: 622). Although he correctly cited the use of oil for other purposes, its use either for those purposes or for administering to the sick occurred no earlier than November 1835, not in 1830 as he claimed.

104. HC, 2:304-307.

105. See G. Vale, *Fanaticism; Its Source and Influenze, Illustrated by the Simple Narrative of Isabelle, In the Case of MATTHIAS . . .* (New York: G. Vale, 1835).

106. The earliest known instance occurred on 28 November 1835. Smith reported, "We prayed for and layed our hands on him [Elder Clark] in the name of the Lord Jesus Christ and anointed him with oil

The use of oil became commonplace though not mandatory. For example, nearly two years after oil was first used Willard Richards was healed by Apostles Heber C. Kimball and Orson Hyde who laid hands on him but did not use oil.[107] One year later Samuel Tyler, seeing for the first time a sick man anointed with oil, wrote, "this is the first time I ever witness'd this ordinance."[108] By the time of Smith's death, other variations had arisen, including taking the oil internally.[109]

Although hands were usually placed on the head of the afflicted, occasionally the officiator merely took the afflicted by the hand. In one instance Jared Carter "took him by the hand and commanded him in the name of Christ to walk and by the power of Christ he was enabled to walk."[110] Yet another variation consisted in placing hands on the afflicted portion of the body: "Elder G. Snow observing that I was in pain & without my speaking a word he laid his hand upon my legs & spake in an unknown tongue perhaps 15 or twenty words; he then said Amen. Is the pain gone, said he? At that moment I first perceived that I was entirely free of the pain."[111]

Another form of healing involved no physical contact at all and was sometimes performed from a distance, similar to the example of Jesus[112] and to the healing of Zeezrom described in the Book of Mormon (BM, LDS, Alma 15:8-11). In 1832, David Patten's wife was sick with a fever. He wrote, "I perceiving that she had faith to be healed I went to her and sed in the name of Jesus Christ I

---

and rebuked his affliction, praying our Heavenly Father to hear and answer our prayers according to our faith" (*Joseph Smith Diary*, 68, 28 Nov. 1835).

107. Willard Richards diary, 16 July 1837, LDS archives.

108. Samuel D. Tyler, "A daily journal of the traveling of the Camp of Latter-day Saints which went out from Kirtland for Zion, July 6th, 1838," 23 Aug. 1838, in Journal History, 4 Oct. 1838.

109. "The Society Islands Mission," *Utah Genealogical and Historical Magazine* 5 (Apr. 1914): 66.

110. Jared Carter journal, Sept., 10 Oct. 1832.

111. Tyler, 23 Aug. 1838.

112. Examples of this type include the paralytic man (Matt. 9:1-8, Mark 2:1-12, Luke 5:17-26, John 5:6-9), the man with a withered hand (Matt. 12:9-14, Mark 3:1-6, Luke 6:6-11), and the ten lepers (Luke 17:11-14).

command you to arise and make your bed and she would and was made whole from that very hour."[113] Patten performed another healing in a similar fashion when a man whose son had been injured came to him requesting him "to go and heal his sores[.] I asked him if he believed that the Lord could heel him[.] he sed he did and I sed unto him in the name of Jesus Christ be it acording to your faith and he went his way."[114]

An uncommon form involved the intercession of the afflicted in his own behalf. This possibility was suggested by an early revelation which stated that those who "have not faith to be healed, but believeth" should call for the Elders to lay on hands,[115] implying that those with sufficient faith would not require intervention. A revelation the following month gave further endorsement to self-healing, stating that "to some it is given to have faith to be healed" (BC XLIX:18). Jared Carter wrote of several occasions when "I knew that the Lord had heard my prayer and relieved me."[116] Although this form of healing appears to have been uncommon, references to it attest to its validity. For example, First Presidency member Heber C. Kimball "touched upon the power which individuals possess, who have received the Priesthood, to bless themselves and to exercise faith for the removal of disease from their own tabernacles."[117]

George Q. Cannon, of the First Presidency, later defended the self-administration of consecrated oil,[118] and Apostle Orson F. Whitney, speaking in general conference, described an instance in which he had administered to himself:

> There was some consecrated oil in the house, but my green inexperience had made me think that it would be improper to use it on myself, there being no other elder present. But suffering had opened my eyes, and my faith was strong, for I felt that the pain had no business there. That night I carefully washed off the liniment, applied the

113. Patten journal, autumn 1832.

114. Ibid., Dec. 1832.

115. *Painesville Telegraph*, 13 Sept. 1831; also BC XLIV:35.

116. Jared Carter journal, 27 Sept. 1831.

117. Minutes of Sabbath meeting, 17 June 1866, in *Deseret Weekly News*, 21 June 1866, 229.

118. *Juvenile Instructor* 29 (15 Apr. 1894): 242.

Self-healing

holy oil, and rebuked the pain in the name of Jesus. The effect was instantaneous. I turned my arm over—the pain was gone; and I have never felt a vestige of it since.[119]

One form of healing reached to the Old Testament for a model, where Moses made a metal serpent on a pole and told the Israelites they could be healed by gazing upon it (Num. 21:9). This was cited twice in the Book of Mormon (BM, LDS, 1 Ne. 17:41; Alma 33:19-21). The first known LDS healing through the use of artifacts was in the patriarchal blessing of Lorenzo Snow: "Thy shadow shall restore the Sick; the diseased shall send to thee their aprons and handkershiefs and by thy touch their owners may be made whole."[120]

Of particular value were relics which had been associated with Smith, both in life and in death. Kimball explained:

> How much would you give for even a cane that Father Abraham had used? or a coat or ring that the Saviour had worn? The rough oak boxes in which the bodies of Joseph and Hyrum were brought from Carthage, were made into canes and other articles. I have a cane made from the plank of one of those boxes, so as brother Brigham and a great many others, and we prize them highly, and esteem them a great blessing. I want to carefully preserve my cane, and when I am done with it here, I shall hand it down to my heir, with instructions to him to do the same. And the day will come when there will be multitudes who will be healed through the instrumentality of those canes, and the devil cannot overcome those who have them, in consequence of their faith and confidence in the virtues connected with them. . . .
> I have known [of] Joseph, hundreds of times, [to] send his handkerchief to the sick, and they have been healed.[121]

One of those handkerchiefs came into the possession of Wilford

---

119. General conference address, 4 Apr. 1925, in *Ninety-fifth Annual Conference of the Church of Jesus Christ of Latter-day Saints* (Salt Lake City: Church of Jesus Christ of Latter-day Saints, 1925), 20-21.

120. Patriarchal Blessing of Lorenzo Snow, given by Joseph Smith, Sr., 15 Dec. 1836, LDS archives.

121. Heber C. Kimball discourse, 15 Mar. 1857, in *Journal of Discourses* (Liverpool, Eng.: S. W. Richards, 1857), 4:294.

Woodruff in 1839. He later used it to heal his daughter of "a vary Severe attack of inflamation on the lungs" by placing it on her stomach.[122]

As has been shown, some men appear to have possessed a gift for healing. While there is no record of such a gift having been formally bestowed upon these men, the patriarchal blessing later served as a conduit through which occasionally came the promise of healing powers. It is important to note that women as well as men were thus blessed. The promise to Elizabeth Ann Whitney was, "Behold, when thy husband is far from thee and thy little ones are afflicted thou shalt have power to prevail and they shall be healed."[123] Flora Jacobs was told, "Thou shalt have authority to lay thy hands on thy children when the Elders cannot be had and they shall recover[,] diseases shall stand rebuked."[124] Edna Rogers was similarly advised, "In the absence of thy husband thou must pray with thy family. When they are sick thou shall lay hands on them, and they shall recover. Sickness shall stand back."[125] And Louisa C. Jackson was assured that "Inasmuch as thou art faithful in the Covenant thou shalt have power to heal the sick in their own houses."[126]

Cursing

Not to be confused with profanity, the ordinance of cursing consisted of a formal act with the intent of causing an adverse effect

---

122. *Wilford Woodruff's Journal*, 5:53, 25 and 26 May 1857.

123. Patriarchal Blessing of Elizabeth Ann Whitney, given by Joseph Smith, Sr., 14 Sept. 1835, Newel K. Whitney Papers, Harold B. Lee Library, Brigham Young University.

124. Patriarchal Blessing of Flora Jacobs, given by Joseph Smith, Sr., 13 June 1837, William Smith Patriarchal Blessing Book, 177-78, RLDS Library-Archives.

125. Patriarchal Blessing of Edna Rogers, given by Joseph Smith, Sr., 1837, in Linda King Newell and Valeen Tippetts Avery, "Sweet Counsel and Seas of Tribulation: The Religious Life of Women in Kirtland," *Brigham Young University Studies* 20 (Winter 1980): 158.

126. Patriarchal Blessing of Louisa C. Jackson, given by John Smith, 6 Feb. 1844, RLDS archives. There are undoubtedly more instances of women being given the gift of healing, but access to the patriarchal blessings books for the years of Joseph Smith's ministry (1834-44) is not allowed under current LDS archival policy.

on an individual or group. The anticipated effect could be expected to occur either in this life or in the life to come. There are several biblical references to cursing (Matt. 10:14; Mark 6:11; Luke 9:5, 10:11; Acts 13:51), but none in the Book of Mormon. The earliest mention of it in the Restoration occurred in a revelation two months after the church was formally organized: "And in whatsoever place ye shall enter, and they receive you not, in my name, ye shall leave a cursing instead of a blessing, by casting off the dust of your feet against them as a testimony, and cleansing your feet by the wayside" (BC XXV:25, July 1830).

Although cursing is not considered an ordinance in the Latter-day Saint church today,[127] it was important enough to be mentioned in eight published revelations:

> And shake off the dust of thy feet against those who receive thee not, not in their presence, lest thou provoke them, but in secret, and wash thy feet as a testimony against them in the day of judgment (BC LXI:22, 8 Aug. 1831).

> To them is power given, to seal both on earth and in heaven, the unbelieving and rebellious; yea, verily, to seal them up unto the day when the wrath of God shall be poured out upon the wicked (BC I:2, 1 Nov. 1831).

> In whatsoever house ye enter, and they receive you not, ye shall depart speedily from that house, and shake off the dust of your feet as a testimony against them; and you shall be filled with joy and gladness and know this, that in the day of judgement you shall be judges of that house, and condemn them; and it shall be more tolerable for the heathen in the day of judgment, than for that house (DC, 1835 LXXXVII:3, 25 Jan. 1832).

> He that receiveth you not, go away from him alone by your-selves, and cleanse your feet, even with water, pure water, whether in heat or in cold, and bear testimony of it unto your Father which is in heaven, and return not again unto that man. And in whatsoever village or city ye enter, do likewise. Nevertheless, search diligently and spare not; and wo unto that house, or that village, or city, that rejecteth you, or your words, or testimony concerning me (DC, 1835 IV:16, 22/23 Sept. 1832).

> And whoso rejecteth you shall be rejected of my Father, and his

---

127. That is, no church handbook or manual lists it among official ordinances.

house; and you shall cleanse your feet in the secret places by the way for a testimony against them (DC, 1835 LXXXVIII:1, Aug. 1833).

And inasmuch as mine enemies come against you to drive you from my goodly land, . . . ye shall curse them. And whomsoever ye curse, I will curse, and ye shall avenge me of mine enemies.[128]

Whosoever he [Hyrum Smith] curses shall be cursed (DC, LDS, 124:93, 19 Jan. 1841).

Whatsoever you seal on earth shall be sealed in heaven; . . . and whomsoever you curse I will curse (DC, LDS, 132:46-47, 12 July 1843).

As early as 1831 missionaries began to practice this ordinance. The earliest known account reflects some impatience on the part of the missionaries, who cursed the entire city of Detroit within one day of their arrival:

> We left the boat immediately and took lodging in a tavern; we breakfasted and dined freely with a merchant's wife, a sister to Almira Mack. We four brethren [John Murdock, Hyrum Smith, Lyman Wight and John Corrill] labored from morning till noon endeavoring to get a chance to preach, but we were not successful. I was turned out of doors for calling on the wool-carder to repent. After dinner we took leave of the two ladies and the family with which we had dined and wiped our feet as a testimony against that city.[129]

Later that year two of these same missionaries, John Murdock and Hyrum Smith, pronounced a similar curse against the city of Chicago.[130] Periodic cursings throughout the 1830s suggest that many individuals, communities, and cities were sentenced to a similar fate.[131]

---

128. Doctrine and Covenants of the Church of Jesus Christ of Latter-day Saints (Salt Lake City: Church of Jesus Christ of Latter-day Saints, 1981), 103:24-25, 24 Feb. 1834 (hereafter cited in the text as DC, LDS).

129. John Murdock journal, in Journal History, 14 June 1831.

130. John Murdock journal, late 1831.

131. For example, see Joseph Coe journal, in Journal History, 12 Oct. 1831; Orson Hyde diary, 19 Mar. 1832, Bancroft Library, University of California, Berkeley; Orson Pratt diary, 27 Feb., 20, 21 Mar. 1834, in *Utah Genealogical and Historical Magazine* 28 (Apr. 1937): 92-93; *Wilford Woodruff's Journal*, 1:100-101, 12 Oct. 1836; and *Heber C. Kimball Diary*,

POWER FROM ON HIGH

A letter from Joseph Smith and other church leaders in 1835 suggests that the ordinance was practiced too frequently, as it cautioned, "Pray for your enemies in the Church and curse not your foes without; for vengeance belongs to God."[132]

In spite of the call for moderation, a zenith of cursing occurred less than a year later at the solemn assembly after the dedication of the Kirtland House of the Lord. One participant, William Harris, described the scene:

> They [the Elders] began to prophesy, pronouncing blessings upon their friends, and curses upon their enemies. If I should be so unhappy as to go to the regions of the damned, I never expect to hear language more awful, or more becoming the infernal pit, than was uttered that night. The curses were pronounced principally upon the Jackson county mob in Missouri. After spending the night in alternate blessings and cursings, the meeting adjourned.[133]

That the Saints took this ordinance seriously and expected literal fulfilment is shown by an article in the church newspaper in 1840:

> Question 6th.—Ought the Elders and Priests, when their testimony is rejected, to wash their feet, &c., and is there no hope of those against whom they wash their feet? An idea has gone out that we consider such sealed up for destruction. Is the washing of feet, in this way, anything more than a testimony that we are clear of their blood, when we bear testimony of it before God?
> Answer.—Certainly . . . when the Elders and Priests have borne a faithful testimony to any city, town, village or person, and that testimony is rejected, and they have fulfilled the revelation [i.e., washing their feet], that city, town, village or person is in the hands of a right-

---

132. Letter of Joseph Smith, Oliver Cowdery, W. W. Phelps and John Whitmer (Kirtland, Ohio) to John M. Burk (Liberty, Clay County, Missouri), 1 June 1835, in Journal History, 1 June 1835.

133. In John C. Bennett, *The History of the Saints; or an Expose of Joe Smith and Mormonism* (Boston: Leland & Whiting, 1842), 136. Although Harris had left the church prior to writing his account, its accuracy is confirmed by Smith's own record: "The brethren began to prophesy upon each others heads, and cursings upon the enimies of Christ who inhabit Jackson county Missouri" (*Joseph Smith Diary*, 154, 30 Mar. 1836).

eous God, who will do with them according to his own pleasure; we are clear from their blood.[134]

In the later years of Smith's ministry, as well as thereafter, cursing took on a more personal profile. In 1840, for example, the Kirtland Elders' Quorum met to consider a complaint filed by Charles Thompson against Henry Moore, one of the charges being that Moore had "pronounc[ed] curses upon Elder Charles Thompson because he would not uphold him in the above abominations and wash[ed] his feet against me for the same reason."[135]

Cursing continued after Smith's death, with occasional noteworthy instances such as the action of the Salt Lake Stake presidency and high council in 1847: "Pres. John Smith sealed a curse upon the person or persons who killed [Albert] Carrington's cow until they came forward and made restitution. The curse was sanctioned unanimously by the council."[136] Because the recipient of this curse was anonymous, it is unlikely that one can determine if it was fulfilled. Indeed, there is no indication that any of the prior curses bore the expected fruit—at least during the mortal life of the recipients. The single apparent exception occurred in 1853 in the West Indies: "The Elders cursed the Mayor, Hector Michell, whose duty it was to have protected them in their person and position as ministers, in the name of the Lord Jesus Christ. Subsequently they learned that the mayor's toes and fingers rotted off and that he soon died with the rot and scabs."[137]

Casting out Evil Spirits

It was common knowledge among New Testament cultures that evil spirits could take possession of human bodies and thus cause disease. One of the signs of Jesus' divinity was his ability to overrule the power of such spirits, causing them to leave the body and restore health (e.g., Matt. 8:16-17; Luke 4:31-37, 8:26-39). The Book of

---

134. "Questions and Answers," *Millennial Star* 1 (Aug. 1840): 95; questions were submitted by Joseph Fielding and answered by the editor, Parley P. Pratt.

135. Kirtland Elders' Quorum minutes, 22 Oct. 1840, in Lyndon W. Cook and Milton V. Backman, Jr., eds., *Kirtland Elders' Quorum Record, 1836-1841* (Provo, UT: Grandin Book Co., 1985), 50-51.

136. Journal History, 18 Dec. 1847.

137. Report of Aaron F. Farr, in Journal History, 11 Feb. 1853.

Mormon spoke of this ability, both during Jesus' mortal ministry (BM, LDS, 1 Ne. 11:31; Mosiah 3:6) and his post-mortal ministry among the Nephites (BM, LDS, 3 Ne. 7:19), and recorded that similar power was promised to believers (BM, LDS, Morm. 9:24).

Shortly after the LDS church was organized, what is generally regarded as the first miracle performed in the new religion consisted of Joseph Smith casting a "devil" out of Newel Knight.[138] A revelation warned against seeking miracles yet made several exceptions, including "casting out devils" (BC XXV:23-24, July 1830). Another revelation that December promised that "whoso shall ask in my name, in faith, they shall cast out devils."[139]

The most dramatic and well-attested example occurred in June 1831 general conference. Levi Hancock described the scene:

> Joseph [Smith] put his hands on Harvey Whitlock and ordained him to the high priesthood. He turned as black as Lyman was white. His fingers were set like claws. He went around the room and showed his hands and tried to speak, his eyes were in the shape of oval O's. Hyrum Smith said, "Joseph, that is not of God." Joseph said "do not speak against this." "I will not believe," said Hyrum, "unless you inquire of God and he ownes it." Joseph bowed his head, and in a short time got up and commanded Satan to leave Harvey, laying his hands upon his head at the same time. At that very instant an old man said to weigh two hundred and fourteen pounds sitting in the window turned a complete summersault in the house and came his back across a bench and lay helpless. Joseph told Lyman to cast Satan out. He did. The man's name was Leamon Coply, formally [sic] a Quaker. The evil spirit left him and as quick as lightening Harvey Green fell bound and screamed like a panther. Satan was cast out of him. But immediately entered someone else. This continued all day and the greater part of the night.[140]

Perhaps because of the notoriety of this event, the Saints' power to

---

138. HC, 1:82-84.

139. *Painesville Telegraph*, 17 Jan. 1832; also BC XXXVII:10.

140. Levi Ward Hancock diary, 4 June 1831, LDS archives. Other participants in the conference who wrote of the same event included Ezra Booth (*Painesville Telegraph*, 15 Nov. 1831), John Corrill (*A Brief History* . . ., chap. 10), John Whitmer ("The Book of John Whitmer, Kept by Commandment," chap. 7), and Philo Dibble (*Juvenile Instructor* 27 [15 May 1892]: 303).

cast out devils was reported shortly thereafter in places as distant as Missouri and Vermont.[141]

In 1834 Lyman Wight taught that "all disease in this Church is of the Devil and that medicine administered to the sick is of the Devil, for the sick in the Church ought to live by faith."[142] Inasmuch as other church members disagreed, the matter was brought before the high council which ruled that "it is not lawful to teach the Church that all disease is of the devil."[143] After 1834 the casting out of evil spirits was not a prominent theme in the Restoration. Occasionally, individuals or groups promised power over evil spirits,[144] but few reports of the use of such power exist.

Although it is not known if any women were promised power over evil spirits, Smith endorsed its potential use by women: "Prest. Smith continued the subject by adverting to the commission given to the ancient apostles 'Go ye into all the world' &c. No matter who believeth; these signs such as healing the sick, casting out devils &c. should follow all that believe whether male or female."[145] No accounts exist of women exercising such power during Smith's lifetime.

141. *Missouri Intelligencer & Bon's Lick Advertiser*, 17 Sept. 1831; *Vermont Patriot and State Gazette*, 18 Sept. 1831.

142. *Far West Record*, 96, 21 Aug. 1834.

143. Ibid.

144. For instance, the newly called Quorum of Twelve Apostles was promised such power (*Heber C. Kimball Diary*, 207), as were Simeon Dunn (22 June 1840) and Howard Coray (20 Oct. 1840) in their patriarchal blessings.

145. "Nauvoo Relief Society Minutes," 28 Apr. 1842.

Chapter Four

Ordinances:
The Endowment

The final scene of the Savior's earthly ministry, according to the Gospel of St. Luke, was the injunction by the resurrected Christ to his closest disciples to take the gospel message to all nations. Before they could begin their missionary journeys, however, they were directed to remain in Jerusalem until they were endowed with "power from on high" (Luke 24:48). Jesus previously had called and ordained these men, thus authorizing them to act in his name, but their failure to work miracles demonstrated that authority alone was insufficient.[1] The admonition to remain in Jerusalem underscored the necessity of both authority and power.

The Latter-day Saint experience was similar to the New Testament antecedent. Joseph Smith and Oliver Cowdery received divine authority in 1829 and immediately began a ministry. By late 1830, however, unsuccessful attempts to work miracles made it clear that a second dimension was necessary. A revelation in January 1831 invoked the memory of the ancient disciples, promising the elders an endowment of power. The fulfillment of that promise came that June, as a pentecostal outpouring followed ordination to the "order of Melchizedek" or "high priesthood." Thereafter the elders were both authorized and empowered to perform supernatural works. By late 1832 Smith recognized a need for further empowerment of mission-

---

1. The most poignant example of this was their failure to cast an evil spirit out of a child. The child's father, speaking to Jesus, lamented, "I spake to thy disciples that they should cast him out; and they could not" (Mark 9:14-26).

115

aries and established a School of the Prophets through which a second pentecostal experience occurred early the following year. Yet another endowment of "power from on high" occurred upon completion of the Kirtland House of the Lord in 1836. The final stage in the development of the Latter-day Saint doctrine of endowment occurred in Nauvoo, Illinois, from 1842 to 1844. Although several new elements were present in the Nauvoo endowment, its primary focus remained unchanged: the empowerment of the elders in preparation to carry the gospel message to all nations.

The most ambitious missionary effort of the early church occurred in 1830 when Oliver Cowdery, Ziba Peterson, Parley P. Pratt, and Peter Whitmer traveled from New York to the western border of the United States to preach to indigenous Native Americans. Because the missionaries breached protocol by not obtaining approval of their plans from General William Clark, Superintendent of Indian Affairs in St. Louis, their unauthorized preaching to the tribes around Independence, Missouri, led to a quick reprimand from the local Indian Agent and a proscription of further preaching to the tribes.[2] Thus the purpose of the journey was thwarted. However, the expedition proved to be significant. Because Pratt had lived in Kirtland, Ohio, the missionaries visited that town on their way to Missouri, baptizing the most important convert of their journey, Campbellite preacher Sidney Rigdon.

While Rigdon was convinced that their message was of God, he was troubled by the apparent limits to their power. According to a local newspaper account, Cowdery attempted without success to work miracles in Kirtland, which Rigdon criticized.[3] As the

---

2. Richard W. Cummins to William Clark, 15 Feb. 1831, in William Clark letterbook, 1831, Kansas State Historical Society.

3. *Painesville* [Ohio] *Telegraph,* 7 Dec. 1830, reported: "When Jesus sent his disciples to preach, he gave them power against all unclean spirits, to cast them out to heal all manner of diseases, and to raise the dead. But these newly commissioned disciples have totally failed thus far in their attempts to heal, and as far as can be ascertained their prophecys have also failed." The same newspaper, in an article dated 15 Feb. 1831, spoke in detail of an unsuccessful attempt by Cowdery to heal a crippled woman, concluding by stating that "one of these people a few days ago, when put to the worst upon the subject, said that he did not think Cowdery would have attempted to do any miracles, had he have known how things would turn out. . . . Mr. R[igdon]. now blames Cowdery

missionaries continued west, Rigdon traveled to New York to meet Smith.

Rigdon arrived in New York in December 1830.[4] A revelation through Smith, occurring days after Rigdon arrived and for which Rigdon served as scribe, addressed the empowerment of missionaries, implicitly acknowledging their lack of power:

> And that ye might escape the power of the enemy, and be gathered unto me a righteous people, without spot and blameless:
> Wherefore, for this cause I gave unto you the commandment, that ye should go to the Ohio: and there I will give unto you my law, and there you shall be endowed with power from on high, and from thence, whomsoever I will shall go forth among all nations, and it shall be told them what they shall do, for I have a great work laid up in store:
> For Israel shall be saved, and I will lead them whithersoever I will, and no power shall stay my hand (BC XL:27-29, 2 Jan. 1831).

This revelation clearly parallels the injunction given by Christ to his disciples, as recorded in the Gospel of Luke:

> Thus it is written, and thus it behooved Christ to suffer, and to rise from the dead the third day;
> And that repentance and remission of sins should be preached in his name among all nations, beginning at Jerusalem.
> And ye are witnesses of these things.
> And, behold, I send the promise of my Father upon you; but

---

for *attempting* to work miracles, and says it was not intended to be confirmed in that way." Smith was also accused of attempting without success to work miracles, most pointedly in the case of Warner Doty, a church member who allegedly died in spite of Smith's promises to the contrary (*Painesville Telegraph*, 5 Apr. 1831; the same incident was referred to in the *Independent Chronicle & Boston Patriot*, 7 May 1831).

4. A revelation to Joseph Smith in December 1830, only days after Rigdon arrived in New York, stated: "Behold, verily, verily, I say unto my servant Sidney, I have looked upon thee and thy works. I have heard thy prayers and prepared thee for a greater work. Thou are blessed, for thou shalt do great things. Behold thou wast sent forth, even as John, to prepare the way before me, and before Elijah which should come, and thou knew it not" (*A Book of Commandments, for the Government of the Church of Christ, Organized According to Law, on the 6th of April, 1830* [Independence, MO: W. W. Phelps & Co., 1833], XXXVII:3-6; hereafter cited in the text as BC).

tarry ye in the city of Jerusalem, until ye be endued with power from on high (24:45-48).[5]

By February 1831 the Latter-day Saint community had migrated to Kirtland. Shortly after arriving there, Smith received two revelations concerning the anticipated endowment. The first indicated that personal preparation would be necessary: "Sanctify yourselves and ye shall be endowed with power" (BC XLV:16). The second reinforced the continuity between ancient and modern by emphasizing both the pentecostal nature of the endowment and its empowerment of missionaries: "Inasmuch as they are faithful, and exercise faith in me, I will pour out my Spirit upon them in the day that they assemble themselves together. And it shall come to pass that they shall go forth into the regions round about, and preach repentance unto the people; And many shall be converted . . ." (BC XLVI:2-4).

Coincident to these revelations, Smith, with Rigdon as his scribe, was revising the King James Bible. In Genesis, Chapter 14, he added sixteen new verses describing the ancient order of Melchizedek and its extraordinary powers[6]: "Every one being ordained after this order and calling should have power, by faith, to break mountains, to divide the seas, to dry up waters, to turn them out of their course; To put at defiance the armies of nations, to divide the earth, to break every band, to stand in the presence of God . . ."[7]

As the time of the endowment approached, it became apparent

---

5. The disciples waited at Jerusalem, as instructed, until the Day of Pentecost, at which time the Holy Ghost, as cloven tongues of fire, conferred the promised power. Thereafter they began their missionary labors. Note that the word "endue" is an infrequently used synonym for "endow" (see *Oxford English Dictionary*). Of the common English translations of the Bible, only the King James Version of this passage uses "endue," while others used "clothed," "armed," or "invested." Latter-day Saint sources prefer "endow," although some retain "endue."

6. Robert J. Matthews, in *"A Plainer Translation:" Joseph Smith's Translation of the Bible, A History and Commentary* (Provo, UT: Brigham Young University Press, 1975), 96, states that Genesis 14 was revised between 1 Feb.-8 Mar. 1831.

7. Gen. 14:30-31, Joseph Smith's revision, commonly referred to as the "Inspired Version." For a comparison with the King James text, see *Joseph Smith's "New Translation" of the Bible* (Independence, MO: Herald Publishing House, 1970), 78.

that it would embody two biblical themes: the New Testament Pentecostal outpouring of "power from on high" and the Old Testament order through which such power would be conferred. The linking of the two was explicit in a subsequent revelation through Smith to Ezra Thayre, which coupled "endowment" with "ordination": "Let my servant Ezra humble himself and at the conference meeting he shall be ordained unto power from on high and he shall go from thence (if he be obedient unto my commandments) and proclaim my gospel unto the western regions with my servants that must go forth even unto the borders by the Lamanites for behold I have a great work for them to do and it shall be given unto you to know what ye shall do at the conference meeting even so amen."[8]

The much anticipated conference began on 3 June 1831, lasted for several days, and involved most of the elders then belonging to the church.[9] Several participants wrote of the experience, giving a generally consistent account of pentecostal experiences.[10] The endowment culminated in the ordination of several elders to the "order of Melchizedek."[11] Having "tarried at Kirtland," they now felt empowered

---

8. Unpublished revelation, dated May 1831, "Kirtland Revelation Book," 91-92, archives, Historical Department, Church of Jesus Christ of Latter-day Saints, Salt Lake City, Utah (hereafter LDS archives). Note that the ordination is to "power" not to a specified office.

9. John Corrill, *Brief History of the Church of Christ of Latter Day Saints . . .* (St. Louis: Printed for the Author, 1839), chap. 10.

10. The most informative of the accounts of the conference were: Corrill; Joseph Smith: "History of Joseph Smith," *Times and Seasons* 5 (1 Feb. 1844): 416; Parley P. Pratt: *Autobiography of Parley Parker Pratt* (Salt Lake City: Deseret Book, 1976), 68; Lyman Wight: Letter to Wilford Woodruff, 24 Aug. 1857, Lyman Wight Letterbook, Library and Archives, The Auditorium, Reorganized Church of Jesus Christ of Latter Day Saints, Independence, Missouri (hereafter RLDS Library-Archives); Newel Knight: "Autobiographical Sketch," LDS archives; Ezra Booth: Letter to Rev. Ira Eddy, Sept. 1831, in E. D. Howe: *Mormonism Unvailed, or, A Faithful Account of that Singular Imposition and Delusion, From its Rise to the Present Time* (Painesville, Ohio, 1834), 110; Philo Dibble: *Juvenile Instructor* 27 (15 May 1892): 303; Levi Ward Hancock: Diary, LDS archives; and Zebedee Coltrin: "Autobiography," LDS archives. An attempt to raise the dead was described by Booth.

11. Corrill. This was also called the "high priesthood." It is essential to understand that at the time of the June 1831 conference, ordination to the "high priesthood" meant neither the Melchizedek

to proceed with their missionary labors, confident that they were on par with the ancient disciples.[12]

The empowered elders undertook, as their first task, a journey to Zion (Independence). A local newspaper chronicled their enthusiasm as they set out for Missouri, stating, "They still persist in their power to work miracles. They say they have often seen them done—the sick are healed—the lame walk—devils are cast out;—and these assertions are made by men heretofore considered rational men, and men of truth."[13] In spite of the anticipation, the aftermath of the endowment appears to have fallen short of expectations, causing some members of the new order to leave the church. One of them, Ezra Booth, wrote shortly after the return from Missouri: "They have been hitherto unsuccessful in finding the lame, the halt, and the blind, who had faith sufficient to become the subjects of their miracles; and it is now concluded that this work must be postponed . . ."[14]

Although Booth had left the church by the time he wrote this letter, the minutes of a general conference held shortly after the elders returned from Missouri lend credence to his account. During that conference Smith stated "that the order of the High-priesthood is that they have power given them to seal up the Saints unto eternal life."[15] This statement signalled two important theological changes. First, the

---

Priesthood nor the office of High Priest. The latter office did not emerge for several months following the conference, while the Melchizedek Priesthood was first formulated in 1835. See chap. 1.

12. Ezra Booth, a participant in the conference who was ordained to the High Priesthood, wrote that "many of them have been ordained to the High Priesthood, or the order of Melchisedec; and profess to be endowed with the same power as the ancient apostles were" (Ezra Booth to Rev. Ira Eddy, Sept. 1831, in Howe, 180-81). The week after the conference an article in the *Painesville Telegraph* stated: "The ceremony of endowing them with miraculous gifts, or supernatural power, was then performed, and they were commanded to take up a line of march; preaching their gospel, (Jo's Bible), raising the dead, healing the sick, casting out devils, &c." (14 June 1831).

13. *Geauga Gazette* (Painesville, Ohio), 21 June 1831.

14. Ezra Booth to Rev. I. Eddy, 2 Oct. 1831, in *Painesville Telegraph*, 1 Nov. 1831.

15. Donald Q. Cannon and Lyndon W. Cook, eds., *Far West Record: Minutes of the Church of Jesus Christ of Latter-day Saints, 1830-1844* (Salt Lake City: Deseret Book Co., 1983), 20.

power inherent in high priesthood was now viewed primarily in an "other worldly" context. That is, rather than focusing on present, verifiable phenomena, it shifted to the there-and-then, marking the beginning of the unique Latter-day Saint theology of afterlife. Second, it separated the concepts of endowment and high priesthood. Whereas the June 1831 endowment included ordination to the high priesthood, such priesthood now began to develop independently. The concept of endowment lay dormant for a full year thereafter.

In spite of the 1831 revelation that the endowed would "go forth among all nations," the work of the elders remained confined to the United States and Canada. A revelation late in 1832 called for these elders to return to Kirtland for further preparation, implying that the 1831 endowment was no longer sufficient. The elders were instructed to assemble themselves for intense preparation, both spiritual and intellectual, for their "ministry to go forth among the gentiles, for the last time."[16] To comply with this mandate, Smith organized a School of the Prophets.

The school opened in January 1833, an event marked by washing the feet of the students,[17] fasting and prayer, and a pentecostal outpouring similar to that accompanying the June 1831 endowment.[18] Although the term "endowment" was not used, the school's continuity with the 1831 endowment and with later Kirtland and Nauvoo endowments is evident. Its purpose was to prepare the elders as missionaries and to receive a pentecostal outpouring.

Another feature of the school eventually became an integral part of endowment theology. The revelation initiating the school mandated construction of "an house of God" in which the elders would meet.[19] Details of the proposed structure developed over the next few months. In a meeting in May 1833 Jared Carter proposed that a school

---

16. "Kirtland Revelation Book," 41.

17. *Doctrine and Covenants of the Church of the Latter Day Saints: Carefully Selected from the Revelations of God* (Kirtland, OH: F. G. Williams & Co., 1835), 7:45-46 (hereafter abbreviated DC, 1835).

18. One account described "many powerful manifestation[s] of the holy spirit . . . the gift of tongues and the interpretation thereof" (Zebedee Coltrin diary, 24 Jan. 1833, LDS archives). Smith's mother later referred to the event as a "day of penticost" (Lucy Mack Smith, manuscript history, LDS archives).

19. "Kirtland Revelation Book," 46.

house be constructed "for the purpose of accomodating the Elders who should come in to receive their education for the ministry."[20] Smith countered that "the Lord would not except [accept] it," and insisted instead on a house of worship.[21] Two days later such a building was endorsed by revelation.[22] A revelation the following month specified the design and dimensions and reinforced the relationship between the ancient and modern disciples: "Yea verily I say unto you I gave unto you a commandment that you should build an house in the which house I design to endow those whom I have chosen with power from on high, for this is the promise of the Father unto you. Therefore, I commanded you to tarry even as mine Apostles at Jerusalem."[23]

The new endowment, then, would bear strong similarities to the 1831 endowment. It was to be exclusively for the elders carrying the gospel to all nations; it would require a gathering at Kirtland; and it would involve a pentecostal outpouring. It went beyond the 1831 endowment by requiring the construction of sacred space in which the event would occur. Construction of the Kirtland "House of the Lord"[24] began in June 1833 and continued for nearly three years.

---

20. "Kirtland Council Minute Book," 4 May 1833, LDS archives.

21. Levi W. Hancock autobiography, LDS archives.

22. B. H. Roberts, ed., *History of the Church of Jesus Christ of Latter-day Saints* (Salt Lake City: Deseret Book Co., 1971), 1:346-47 (hereafter cited as HC).

23. Revelation dated 1 June 1833, in "Kirtland Revelation Book," 59-60.

24. The word "temple" was not associated with the Kirtland building until several years after its completion, whereupon later writers, including Levi Hancock (quoted above) commonly used it. The idea of a Latter-day Saint temple had been present at least as early as October 1830 when Oliver Cowdery wrote that "the temple of God shall be built" in the lands to which the missionaries would travel (Journal History, 17 Oct. 1830). It was understood that there would be a temple in Missouri but nowhere else. Orson Hyde and Hyrum Smith wrote in January 1833 that "Zion is the place where the temple will be built, and the people gathered" (HC, 1:320). A year later, J. C. Chauncey, a non-Mormon describing the encampment of "Zion's Camp" a mile from his house, wrote that "God directed them there and there alone to build up his holy temple for the gathering of the scattered tribes of Israel" (J. C. Chauncey to "Dr. Sir," Liberty, Clay County, Missouri, 27 June 1834, RLDS Library-Archives). After 1838, when it became apparent

While the work proceeded in Kirtland, harassment in Missouri prompted the formation of Zion's Camp, a body of elders whose intent was to march to Independence and, by military action, "redeem Zion."[25] The expedition failed. As this became apparent, a revelation assigned blame for the failure, then linked the future redemption of the Missouri settlement to the empowerment which would be part of the new endowment:

> Behold, I say unto you, were it not for the transgressions of my people, speaking concerning the church, and not individuals, they might have been redeemed, even now . . .
> Therefore, in consequence of the transgressions of my people, it is expedient in me that mine elders should wait for a little season for the redemption of Zion . . .
> And this cannot be brought to pass until mine elders are endowed with power from on high; for, behold, I have prepared a greater endowment and blessing to be poured out upon them . . ."[26]

The wording of the latter verse is significant, for by a "greater endowment" it signaled continuity with its 1831 predecessor yet allowed for expansion of the theology.[27] Two months later, following his return to Kirtland, Smith cautioned patience on the part of his Missouri brethren, reminding them of the link between the endowment and the redemption of Zion: "You will recollect that the first elders are to receive their endowment in Kirtland before the redemption of Zion."[28] The following year Smith reminded the high council

---

that the Saints would not be able to maintain a permanent foothold in Missouri, the term "temple" was applied to other buildings.

25. Detailed studies of Zion's Camp have been written by Roger Launius, *Zion's Camp: Expedition to Missouri, 1834* (Independence, MO: Herald Publishing House, 1984), and James L. Bradley, *Zion's Camp 1834: Prelude to the Civil War* (Salt Lake City: Publishers Press, 1990).

26. "Kirtland Revelation Book," 97-98 (22 June 1834).

27. The word "greater" in the "Kirtland Revelation Book," the earliest manuscript version of this revelation, was changed in later published versions (the first being in DC, 1844 ed.) to "great" without explanation.

28. Joseph Smith to Lyman Wight, Edward Partridge, John Corrill, Isaac Morley, and others of the High Council, 16 Aug. 1834, in Dean C. Jessee, ed., *The Personal Writings of Joseph Smith* (Salt Lake City: Deseret Book Co., 1984), 329.

in Kirtland: "the Lord has commanded us to build a house, in which to receive an endowment, previous to the redemption of Zion; and that Zion could not be redeemed until this takes place."[29]

In the winter of 1835-36, as the Saints awaited completion of the building, they anticipated a second expedition to Missouri during the summer of 1836: "I expect that the elders will be sent out as soon [as] the endowment takes place and I think likely that Roger [Orton] will goe east but don't know wether he wil come that way or not[.] they intend to get all they can to go up to Misouri next sumer to redeem Zion."[30]

At the solemn assembly in late March 1836, during which the endowment would occur, the redemption of Missouri would be a prominent theme: "Presidents Joseph Smith, Jun, Frederick G. Williams, Sidney Rigdon, Hyrum Smith, and Oliver Cowdery met in the Most Holy Place in the Lord's House and sought for a revelation from Him to teach us concerning our going to Zion and other important matters."[31] The following day leaders would "prophesy upon each others heads, and [pronounce] cursings upon the enimies of Christ who inhabit Jackson county Missouri."[32] In spite of the expectations, Jackson County would remain out of reach of the Saints and the redemption of Zion would cease to be part of endowment theology.

Although Zion's Camp failed, it served as a proving ground for a generation of church leaders. Following the expedition, with completion of the House of the Lord and the endowment still a year away, Smith was shown in vision the lofty reward given to camp members who had died. Furthermore, he was admonished to organize two groups of leaders, the Quorum of Twelve Apostles and the seventy.[33]

---

29. HC, 2:239 (4 Aug. 1835).

30. Clarissa Bicknell Orton (Kirtland) to "Dear Parents," Jan. 1836, in L. B. Johnson, ed., *The Pines Letters* (n.p., 1954), 22. I am indebted to Rick Grunder for bringing this book to my attention and for providing me with a photographic copy of the third chapter, entitled "The Mormons."

31. Scott H. Faulring, ed., *An American Prophet's Record: The Diaries and Journals of Joseph Smith* (Salt Lake City: Signature Books in association with Smith Research Associates, 1987), 152-53, 29 Mar. 1836.

32. Ibid., 153-55, 30 Mar. 1836.

33. Joseph Young, *History of the Organization of the Seventies* (Salt

The following week he called a meeting of Zion's Camp veterans and instructed the three witnesses of the Book of Mormon "to pray each one and then proceed to choose twelve men from the Church as Apostles to go to all nations, Kindred tongue and people."[34] Although the injunction to travel to foreign nations had been given several years earlier, this was the first time a group of men was designated for the task. It has remained the primary responsibility of the twelve ever since.

One week later Cowdery gave a charge to the twelve, telling them that they would now be required "to preach the gospel to every nation," but that, like the ancient apostles, "you are not to go to other nations, till you receive your endowment. Tarry at Kirtland until you are endowed with power from on high."[35] Although other men would participate in the new endowment, it became clear that the most important recipients would be the twelve. Early in November 1835 Smith wrote to the twelve: "Thus came the word of the Lord unto me concerning the Twelve saying . . . they must all humble themselves before me, before they will be accounted worthy to receive an endowment to go forth in my name unto all nations."[36]

A week later, at their request, Smith met with the twelve and promised that this endowment, like its 1831 predecessor, would confer power over tangible things, though adding a caveat:

> You need an Endowment brethren in order that you may be prepared and able to over come all things. Those that reject your testimony will be damned. The sick will be healed, the lame made to walk, the deaf to hear and the blind to see through your instrumentality. But let me tell you that you will not have power after the Endowment to heal those who have not faith, nor to benifit them. . . . But when you are endowed and prepared to preach the gospel to all nations, kindred and toungs in there own languages you must faithfully warn all and bind up the testimony and seal up the law.[37]

Throughout the winter of 1835-36, the twelve and other officers in Kirtland prepared themselves while working to complete the

Lake City: Deseret News Steam Printing Establishment, 1878), 1-2.
   34. "Kirtland Council Minute Book," 14 Feb. 1835.
   35. Ibid., 21 Feb. 1835.
   36. *Joseph Smith Diary*, 46-47, 3 Nov. 1835.
   37. Ibid., 55-58, 12 Nov. 1835.

House of the Lord.[38] Unlike 1831, when the endowment culminated in an ordinance, this time several ordinances were prescribed
to prepare for the endowment. In January, as they were about to
begin the preparatory ordinances, Cowdery wrote, "O may we be
prepared for the endowment,—being sanctified and cleansed from
all sin."[39] Four days later the First Presidency and other church
leaders met in the attic of the printing office. After washing and
perfuming their bodies, they moved to the House of the Lord to
attend to the ordinance of anointing their heads with holy oil. After
Smith was anointed, the rest of the First Presidency placed their
hands on his head and pronounced prophecies and blessings, whereupon he experienced a vision of the Celestial Kingdom.[40] Two
weeks later another preparatory ordinance was begun, the "sealing"
of the anointing blessing with uplifted hands.[41] Participation in the
preparatory ordinances would continue throughout the winter and
involve male church officers of all ranks, including priests, teachers,
and deacons.[42]

---

38. It appears unlikely that a target date had been set for completion of the building and the Solemn Assembly. In January W. W. Phelps
wrote to his wife: "The whole work continually progresses, though
somewhat slowly. I cannot tell when the Endowment will take place"
(W. W. Phelps to Sally Phelps, 5 Jan. 1836, in Journal History, 5 Jan.
1836).

39. "Oliver Cowdery's Kirtland, Ohio, 'Sketch Book,'" *Brigham
Young University Studies* 12 (1972): 416 (17 Jan. 1836).

40. This vision was canonized in 1978 and now comprises sec. 137
of Doctrine and Covenants (Salt Lake City: Church of Jesus Christ of
Latter-day Saints, 1981) (hereafter cited in the text as DC, LDS). It is
significant, for it contradicts a portion of an earlier vision (16 Feb. 1832;
DC, LDS, 76). The earlier vision consigned all who died without baptism
to a lesser kingdom, the later one included Alvin Smith in the Celestial
Kingdom. Smith "marveled" that his brother was there, since he had died
before being baptized. While the LDS doctrine of baptism for the dead
now responds to the fate of those dying without baptism, it took four
years of reflection on Smith's part, following this vision, to conclude that
ordinances performed in behalf of the dead could assist in effecting their
salvation.

41. *Joseph Smith Diary,* 123-24, 28 Jan. 1836.

42. For example, see Edward Partridge diary for this period (LDS
archives).

As the time of the solemn assembly approached, enthusiasm and expectations increased, spilling over into the non-Mormon press in a manner similar to the 1831 endowment: "They assure you, with the utmost confidence, that they shall soon be able to raise the dead, to heal the sick, the deaf, the dumb, and the blind, &c. Indeed, more than one assured me, that they had, themselves, by the laying on of their hands, restored the sick to health."[43]

The Kirtland House of the Lord was dedicated on 27 March 1836 in a ceremony attended by hundreds of men, women, and children. Two days later the solemn assembly began. Inasmuch as its purpose was the endowment of elders to pursue their missionary labors, only men attended. The assembly began on 29 March with Joseph Smith, Frederick G. Williams, Sidney Rigdon, Hyrum Smith, and Oliver Cowdery meeting for prayer. A small group of other church leaders joined them later in the day, and Smith told them that "the word of the Lord" required that they remain in the building throughout the day and night to prepare for the activities of the following day. Accordingly, they spent the day and evening in prayer, in the final preparatory ordinance of washing each other's feet, and in partaking of bread and wine.[44] Thereafter they "prophesied and spoke in tongues and shouted Hosannas the meeting lasting till day light."[45]

The following morning, 30 March, most of the officers of the church, about 300 men, met in the House of the Lord. The washing of feet proceeded throughout the morning, being completed by noon, whereupon

> the brethren began . . . prophesying and blessing and sealing them with Hosanna and Amen until nearly 7 o clock P.M. the bread and wine was then brought in, and I [Smith] observed that we had fasted all the day, and lest we faint; as the Saviour did[,] so shall we do on this occasion, we shall bless the bread and give it to the 12 and they to the multitude, after which we shall bless the wine and do likewise; while waiting I made the following remarks, that the time we were required to tarry in Kirtland to be endued would be fulfilled in a few days, and then the Elders would go forth . . .[46]

---

43. Letter published in *Ohio Atlas*, 16 Mar. 1836; reprinted in *Painesville Telegraph*, 20 May 1836.

44. *Joseph Smith Diary*, 152-53, 29 Mar. 1836.

45. Edward Partridge diary, 29 Mar. 1836, LDS archives.

46. *Joseph Smith Diary*, 153-55, 30 Mar. 1836.

Having spent two days in the building without a break, Smith then left the meeting in the charge of the twelve and went home to sleep. The rest of the men remained, exhorting, prophesying, and speaking in tongues until 5:00 a.m. the following morning (31 March): "The Saviour made his appearance to some, while angels minestered unto others, and it was a penticost and enduement indeed, long to be remembered for the sound shall go forth from this place into all the world, and the occurrences of this day shall be hande[d] down upon the pages of sacred history to all generations, as the day of Pentecost . . .,"[47]

Several participants recorded these events. Milo Andrus "saw the Spirit in the form of cloven tongues as a fire descend in thousands, and rest upon the heads of the Elders, and they spoke with tongues and prophesyed."[48] David Patten said that "the heavens Was opened unto them. Angels & Jesus Christ was seen of them sitting at the right hand of the Father."[49] Erastus Snow recorded that "the angels came & worshipped with us & some saw them yea even twelve legions of them[,] the charriots of Israel & the horseman thereof."[50]

Other participants, while clearly a minority, were not as impressed, and two prominent leaders later denounced the proceedings. William McLellin, a member of the Quorum of the Twelve, wrote that "it was no endowment from God. Not only myself was not endowed, but no other man of the five hundred who was present—except it was with wine!"[51] David Whitmer, one of the three witnesses of the Book of Mormon, described the event as a "grand fizzle," denying any angelic visitations.[52] While it may be that these reminiscences were clouded by time and disaffection, a contemporary account by Church Historian John Corrill echoes the interpretation without the bias: "The sacra-

47. Ibid.

48. "Autobiography of Milo Andrus, 1814-1875," LDS archives.

49. Scott G. Kenney, ed., *Wilford Woodruff's Journal* (Midvale, UT: Signature Books, 1983), 1:67, 19 Apr. 1836. Woodruff was not at the solemn assembly but recorded in his diary the account of David Patten, one of the twelve.

50. "E[rastus]. Snows Sketch book No. 1," 9 Nov. 1818-5 Dec. 1837, typescript at Huntington Library.

51. William McLellin to M. H. Forscutt, Oct. 1870, RLDS Library-Archives.

52. *Chicago Inter-Ocean*, 17 Oct. 1886.

ment was then administered, in which they partook of the bread and wine freely, and a report went abroad that some of them got drunk: as to that every man must answer for himself. A similar report, the reader will recollect, went out concerning the disciples, at Jerusalem, on the day of pentecost."[53]

There was a general understanding, both then and later, that the purpose of the endowment had been accomplished and that the elders were now enabled to take the gospel abroad. At the time Smith told the men at the solemn assembly "that they now were at liberty after obtaining their lisences to go forth and build up the kingdom of God."[54] Parley P. Pratt, writing a short time later, addressed the same issue and made the clearest distinction among early writers between authority and power: "The Saviour, having given them their authority, commands them to tarry, and not undertake their mission, until they were endowed with power from on high. But why this delay? Because no man was ever qualified, or ever will be, to preach that Gospel, and teach all things whatsoever Jesus commanded him, without the Holy Ghost."[55] Similarly, Corrill reiterated the connection between endowment and missionary labor when he wrote, "At the close of the solemn assembly meetings in Kirtland, Smith told the elders that they were now endowed with power to go forth and build up the Kingdom."[56] Decades after the event, a church catechism reflected the importance to missionary labors: "What was the endowment which the elders there received? It caused the work of God to take a mighty stride, and from that time the preaching of the gospel took a much wider range."[57]

Although the expectation may have been to send missionaries to

---

53. Corrill, chap. 12. This account was published in 1839. See also the account of participant William Harris, in *Mormonism Portrayed; Its Errors and Absurdities Exposed, and the Spirit and Designs of its Authors Made Manifest* (Warsaw, IL: Sharp & Gamble, 1841), quoted in John C. Bennett, *History of the Saints: or, an Expose of Joe Smith and Mormonism* (Boston: Leland & Whiting, 1842), 136.

54. *Joseph Smith Diary,* 153-55, 30 Mar. 1836.

55. Parley P. Pratt (1837) in *A Voice of Warning and Instruction to All People, Containing a Declaration of the Faith and Doctrine of the Church of the Latter-day Saints, Commonly Called Mormons* (1857 ed.), 72-73.

56. Corrill, chap. 14.

57. "Catechism for our Juveniles to Answer," *Juvenile Instructor* 3 (15 Mar. 1868): 44.

foreign lands immediately, more than a year passed before Heber C. Kimball, a member of the Quorum of the Twelve, "was unanimously appointed, set a part, and Ordained to go at the he[a]d of this mission to England to proclaim the Gospel of Jesus Christ to the people of that nation."[58] One other member of the quorum, Orson Hyde, accompanied Kimball. Over the next four years nine members of the quorum would serve as missionaries in England, reinforcing their primary role in taking the gospel to all nations.

The original intent was that there would be but one solemn assembly and endowment in the House of the Lord, as reflected not only in the revelations pointing towards the event but also in the perception of church members, one of whom wrote: "Brother Joseph Smith ses whoever is Her[e] at the endowment will always regois [rejoice] and whoever is not will a[l]way[s] be Sorry[.] this thi[n]g will not take place a gain whil time last[s]."[59] It became apparent, however, that not all who required endowment had been present. Therefore, it was repeated at least three times during the following month and at least once in 1837.[60] Although involving far fewer men, it included the same itinerary. Charles C. Rich wrote of his experience on 16 April: "We then continued to fast and pray until the setting of the sun when we Broke Bread and Drank wine[.] we prophesied all night pronouncing blessings and cursings until the morning light[.] there was Great manifestations of the power of God . . . and I was filled with the spirit of prophesy and I was endued with power from on high."[61] Wilford Woodruff, who had been away from Kirtland during the spring of 1836, participated in the endowment a year later: "April 3rd [1837]. The day had now arrived for preperations of the Elders of Israel

58. Stanley B. Kimball, ed., *On the Potter's Wheel: The Diaries of Heber C. Kimball* (Salt Lake City: Signature Books in association with Smith Research Associates, 1987), 5, 13 June 1837, describing a conference of elders held in Kirtland on 2 June 1837.

59. Roger Orton (Kirtland) to "Deer Father," Jan. 1836, in *The Pines Letters*, 22.

60. Such events were recorded for 6 April (HC, 2:475-77), 16 April (Charles Coulson Rich diary, vol. 5, LDS archives), and 30 April (Lyndon W. Cook and Milton V. Backman, eds., *Kirtland Elders' Quorum Record, 1836-1841* [Provo, UT: Grandin Book Co., 1985]).

61. Charles C. Rich diary, vol. 5, LDS archives.

or at least for those that were not endowed in Kirtland[,] the strong hold of the daught[ers] of Zion[,] in the spring of 1836."[62]

The departure of most of the Saints from Kirtland between December 1837 and July 1838 resulted in the cessation of further endowments.[63] Upon arriving in Missouri, Smith and his followers built homes, founded new settlements, and engaged in political, legal, and paramilitary skirmishes with neighbors. Smith and other church leaders were soon imprisoned, and the Missouri governor ordered all Mormons from the state. No significant developments in endowment theology occurred during this troubled period.[64]

After Smith and the Saints settled in Illinois, endowment theology and practice resumed their development. In an 1839 letter, Smith revisited a concept he had first articulated in 1831: the power to seal. Whereas the earlier context of sealing had been its link to High Priesthood, he now equated it with "being endowed with power," a concept no longer synonymous with ordination to that priesthood.[65]

---

62. *Wilford Woodruff's Journal*, 1:128-29, 3 Apr. 1837.

63. The single known exception occurred in November 1839. John Taylor had joined the church in May 1836 and consequently missed the solemn assembly and endowment. Called to the Quorum of the Twelve in July 1838, he was now on his way from Missouri to England with other members of the quorum. He and fellow apostles Brigham Young, Heber C. Kimball, and George A. Smith met in Kirtland, and on 17 November a small congregation convened in the House of the Lord. Taylor and Theodore Turley, a seventy, then received the endowment, consisting as before of washing and anointing, sealing the anointing, washing the feet, and a spiritual outpouring (see "Manuscript History of Brigham Young," 17 Nov. 1839). The only member of the quorum who had not previously participated in the endowment, Taylor was now empowered to proceed on his journey to the British Isles.

64. A revelation on 26 April 1838 called for construction in Far West, Missouri, of "an house unto me for the gathering together of my Saints that they may worship me" (*Joseph Smith Diary*, 175-76, 26 Apr. 1838; also DC, LDS, 115:8). Unlike the Kirtland House of the Lord, however, the proposed building was never associated with the concept of endowment. Its cornerstones were laid on 4 July 1838, but no further construction was accomplished.

65. Joseph Smith to Isaac Galland, 22 Mar. 1839, in Dean C. Jessee, ed., *The Personal Writings of Joseph Smith* (Salt Lake City: Deseret Book Co., 1984), 422.

A year later Smith announced construction of a temple in Nauvoo. Although the connection between the endowment and the Kirtland House of the Lord was explicit prior to its construction, no such relationship was expressed in the announcement of the Nauvoo temple. Rather, it was to be a monument, "as great a temple as ever Solomon did," which would be visited by the curious "from all parts of the world" and would enrich the Saints by "the money of these proud men received from such as come and dwell with us."[66]

The following month a more religious purpose was ascribed to the temple, "a place for the Lord to meet with his people and give revelations."[67] A week later the First Presidency stated it would also be a place "where the ordinances can be attended to agreeably to His divine will."[68] These included the endowment and baptism for the dead. Below ground level it would contain a baptism font for baptisms. Above ground the Kirtland and Nauvoo buildings were similar, each consisting of large assembly halls on the first and second floors and a third-floor attic.[69] Unlike the design of current Latter-day Saint temples, which revolves around specialized rooms to accommodate the endowment, the Nauvoo temple was designed like the Kirtland House of the Lord for the simple reason that as late as April 1842 no differences between the Kirtland and Nauvoo endowments were anticipated. Even when the Nauvoo endowment had developed well beyond its predecessor, no structural features were included in the building to reflect the evolved ordinance, and the endowments which were finally performed a year and a half after Smith's death occurred in hastily arranged attic quarters.

For nearly two years after announcement of the temple, it was clear that the Nauvoo endowment would duplicate Kirtland and that only those men who had missed the one would require the other: "The Elders of Israel, who have not yet received their endowment, must

---

66. Joseph Smith discourse, 19 July 1840, Martha Jane Knowlton transcript, in *Brigham Young University Studies* 19 (1979): 393-94.

67. John Smith (Iowa) to his son, George A. Smith (England), in *Journal History*, 24 Aug. 1840.

68. HC, 4:186 (31 Aug. 1840).

69. A detailed study of these buildings is contained in Laurel B. Andrew, *The Early Temples of the Mormons* (Albany: State University of New York Press, 1978).

indeed look forward to the completion of the building with feelings of no ordinary kind, and inasmuch as they anticipate great blessings, let them make such efforts to facilitate the work as are worthy of them."[70]

As was the case in Kirtland, the Nauvoo endowment would serve to empower new missionaries. Women would be excluded.[71] In the April 1842 general conference Hyrum Smith reiterated that the Nauvoo endowment would not differ from the earlier one and that men previously endowed would not need attend:

> Pres't. H. Smith spoke concerning the elders who went forth to preach from Kirtland, and were afterwards called in for the washing and anointing at the dedication of the House, and those who go now will be called in also, when this Temple is about to be dedicated, and will then be endowed to go forth with mighty power having the same anointing, that all may go forth and have the same power, the first, second, and so on, of the seventies and all those formerly ordained.[72]

Only four weeks later, a new endowment was presented to a few select men including Hyrum Smith, and, contrary to Hyrum's discourse, it differed markedly from the Kirtland endowment. In attempting to understand the dramatic and apparently unanticipated evolution, one needs to focus on a key personality of this period of Latter-day Saint history, John C. Bennett.

Bennett joined the church in 1840. A politician, he shepherded through the Illinois state legislature the Nauvoo Charter, a document which gave Nauvoo the legal powers of a virtual city-state. Bennett's political skills extended into religious circles, and in April 1841, only six months after his conversion to Mormonism, he was appointed assistant president of the church. His relationship with Smith soon

---

70. *Times and Seasons* 2 (1 July 1841): 455-56.

71. A graphic example is in the patriarchal blessings of the Gribble family. On 4 October 1841 Levi Gribble, his wife Polly, and his daughter Patience all received blessings from Hyrum Smith. Levi was told, "Then shall you be a chosen vessel having received the anointing, & the enduements, in the Lords House." Polly was "sealed with Eternal Life from this very Hour," and Patience was sealed "up unto Eternal Life." All three blessings are in RLDS Library-Archives, P8 f9.

72. Hyrum Smith discourse, 7 Apr. 1842, in *Times and Seasons* 3 (15 Apr. 1842): 763.

soured over allegations of illicit sexual relationships.[73] Although Bennett was not formally excommunicated until mid-1842, his relationship with Smith had disintegrated by late 1841. Charges and counter-charges flew between the two men, and Bennett, who was privy to the fact that Smith was practicing plural marriage, vowed to expose him and thus destroy the church. It was against this backdrop that Smith stated: "Some say Joseph is a fallen prophet because he does not bring forth more of the word of the Lord. . . . The reason we do not have the secrets of the Lord revealed unto us is because we do not keep our own secrets but reveal our difficulties to the world even to our enemies[.] [T]hen how would we keep the secrets of the Lord[? . . .] I can keep a secret till dooms day."[74]

Three weeks later Bennett extended his campaign by appealing to two prominent church leaders, First Presidency member Sidney Rigdon and Apostle Orson Pratt:

> We shall try Smith on the Boggs case when we get him into Missouri. The war goes bravely on, and although Smith thinks he is now safe, the enemy is near, even at the door. He has awoke the wrong passenger. The Governor will relinquish Joe up at once on the new requisition—there is but one opinion in the case, and that is nothing can save Joe on a new requisition and demand predicated on the old charges, on the institution of new suits.[75]

Faced with the most serious crisis of his ministry, initiated by one of his closest confidants, Smith turned his attention to an institution renowned for keeping a secret: Freemasonry.[76] Less than two weeks after denouncing those who "do not keep our own secrets," he petitioned to become a Mason.[77]

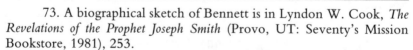

---

73. A biographical sketch of Bennett is in Lyndon W. Cook, *The Revelations of the Prophet Joseph Smith* (Provo, UT: Seventy's Mission Bookstore, 1981), 253.

74. Joseph Smith discourse, 19 Dec. 1841, in Andrew F. Ehat and Lyndon W. Cook, eds., *The Words of Joseph Smith* (Provo, UT: Religious Studies Center, Brigham Young University, 1980), 81.

75. John C. Bennett to Sidney Rigdon and Orson Pratt, 10 Jan. 1842, in Journal History, 10 Jan. 1842.

76. He later said, "The secrets of Masonry is to keep a secret" (*Joseph Smith Diary*, 420-22, 15 Oct. 1843).

77. His petition was filed 30 December 1841. See Mervin B. Hogan, ed., *The Founding Minutes of Nauvoo Lodge* (Des Moines, IA:

Although he had no formal ties to Freemasonry prior to 1842, Smith was no stranger to the fraternity. His brother Hyrum had been a Mason since 1821,[78] and in September 1826, one year before Smith obtained the gold plates, an incident occurred only a few miles from the Smith home which thrust the Masonic movement into the consciousness of the entire nation. William Morgan had written and published an expose of Masonic ritual, as a consequence of which he was abducted and allegedly murdered. Public outrage was fierce and long-lived, resulting in a national anti-Masonic movement and the formation of the Antimasonic Party, the first influential third political party in the United States.[79] By 1831 three important exposes of Freemasonry had been published and circulated widely in this country, thus providing the uninitiated ready access to the secret ceremonies.[80]

On 15 March 1842 Smith was inducted into the first degree of Freemasonry, Entered Apprentice. The following day he advanced to the second (Fellow Craft) and third (Master Mason) degrees.[81] In a public discourse within days of his induction, Smith first spoke of "certain key words & signs belonging to the priesthood which must be observed in order to obtaine the Blessings."[82] "Key words and signs" are concepts central to Freemasonry, and their use in the context of priesthood suggests that Smith saw a continuity between Masonic symbolism and priesthood. However, he did not yet link the symbols of Freemasonry with the concept of endowment, and Hyrum Smith's statement two weeks later that the Nauvoo and Kirtland endowments

---

Research Lodge No. 2, n.d.), 8. An extensive discussion of the relationship betweeen Mormonism and Freemasonry is Michael W. Homer, "Similarity of Priesthood in Masonry," *Dialogue: A Journal of Mormon Thought* 27 (Fall 1994): 1-116.

78. Hogan, 8.

79. William Preston Vaughn, *The Antimasonic Party in the United States, 1826-1843* (Lexington, KY: University of Kentucky Press, 1983).

80. William Morgan's *Illustrations of Masonry by One of the Fraternity Who has Devoted Thirty Years to the Subject* was published in 1827; David Bernard's *Light on Masonry: A Collection of All the Most Important Documents on the Subject of Speculative Free Masonry* in 1829; and Avery Allyn's *A Ritual of Freemasonry* in 1831.

81. HC, 4:550-52. Smith never advanced to any of the higher degrees of Freemasonry.

82. *Wilford Woodruff's Journal*, 2:162, 20 Mar. 1842.

were to be the same suggests that it took several more weeks for the linkage to be made.[83]

A public discourse by Smith on 1 May 1842 suggested that the symbolism of Freemasonry, which Smith held to be an authentic vestige of an ancient endowment, had now been fused with the modern endowment and with the temple:

> The keys are certain signs and words by which false spirits and personages may be detected from true, which cannot be revealed to the Elders till the Temple is completed—the rich can only get them in the Temple—the poor may get them on the Mountain top as did Moses. . . . There are signs in heaven, earth and hell, the Elders must know them all to be endowed with power . . .[84]

Two days later Smith summoned a half-dozen men to the top floor of his red brick store, where he directed them in preparing the room for "giving endowments to a few Elders."[85] The following day he gathered nine close associates, all of whom were Masons,[86] and

---

83. Shortly after the 1842 endowment, Heber C. Kimball wrote to fellow Apostle Parley P. Pratt (in England), "Thare is a similarity of preast hood in masonary. Br Joseph Ses Masonary was taken from preasthood but has become degenrated. but menny things are perfect" (Kimball to Pratt, 17 June 1842, LDS archives). Brigham Young later said of the 1842 endowment that "key words, signs, tokens and penalties" were an integral part of the ceremony (L. John Nuttall diary, 7 Feb. 1877, LDS archives).

84. Joseph Smith discourse, 1 May 1842, in Ehat and Cook, 119-20.

85. Lucius N. Scovill, in *Deseret News Semi-Weekly*, 15 Feb. 1884, 2.

86. James Adams was Deputy Grand Master Mason of Illinois and had been the first master of the Springfield Lodge when the lodge was under dispensation from Missouri (Newton Bateman, ed., *Historical Encyclopedia of Illinois* [Chicago: Munsell Pub. Co., 1912], 2:997). George Miller, Worshipful Master of the Nauvoo Lodge, was a Mason in 1819 (H. W. Mills, "De Tal Palo Tal Astilla," *Annual Publications—Historical Society of Southern California* 10 [1917]: 120-21). Hyrum Smith, Senior Warden and Worshipful Master, pro tem., had been a Mason at least since 1821 (Hogan). Heber C. Kimball had been a Mason since 1823 (Stanley B. Kimball, *Heber C. Kimball—Mormon Patriarch and Pioneer* [Urbana: University of Illinois Press, 1982], 12). Newel K. Whitney had been a member of the Meridian No. 10 Lodge of Ohio (Hogan, 9). William Law, William Marks, Brigham Young, and Willard Richards

administered to them an endowment which maintained continuity with its Kirtland antecedent but added several new dimensions. Smith's own record described the proceedings, including his

> instructing them in the principles and order of the priesthood, attending to washings & anointings, endowments, and the communications of keys, pertaining to the Aaronic Priesthood, and so on to the Highest order of the Melchisedec Priesthood, setting forth the order pertaining to the Ancient of days & all those plans & principles by which any one is enabled to secure the fulness of those blessings which has been prepared for the church of the firstborn, and come up and abide in the presence of . . . Eloheim in the eternal worlds. In this council was instituted the Ancient order of things for the first time in these last days. And the communications I made to this Council were of things spiritual, and to be received only by the spiritual minded: and there was nothing made known to these men but will be made known to all Saints, of the last days, so soon as they are prepared to receive, and a proper place is prepared to communicate them, even to the weakest of the Saints: therefore let the Saints be diligent in building the temple and all houses which they have been or shall hereafter be commanded of god to build, and wait their time with patience, in all meekness and faith, & perserverance unto the end.[87]

Analysis of the Nauvoo endowment, as it was first given by Smith, is difficult because of the scarcity of contemporary records. The ceremony was not written by church leaders until 1877[88] and by that time reflected changes made in the intervening decades.[89] Exposes by disaffected church members who had been initiated into the endowment were not written until 1846 and reflected the ceremony given in the Nauvoo temple a year and a half after Smith's death. In spite of

---

were all Masons but of recent initiation (Hogan, 15, 21, 24).

87. Joseph Smith, draft sheet of "Manuscript History of the Church," in the hand of Willard Richards, 4 May 1842, Historian's Office Church Records Group, LDS archives. This date is not when this document was written. A more contemporary account is in "The Book of the Law of the Lord," in Dean C. Jessee, ed., *The Papers of Joseph Smith* (Salt Lake City: Deseret Book Co., 1992), 2:380, 4 May 1842.

88. See entries in *Wilford Woodruff's Journal,* 7:322-27, between January and February 1877.

89. L. John Nuttall diary, 7 Feb. 1877.

these limitations, records of four of the participants allow several observations.[90] The continuity between the Kirtland and Nauvoo endowments was clear. The Nauvoo ceremony included washings, anointings, and sealings, and, although a special exception was made until completion of the Nauvoo structure, it was explicitly stated that future endowments could occur only in a temple. Although no pentecostal outpouring was described in connection with the initial Nauvoo ceremony, later statements by church leaders in anticipation of the completion of the temple made it clear that a Pentecost was expected to be part of the temple endowment.[91] The fact that the Nauvoo endowment went well beyond the Kirtland antecedent made it necessary that recipients of the earlier endowment participate in the new one. Furthermore, Smith's statement that this eventually "will be made known to all Saints" extended the benefits of the endowment beyond the missionary ranks. Whereas the Kirtland endowment was patterned after the New Testament Day of Pentecost, the Nauvoo endowment reached into the Old Testament era, claiming continuity with an Adamic order which was now embodied in the endowment "for the first time in these last days."[92] The new endowment also extended to the future, into the afterlife. While the earlier endowment had emphasized here-and-now empowerment, the new ritual introduced "knowledge" as an essential element, "plans & principles by which any one is enabled to secure the fulness of those blessings . . . and come up and abide in the presence of . . . Eloheim in the eternal worlds." And, of course, the similarities between Freemasonry and the

---

90. See Smith, draft sheet of "Manuscript History . . . "; Brigham Young Manuscript History, 4 May 1842; L. John Nuttall diary, 7 Feb. 1877; Heber C. Kimball diary, June 1842; Heber C. Kimball to Parley P. Pratt; George Miller to James J. Strang, 26 June 1855, in Mills.

91. The remaining element of the Kirtland endowment, the washing of feet, was not mentioned in any account of the 1842 ceremony.

92. A revelation dated 19 Jan. 1841 (DC, LDS, 124) speaks of "things which have been kept hid from before the foundation of the world" (v. 41). Although this sounds similar to the statement concerning the 1842 endowment, the fact that it reaches *farther* back than Adam ("*before* the foundation of the world") and makes no mention of endowment suggests that it did not anticipate a newer version of the Kirtland endowment.

1842 endowment are obvious. In addition to "key words, signs, tokens and penalties," the ceremonial clothing and strict obligation of loyalty and secrecy were Masonic.

Smith was now confident that through this initiative he had reestablished his inner circle of confidants. This is indicated by the Kimball letter:

> Brother Joseph feels as well as I Ever see him. One reason is he has got a Small company. that he feels safe in thare ha[n]ds. and that is not all[,] he can open his bosom to [them] and feel him Self safe[.] I wish you was here so as to feel and hear for your Self. we have recieved some pressious things through the Prophet on the preasthood that would caus your soul to rejoice[.] I can not give them to you on paper fore they are not to be riten.[93]

Smith made it clear that the ceremony was incomplete. He instructed Brigham Young "to take this matter in hand organize and systematize all these ceremonies." By the time the Nauvoo temple was ready for the endowment, Young stated, "we had our ceremonies pretty correct." In the year following the 1842 endowment, while the ceremonies were being refined, no other men received the endowment. Nor were there any developments in endowment theology.[94]

On 26 May 1843 eight of the ten men who participated in the 1842 ceremony met again,[95] whereupon Smith "gave them their

---

93. Kimball to Pratt. Ironically, Smith's effort to surround himself with a new inner circle was ultimately frustrated. Two of the nine men receiving the endowment on 4 May 1842, William Law and William Marks, eventually turned against him. When the official *History of the Church* was published, the names of these two were deleted from the record, giving the erroneous impression that Smith first gave the endowment to only seven men.

94. Andrew F. Ehat makes a convincing argument that dissension over the issue of plural marriage made it inadvisable, if not impossible, for Smith to bring additional people into the group or to expand the theology. See Ehat, "Joseph Smith's Introduction of Temple Ordinances and the 1844 Mormon Succession Question," M.A. thesis, Brigham Young University, 1982, 53-54. By May 1843 a reconciliation appears to have been achieved (61).

95. The participants in the reunion were Joseph and Hyrum Smith, Brigham Young, Heber C. Kimball, Willard Richards, James Adams, Newel K. Whitney, and William Law. No explanation was given for the absence of George Miller and William Marks (HC, 5:409).

endowments and also instructions in the priesthood on the new and everlasting covenant."[96] Because all of these men had received the 1842 endowment, it seems certain that the reason they met again was that the new form went beyond the old. Furthermore, the use of the term "new and everlasting covenant" in connection with the endowment suggests that plural marriage (synonymous at the time with "new and everlasting covenant") accounted for the need to update the ceremony. No other records are known, however, which would shed additional light on the details of this development.

During 1843 completion of the temple was a source of concern to church members largely because they understood that the endowment was accessible to them only in the completed temple. In September, Saints in Boston and in England were urged to contribute to the temple's completion so that two things might occur. First, the Elders might thereby be endowed "with power from on high" to "go forth and gather . . . from the ends of the earth." Second, "those things hid up from the world," including "the ordinances and blessings of His kingdom," would therein be revealed.[97]

By October 1843 women received the endowment for the first time, with Emma Smith apparently the first female recipient. By the middle of the same month, at least one woman had received a patriarchal blessing promising that she would "be endowed with power, as far as ministrations and priesthood was ordained to be given unto man, and unto their help mate."[98] Unlike the endowment of males, which carried no qualification, that of females was conditioned upon sharing it with their husbands.[99] Although women would par-

---

96. Ibid.

97. Minutes of the Manchester, England Conference, 3 Sept. 1843, in *Millennial Star* 4 (Oct. 1843): 83; Brigham Young, Conference of the Twelve, Boylston Hall, Boston, 9 Sept. 1843, in HC, 6:13-14.

98. Patriarchal blessing given to Ann Elisa DeLong by Hyrum Smith, 16 Oct. 1843, LDS archives. This is the earliest mention of an endowment for a woman in the copies of 150 patriarchal blessings prior to 1845 in my possession.

99. DeLong's blessing said, "There are blessings to be received in common with your husband." Several months later Father John Smith gave a patriarchal blessing to Louisa C. Jackson, promising she would "see the Temple finished and in it shall have an endowment with thy Companion" (6 Feb. 1844, RLDS Library-Archives, P8 f16).

ticipate in the endowment, the dominant theme continued to be empowerment of male missionaries.

A new focus now emerged in proselyting strategy, reversing a trend of gathering all new converts to Nauvoo. In an April 1844 general conference address, Smith said:

> I have received instructions from the Lord that from henceforth wherever the Elders of Israel shall build up churches and branches unto the Lord throughout the States, there shall be a stake of Zion. In the great cities, as Boston, New York, &c., there shall be stakes. It is a glorious proclamation, and I reserved it to the last, and designed it to be understood that this work shall commence after the washings, anointings and endowments have been performed here.[100]

In a discourse the following day Brigham Young endorsed Smith's proclamation and extended it to foreign lands: "Let us obey the proclamation of Joseph Smith concerning the Elders going forth into the vineyard to build up the Temple, get their endowments, and be prepared to go forth and preach the Gospel."[101] He "wished to draw the attention of the brethren, first to build the Temple and get your washings, anointings and endowments; after that to build up branches throughout the nations."[102]

Even after Smith's death, when it was apparent that the Saints would be forced from Nauvoo and their primary concern would be survival, Sally Murdock could still write in 1845: "There has been but few elders sent out since the death of the prophet but when the seventies receive their endeument they will go forth with power to all the nations kindreds tongues and people of the earth."[103]

---

100. HC, 6:319-20 (8 Apr. 1844).

101. Brigham Young, HC, 6:321.

102. Hyrum Smith, quoting Brigham Young, HC 6:322-23. The deaths of Joseph and Hyrum Smith two months later ultimately resulted in a decades-long delay in creating branches and stakes throughout the world. Brigham Young's emphasis was to convert people in domestic and foreign lands and encourage them to emigrate to the Great Basin. It was only after the turn of the twentieth century that the emphasis gradually shifted back to Smith's goal of building stakes throughout the world.

103. Sally Murdock (Nauvoo) to William Rhoads (Madison County, New York), 12 Aug. 1845. I am indebted to Rick Grunder for providing me with a photocopy of the original.

The final development during Smith's ministry, which continues to be the driving force behind Latter-day Saint temple activity today, was the realization that it was mandatory that the dead, as well as the living, receive (by proxy) the benefits of the endowment.[104] In order to appreciate the extension of endowment theology to the dead, it is necessary to review the development of this unique Latter-day Saint view of proxy ordinances.

The foundational document, the Book of Mormon, is essentially silent on the subject of salvation of the dead. Although it speaks of the reality of a bodily resurrection, it says nothing of the relative status of beings in the afterlife. While the October 1831 conference introduced the doctrine of "sealing up to eternal life," it was clear that only the living were to be its beneficiaries. There is no record of the subject of salvation of the dead being discussed in the church prior to 1832. On 16 February of that year Smith saw a vision of the afterlife[105] in which several states of postmortal existence were portrayed. In order to inherit the highest ("Celestial") kingdom, it was necessary that one be baptized during mortal life. By contrast, those who were otherwise good people who "died without the law" and received the testimony of Jesus after death but were not baptized while living would inherit an intermediate ("Terrestrial") kingdom, while the remainder were consigned to the lowest ("Telestial") kingdom.

There is no record of any discussion in the church over the next four years regarding the implications of this vision, but a vision in January 1836 made it clear that Smith had resigned himself to the fate of his dead brother, Alvin, who according to the 1832 vision was an heir to the Terrestrial Kingdom:

> I saw father Adam, and Abraham and Michael and my father and mother, my brother Alvin that has long since slept, and marvled how it was that he had obtained an inheritance in that [Celestial] Kingdom, seeing that he had departed this life, before the Lord had set his hand to gather Israel the second time and had not been baptised for the remission of sins—Thus came the voice of the Lord unto me say-

---

104. In 1985, 54,554 endowments for the living were performed, versus 4,857,052 for the dead, a ratio of nearly 100 to 1 (*Conference Report*, Apr. 1986, 23). Since 1986, endowment statistics have not been published by the church.

105. "Kirtland Revelation Book," 1-10; *Evening and Morning Star* 1 (July 1832): 10-11; DC, LDS, 76.

ing all who have died without a knowledge of this gospel, who would have received it, if they had been permitted to tarry, shall be heirs of the celestial Kingdom of God—also all that shall die hense-forth, without a knowledge of it, who would have received it, with all their hearts, shall be heirs of that Kingdom, for I the Lord will judge all men according to their works according to the desires of their hearts.[106]

This vision represented a major shift in Latter-day Saint theology and negated an important point of the 1832 vision, namely that those dying without baptism could not rise above the Terrestrial Kingdom. It gave no hint that anything must be done by the living to allow the dead entrance into the Celestial Kingdom. Rather, the dead would be judged according to desire, and those deemed willing to receive the gospel would become heirs of that kingdom. This theology was consistent with 1 Peter 4:6: "For for this cause was the gospel preached also to them that are dead, that they might be judged according to men in the flesh, but live according to God in the spirit."

That the Saints soon embraced the new doctrine is reflected in a blessing pronounced upon Woodruff in January 1837: "President Z. Coltrin ordained me as a member of the first Seventy & Pronounced great blessings upon my head by the Spirit of Prophecy & Revelation. . . . Also that I should visit COLUB & Preach to the spirits in Prision & that I should bring all of my friends or relatives forth from the Terrestrial Kingdom (who had died) by the Power of the gospel."[107] This statement implies that those who die without the gospel are assigned automatically to the Terrestrial Kingdom. They presumably remain there unless someone intervenes in their behalf. No mention was made of any ordinance to be performed in their behalf.

Later that same year Warren Cowdery, editor of the church newspaper *Messenger and Advocate*, wrote a lengthy article on the subject. Echoing Woodruff's insight, Cowdery wrote that the dead could inherit the Celestial Kingdom on condition that the gospel were preached to them and they accepted its message. He cited 1 Peter 4:6 to defend the concept of preaching to the dead. Once again, however, there was no mention of any requirement for ordinances to be performed in behalf of the dead.[108]

---

106. *Joseph Smith Diary,* 117-20, 21 Jan. 1836; DC, LDS, 137.

107. *Wilford Woodruff's Journal,* 1:118-19, 3 Jan. 1837.

108. *Messenger and Advocate* 3 (Apr. 1837): 470-71.

A year later, Smith addressed the question in print: "Question 16th. If the Mormon doctrine is true what has become of all those who have died since the days of the apostles. [Answer] All those who have not had an opportunity of hearing the Gospel, and being administered unto by an inspired man in the flesh, must have it hereafter, before they can be finally judged."[109]

While it may be claimed that Smith referred obliquely to the performance of baptism and other ordinances in their behalf, nothing else in the historical record for this period supports such an interpretation. Indeed, Apostle Parley P. Pratt, when asked two years later, if "the thief on the cross [was] saved without baptism," answered that he was "included in the same mercy as the heathens, who have never had the offer of the Gospel, and therefore, are under no condemnation for not obeying it."[110]

Later in 1840, in the course of delivering a funeral sermon, Smith announced that the living could participate in the redemption of the dead by being baptized in their behalf.[111] A year later, in commenting on the construction of the Nauvoo Temple, Joseph Fielding confirmed that prior to August 1840 the idea of baptism for the dead had not been part of Latter-day Saint theology:

> The object of the Baptismal Font is also truly interesting to me, and I have no doubt to all the saints: for some time I had thought much on the subject of the redemption of those who died under the broken covenant, it is plain they could not come forth in the king-dom of God, as they had not been adopted, legally [i.e., by baptism] into it, neither could they be while there was no priesthood, they had not been born of water and the spirit, and if they should come into the kingdom without this it would falsify the plain word of Jesus Christ, yet how would those who died martyrs and all those who have lived up to the best light they have had, and would no doubt have rejoiced in the fulness of the gospel had they had it, be denied this privilege? I thought, perhaps those who receive the priesthood in

---

109. Joseph Smith, in *Elders Journal* 1 (July 1838): 43.

110. "The Gospel Illustrated in Questions and Answers," *Millennial Star* 1 (June 1840): 27.

111. Journal History, 15 Aug. 1840. Smith and all subsequent Latter-day Saint commentators have cited 1 Corinthians 15:29 as justification for the doctrine: "Else what shall they do which are baptized for the dead if the dead rise not at all? Why are they then baptized for the dead?"

these last days would baptize them at the coming of the Savior, and this would fulfil the words of the Savior; many shall come from the east and from the west &c., and shall sit down in the kingdom of God,—but the children of the kingdom shall be cast out, as foolish virgins, but a touch of the light of revelation has at once dispelled the darkness and scattered the doubts which once perplexed my mind and I behold the means which God hath devised that his banished ones may be brought back again; every step I take in surveying the plan of heaven, and the wisdom and goodness of God, my heart feels glad, but when I have listened to the teachings of the servants of God under the new covenant and the principles of Baptism for the Dead the feelings of my soul were such as I cannot describe.[112]

At this time baptism was the only ordinance said to be necessary for the dead. That the endowment was not yet considered essential is no surprise, inasmuch as the Kirtland endowment had never been considered an ordinance essential to the living. In October 1842 it was first taught that the endowment was necessary for the living,[113] but an article written later the same month, while reaffirming the necessity of baptism for the dead, spoke of no other ordinance essential to their salvation.[114] The first hint came in December 1843, apparently following a meeting between Smith and other church leaders. Young stated: "When the Temple is done I expect we shall be baptized, washed anointed ordained, & offer up the keys & signs of the priesthood for our dead that they may have a full salvation & we shall be a[s] saviors on mount Zion according to the Scriptures."[115]

The following month, in his first recorded public discourse on the subject, Smith outlined the scope of proxy work expected of the Saints:

The Saints [are] to Come up as Saviors on mount Zion. But how are they to become Saviors on Mount Zion? By building their temples erecting their Baptismal fonts & going forth & receiving all the ordinances, Baptisms, confirmations, washings anointings ordinations, & sealing powers upon our heads in behalf of all our Progenitors who

---

112. Joseph Fielding to Br. Robinson, Nauvoo, 28 Dec. 1841, in *Times and Seasons* 3 (1 Jan. 1842): 648-49.

113. *Times and Seasons* 3 (1 Oct. 1842): 937-39.

114. "The Temple of God in Nauvoo," 28 Oct. 1842, in *Times and Seasons* 4 (15 Nov. 1842): 10-11.

115. Brigham Young, quoted in *Wilford Woodruff's Journal*, 2:333-34, 28 Dec. 1843.

are dead & redeem them that they may come forth in the first resurrection & be exalted to thrones of glory with us.[116]

On at least three occasions during the remaining five months of his life Smith reemphasized the necessity of all ordinances of salvation for the dead.[117] Although endowments were not performed for the dead until the completion of the St. George temple in January 1877, Smith clearly established the need prior to his death.

Freemasonry and the Endowment

The relationship between Mormonism and Freemasonry has been a matter of controversy since 1842. Only one week after the Nauvoo endowment was first given, Bennett wrote that Smith had "established a new lodge of his own, *by inspiration,* called 'ORDER,' in which there are many curious things."[118] In attempting to decipher the relationship between the two traditions, it is important to distinguish between what Smith took to Freemasonry and what he brought from it. As has been shown in this chapter, his betrayal at the hands of Bennett appears to have catalyzed his movement to Freemasonry. By selecting men who were already Masons to constitute the new inner circle, and by placing them under oaths of loyalty and secrecy similar to those they had already taken as Masons, he established some security, at least for the short-term. Because the endowment was part of a larger picture which

---

116. Joseph Smith to a Sunday meeting of the Saints, in *Wilford Woodruff Journal,* 2:341-43, 21 Jan. 1844.

117. These occasions were 10 March (Wilford Woodruff diary for that date); 8 April (William Clayton and Thomas Bullock reports, in Ehat and Cook, 362-64; Wilford Woodruff and Joseph Smith diaries for that date); and 12 May (Thomas Bullock report, George Laub journal, and Samuel W. Richards record, in Ehat and Cook, 368-72). In addition, Joseph Fielding reminisced in his journal, apparently written in the summer of 1844: "Much said on the Subject of the Coming or Spirit of Elijah . . . it is necesary that they [the dead] as well as we who are now alive should be made acquainted with the Ordinances, Signs and Tokens of the Priesthood and the Turms of Admission into the Kingdom in Order that they may come forth with those who have received it here" (Joseph Fielding journal, in *Brigham Young University Studies* 19 [Winter 1979]: 133-66).

118. John C. Bennett letter, dated 11 May 1842, in *Sangamo [Illinois] Journal,* 8 July 1842.

also involved plural marriage, the need for secrecy extended to all new initiates.[119]

Smith saw in Freemasonry the vestige of an ancient ceremony. Though it had no relationship to the pentecostal endowment of the New Testament, he incorporated it into the new endowment, thus transforming it into a chimera of Old and New Testament forms. He told his close friend, Benjamin F. Johnson, that "Freemasonry, as at present, was the apostate endowments."[120] Convinced of its pedigree as a degenerate form of an authentic ancient endowment ceremony, Smith borrowed liberally from the symbolism in giving form to the new ceremony.[121]

While there is no question that Smith believed Freemasonry dated to the construction of Solomon's Temple, contemporary scholarship dates its origins among the trade guilds of the fourteenth century.[122] Like other guilds arising at the same time, it developed for itself an elaborate backdrop of ancient origins and a labyrinth of secret pass-words, signs, and handgrips which assured that as guildsmen traveled in an increasingly mobile Europe they would be able to obtain work in a new town, while non-members would be excluded. By the time of Mormonism, the Masonic legend had existed for two centuries, and all contemporary histories of the movement accepted as authentic the ancient motif, an explanation later known as the "mythical" or "imaginative" school. The first scholar to challenge this was George Kloss. His landmark work, *Geschichte der Freimaurerei in England, Irland und Schottland*, published in 1847, established the "authentic" or

---

119. Prior to 1842 nothing associated with the endowment, either in principle or in practice, was clothed in secrecy. Although plural marriage ceased to be part of the temple experience shortly after the turn of the century, secrecy today remains an integral part of the endowment.

120. In Benjamin F. Johnson, *My Life's Review* (n.p., n.d.), 96 (16 May 1843).

121. Among the borrowed Masonic symbols used openly by Mormonism at various times during its history have been the compass, square, all-seeing eye, and beehive.

122. A definitive scholarly treatment of Masonic history is Douglas Knoop and G. P. Jones, *The Genesis of Freemasonry: An Account of the Rise and Development of Freemasonry in its Operative, Accepted, and Early Specu-lative Phases* (London: Q. C. Correspondence Circle Ltd., 1978).

"verified" school of Freemasonry which demonstrated that the movement began in the Middle Ages not anciently.[123]

There is no evidence to support the claim that Masonic ritual mirrored rites practiced in Solomon's Temple. The Bible itself describes the rituals which bear no resemblance to either Masonic or Latter-day Saint ceremonies. Smith was correct in inferring that Masonic ritual had changed over time. The differences between the earliest known text (1696) and nineteenth-century exposes by Morgan, Bernard, and Allyn (1827, 1829, and 1831) are substantial.[124] One might expect that the earlier Masonic rituals, because they were closer in time to the Solomonic rites, would be closer to the "restored" Latter-day Saint endowment. The opposite is true, however. That is, the similarities between Masonic texts and the Latter-day Saint endowment are most pronounced in the later (1827-31) Masonic rites. Early Masonic texts bear little resemblance to the Latter-day Saint ceremony.

Smith's prophetic genius lay not in his ability to discern what might be called "objective knowledge" but rather in his understanding of "subjective knowledge," coupled with an ability to use symbols with which his community readily identified to bring it into communion with realities that they had experienced. His use of Masonic symbolism sidesteps the issue of historicity. The substance of the endowment was independent of the form. The symbolism conveyed intangible realities totally unrelated to their original Masonic context. One test of any religious leader is his or her ability to provide the community of believers with tangible, finite symbols through which an understanding of and communion with the infinite is facilitated. A century and a half of Latter-day Saint experience with endowment theology and practice attests to Smith's ability to provide his community with such symbols.

---

123. Although Kloss's book was published in 1847, the first Masonic history from the new school published in English was J. G. Findel's *History of Freemasonry* in 1865.

124. A collation of early Masonic rituals from 1696 to 1726 has been reprinted in Douglas Knoop, G. P. Jones, and Douglas Hamer, *The Early Masonic Catechisms* (London: Quatuor Coronati Lodge, No. 2076, 1976).

Chapter Five

Ordinances
1831–36

From 1831 to 1836 several distinctive ordinances emerged in Mormon practice having less to do with everyday religious experience—what one might expect from Sunday worship—and more with extraordinary circumstances and other-worldly expectations. These included raising the dead, prophetic blessings, ceremonies of eternal marriage, and washing one's feet and anointing one's body with oil. Although the context, objectives, and procedures of such ordinances have changed since their inception, the earliest impulses were forerunners to today's versions.

Raising the Dead

Except for his own resurrection, Jesus' crowning miracle was raising Lazarus from the dead. Similarly, the Book of Mormon prophet Nephi raised his brother from the dead (3 Ne. 7:19), and after the resurrected Christ visited the Nephites they too demonstrated this extraordinary power (4 Ne. 1:5). Although the first Mormon elders were promised great spiritual gifts, power over death was not among them. For example, a December 1830 revelation stated: "They shall cast out Devils; they shall heal the sick; they shall cause the blind to receive their sight, and the deaf to hear, and the dumb to speak, & the lame to walk."[1] But as the June 1831 endowment approached, it

---

1. *Painesville Telegraph*, 17 Jan. 1832; also *A Book of Commandments, for the Government of the Church of Christ, Organized According to Law, on the 6th of April, 1830* (Independence, MO: W. W. Phelps & Co., 1833), XXXVII:10; hereafter cited in the text as BC.

became apparent that the elders' expectations now included this power.[2] Ezra Booth, a participant at the June conference, wrote that the elders tried without success to revive "a dead body, which had been retained above ground two or three days."[3] None of the other participants confirmed the report, although three years later an unsympathetic author wrote: "That an attempt was made to raise the child, is denied, of course, as every other attempt has been, after its entire failure was obvious to all."[4]

Regardless of whether an attempt was actually made to raise the dead, reports show that the elders persisted in believing they possessed this power.[5] A Vermont newspaper stated: "It is said they believe their leader to be the real Jesus, and that both he and his disciples have infinite power to work miracles, raise the dead, cleanse the lepers, cast out devils."[6]

These claims may have been put to the test early in 1832. While serving a proselyting mission in Vermont, Joseph Brackenbury died suddenly. A local newspaper, in reporting his death, stated: "In confirmation of their doctrines and divine mission, they *professed* to have power to heal the sick and raise the dead. . . . The company of Brackenbury attempted also to heal him, and since his disease [decease], to raise him from the dead."[7] Similar reports were published in New York and Ohio.[8] Although it may be that these non-Mormon sources exaggerated the truth, a letter written two decades later by a Latter-day Saint apostle lends support to their claim. In compiling the official history of the church, Apostle George A. Smith wrote to Elizabeth Brackenbury for details regarding the death of her husband, including

2. *Western Courier* (Ravenna, Ohio), 26 May 1831; reprinted in *St. Louis Times*, 9 July 1831.

3. Ezra Booth to Rev. Ira Eddy, 31 Oct. 1831, in *Painesville Telegraph*, 15 Nov. 1831.

4. E. D. Howe, *Mormonism Unvailed: or, A Faithful Account of that Singular Imposition and Delusion, from its Rise to the Present Time* (Painesville, OH: Printed and Published by the Author, 1834), 190.

5. *Painesville Telegraph*, 14 June 1831; see also *Niles' Weekly Register*, 16 July 1831.

6. *Vermont Patriot and State Gazette*, 18 Sept. 1831.

7. *Burlington [Vermont] Sentinel*, 23 Mar. 1832; emphasis in original.

8. *Wayne Sentinel*, 11 Apr. 1832; *Ohio Star*, 12 Apr. 1832.

the question, "What were the circumstances of his death, burial, and attempted resurrection?"[9]

If attempts were made in these early years to raise the dead, none were successful. A non-Mormon neighbor wrote that "several of them, however, have died, but none have been raised from the dead."[10] The expectation of such a miracle was revived in February 1835 when the Quorum of the Twelve Apostles was first organized. In ordaining men to the apostleship, the three witnesses to the Book of Mormon "predicted many things which should come to pass, that we should have power to heal the sick, cast out devils, raise the dead, give sight to the blind, have power to remove mountains, and all things should be subject to us through the name of Jesus Christ . . ."[11]

At about this time Joseph Smith, Sr., began to give patriarchal blessings to church members.[12] In blessing Apostle Orson Pratt, he reaffirmed the promise "that thou shalt raise the dead, if needful, to accomplish thy mission."[13] By the following year, as the Kirtland House of the Lord neared completion, the confidence in this promise again attracted the attention of the non-Mormon press: "They assure you, with the utmost confidence, that they shall soon be able to raise the dead . . ."[14] Indeed, a patriarchal blessing given five days before the

---

9. George A. Smith to Elizabeth Brackenbury, 29 Aug. 1855, Henry Stebbins Collection, Library-Archives, The Auditorium, Reorganized Church of Jesus Christ of Latter Day Saints, Independence, Missouri (hereafter RLDS Library-Archives).

10. B. Pixley letter of 12 Oct. 1832, in *Journal and Telegraph* (Albany, New York), 17 Nov. 1832.

11. Stanley B. Kimball, ed., *On the Potter's Wheel: The Diaries of Heber C. Kimball* (Salt Lake City: Signature Books in association with Smith Research Associates, 1987), 207; see also B. H. Roberts, ed., *History of the Church of Jesus Christ of Latter-day Saints, Century I* (Salt Lake City: Deseret Book Co., 1971), 2:188-89 (hereafter cited as HC).

12. Although he was ordained patriarch in December 1833, Smith did not begin to give blessings until December 1834, and then only to members of the Smith family and their spouses.

13. Patriarchal Blessing of Orson Pratt, given by Joseph Smith, Sr., 29 Apr. 1835, Patriarchal Blessing Book A, 21, archives, Historical Department, Church of Jesus Christ of Latter-day Saints, Salt Lake City, Utah (hereafter LDS archives), typescript in my possession.

14. *Ohio Atlas*, 16 Mar. 1836.

dedication promised that "thou shalt receive all the power of the holy priesthood; power to raise the dead . . ."[15]

Over the next few years the promise was periodically repeated, generally through a patriarchal blessing and always to men. For example, in December 1836 Lorenzo Snow was promised, "If expedient the dead shall rise and come forth at thy bidding, even those who have long slept in the dust."[16] Four years later, Arnold Stephens was told, "Thou shalt have great power even to raise the Dead . . ."[17] The final known promise of this power was included in a revelation in January 1841 in which it was said of William Law, "And what if I will that he should raise the dead, let him not withhold his voice."[18] It is not known how many attempts to fulfill this promise may have been made during Smith's lifetime. But in 1891 Apostle Snow revived a young girl who apparently had died several hours earlier—a remarkable event witnessed by several people.[19]

Two related promises, while not considered ordinances, bear inclusion in this section. The first was that an individual, rather than being raised from the dead, would not die. Unlike the power to raise the dead, this promise was given both to women and men. For example, Oliver Harmon was told that "thou Shalt have power over death & the grave & not sleep in the dust,"[20] while Betsy Smith was promised that she would "not see death."[21] In spite of these promises, both died.

---

15. Patriarchal blessing of Ethan Barrows, given by Joseph Smith, Sr., 22 Mar. 1836, in *Journal of History* 15 (1922): 40.

16. Patriarchal blessings given by Joseph Smith, Sr., 15 Dec. 1836, LDS archives.

17. Patriarchal blessing given by Joseph Smith, Sr., 6 July 1840, William Smith Patriarchal Blessing Book, 196-98, RLDS Library-Archives.

18. Doctrine and Covenants (Salt Lake City: Church of Jesus Christ of Latter-day Saints, 1981), 124:100 (hereafter cited in the text as DC, LDS).

19. *Young Woman's Journal* 4 (Jan. 1893): 164-65; *Improvement Era* 32 (Sept. 1929): 883-86.

20. Patriarchal blessing given by Joseph Smith, Sr., 8 Mar. 1836, in "Oliver N. Harmon Reminiscences and Diary," LDS archives.

21. Patriarchal blessing given by Joseph Smith, Sr., 17 June 1836, George A. Smith Family Papers, Marriott Library, University of Utah,

Another promise involved the slain prophet and patriarch, Joseph and Hyrum Smith. One week after their death, Apostle Parley P. Pratt addressed "a great congregation consisting of thousands" upon the subject of the martyrs. He encouraged the Saints to complete the Nauvoo temple so "that when done we might meet our beloved Prophets at the time of the inducement [endowment] of the faithful."[22] Within weeks, apparently in an exaggerated response to this sermon, a report published in the St. Louis New Era and reprinted in Iowa and New York stated that: "A Mormon has arrived in this city who reports that Joe Smith has risen from the dead, and has been seen in Carthage and Nauvoo, mounted on a white horse, and with a drawn sword in his hand."[23]

While such accounts quickly vanished, reports that Smith would return at the dedication of the temple persisted through September. The Burlington [Iowa] Hawkeye stated that "the Temple is progressing very rapidly as the leaders tell the people that when it is finished Joe will appear and dedicate it."[24] Similar accounts were published in Illinois, Iowa, and Ohio,[25] and a national periodical reported that "the Temple is going ahead with astonishing rapidity, all hands being employed at it; it is said, in full faith that Joseph will re-appear at its dedication."[26] No account is known to exist which describes such an appearance either at or prior to the dedication.

Blessing

One of the early accounts of a blessing ordinance occurred at the June 1831 general conference. After Joseph Smith and Lyman Wight ordained several men to the High Priesthood, Bishop Edward Partridge "then proceeded and blessed the above named and others by

---

Salt Lake City.

22. William Huntington diary, 4 July 1844, Huntington Library, San Marino, California.

23. The Davenport [Iowa] Gazette, 22 Aug. 1844; Semi-Weekly Courier and Enquirer (New York), 24 Aug. 1844.

24]. Burlington Hawkeye, 12 Sept. 1844.

25. Sangamo [Illinois] Journal, 12 Sept. 1844; The Davenport [Iowa] Gazette, 19 Sept. 1844; and Buckeye [Ohio] Eagle, 25 Sept. 1844.

26. Niles' National Register, 28 Sept. 1844.

the laying on of hands."[27] In 1834 when the first high council was organized:

> After much good instruction, Joseph, the president, laid his [hands] upon the heads of the two assistant presidents and pronounced a blessing upon them, that they might have the wisdom to magnify their office, and power over all the power of the adversary. He also laid his hands upon the twelve counsellors and commanded a blessing to rest upon them, that they might have wisdom and power to counsel in righteousness upon all subjects that might be laid before them. He also prayed that they might be delivered from those evils to which they were most exposed, and that their lives might be prolonged on the earth.[28]

A year later, the three witnesses of the Book of Mormon were "blessed by the laying on of the hands of the Presidency," whereupon they proceeded to select the members of the first Quorum of Twelve Apostles.[29]

Blessings were sometimes combined with other ordinances. For example, when Wilford Woodruff was ordained a seventy in 1837 Zebedee Coltrin added words of blessing which were not related to the ordination: "President Z. Coltrin ordained me as a member of the first Seventy & Pronounced great blessings upon my head by the Spirit of Prophecy & Revelation."[30]

Occasionally a blessing was pronounced on an individual or group without physical contact between officiator and recipient(s). For example, an 1832 revelation directed missionaries that "in whatsoever house ye enter, and they receive you, leave your blessings upon that house."[31] In the course of preparing for the 1836 endowment, Smith

---

27. John Whitmer, "The Book of John Whitmer," chap. 7, in F. Mark McKiernan and Roger D. Launius, eds., *An Early Latter Day Saint History: The Book of John Whitmer Kept by Commandment* (Independence, MO: Herald House, 1980), 70.

28. "Kirtland Council Minutes," 19 Feb. 1834, LDS archives.

29. HC, 2:186-87.

30. Scott G. Kenney, ed., *Wilford Woodruff's Journal* (Midvale, UT: Signature Books, 1983), 1:118-19, 3 Jan. 1837.

31. *Doctrine and Covenants of The Church of the Latter Day Saints: Carefully Selected from the Revelations of God* (Kirtland, OH: F. G. Williams & Co., 1835), LXXXVII:3 (25 Jan. 1832); hereafter cited in the text as DC, 1835.

blessed "each quorem in the name of the Lord,"[32] and later the same month "pronounced a blessing upon the Sisters for the liberality in giving their servises so cheerfully to make the veil for the Lord's house also upon the congregation and [then] dismissed [them]."[33]

Infrequently a blessing was bestowed on an inanimate object. For instance, the Book of Mormon recorded that Alma "blessed the earth for the righteous' sake."[34] Although there is no record of a similar blessing by Smith, Apostle Heber C. Kimball took literally the blessing of land:

> Do you not see the propriety of our blessing the earth—the earth that we inhabit and cultivate? If you do not see the propriety of it, for heaven's sake do not bless the sacrament again. Do not take a bottle of oil to the prayer circle to be blessed, when you do not believe the earth can be blessed.
>
> If you have got half-an-acre, you can bless it, and dedicate it, and consecrate it to God, and ask him to fill it with life. Well, then, if you can bless half-an-acre, why can you not bless a whole acre? And if you can bless an acre, why can you not bless all this Territory?[35]

Sealing

One of the central doctrines of the Restoration is "sealing," which today is used primarily to join spouse to spouse, child to parent(s) for eternity. However, such context was the last of several to develop during Joseph Smith's ministry. Because the single term, "seal," implied so many different concepts, and because these often existed simultaneously, it is important to distinguish among definitions being used at any given time.

The earliest use of the concept occurred in 1830 and drew upon precedents from the Bible and the Book of Mormon. A revelation that September spoke of Smith's special ability to penetrate ancient "seals":

---

32. Scott H. Faulring, ed., *An American Prophet's Record: The Diaries and Journals of Joseph Smith* (Salt Lake City: Signature Books in association with Smith Research Associates, 1987), 128, 1 Feb. 1836.

33. Ibid., 23 Feb. 1836.

34. Alma 45:15, in The Book of Mormon (Salt Lake City: Church of Jesus Christ of Latter-day Saints, 1981) (hereafter cited in the text as BM, LDS).

35. Heber C. Kimball discourse, 8 Nov. 1857, in *Journal of Discourses* (Liverpool, Eng.: Asa Calkins, 1859), 6:36.

"And thou shalt not command him who is at thy head, and at the head of the church, for I have given him the keys of the mysteries and the revelations which are sealed, until I shall appoint unto them another in his stead" (BC XXX:6). Another revelation three months later reinforced the notion that Smith had special powers to decipher hidden things: "I have given unto him the keys of the mystery of those things which have been sealed" (BC XXXVII:19).

In this context the verb "to seal" means to hide or to remove from access, as employed in a passage from Isaiah which became an important proof text of Smith's divine calling: "And the vision of all is become unto you as the words of a book that is sealed, which men deliver to one that is learned, saying, Read this, I pray thee: and he saith, I cannot; for it is sealed" (Isa. 29:11).

In this scripture the "book" is a metaphor for a vision which, though presented to "one that is learned," is incomprehensible to him. Stated another way, the book is accessible to him but the meaning is not. This passage is referred to in the Book of Mormon, but the book is depicted as a reality—that is, the gold plates which formed the basis of the Book of Mormon—and not as a metaphor:

> And behold the book shall be sealed; and in the book shall be a revelation from God, from the beginning of the world to the ending thereof. . . .
>
> But behold, it shall come to pass that the Lord God shall say unto him to whom he shall deliver the book:
>
> Take these words which are not sealed and deliver them to another, that he may show them unto the learned, saying: Read this, I pray thee.
>
> And the learned shall say: Bring hither the book, and I will read them. . . .
>
> And the man shall say: I cannot bring the book for it is sealed.
>
> Then shall the learned say: I cannot read it (BM, LDS, 2 Ne. 27:7, 15, 17-18).

In this passage there is a slightly different meaning than in Isaiah, for now it is not merely the meaning which is inaccessible to the learned man, but the book itself.

Several other biblical passages employ a similar usage. In some cases the object is concrete: "And I saw in the right hand of him that sat on the throne a book written within and on the backside, sealed with seven seals" (Rev. 5:1). In other cases the object is abstract: "And he said, go thy way, Daniel: for the words are closed up and sealed till the time of the end" (Dan. 12:9). In the case of the Book of Mormon the object is always concrete, as in the Book of Ether: "And behold, when ye shall come unto me, ye shall write them and shall seal them up, that no one can interpret them" (3:22). Obviously, this use of "seal," which predominated prior to 1831, cannot be considered an ordinance, although subsequent uses during Smith's ministry were.

The highlight of the June 1831 general conference was the ordination of several elders to the Order of Melchizedek (or High Priesthood) prior to their journey to Missouri to dedicate a temple site. Upon their return to Kirtland, "Br. Joseph Smith jr. said that the order of the High-priesthood is that they have power given them to seal up the Saints unto eternal life. And said it was the privilege of every Elder present to be ordained to the Highpriesthood."[36]

When Smith made this statement the High Priesthood was an order of elders and referred neither to the office of high priest nor to an umbrella organization encompassing several offices. With the passage of time, however, High Priesthood became synonymous with the office of high priest (late 1831) and eventually with Melchizedek Priesthood (1835), a term encompassing five offices. Statements made after 1835 assigned the sealing power to the Melchizedek Priesthood in general and not to a single office within that priesthood. For example, an editorial in 1841 stated: "The power and authority of the Higher, or Melchizedek Priesthood was to hold the keys of all the spiritual blessings of the Church, as Jesus said, 'I give unto thee the keys of the kingdom of heaven—whatsoever thou shalt bind on earth shall be bound in heaven,' etc."[37] Similarly, Smith wrote to James Arlington Bennett in 1843 of "the sealing power of the Melchizedek priesthood."[38] Indeed, all known examples of sealings during Smith's ministry involved men who had been ordained to offices in the Melchizedek Priesthood.

The most common form of sealing was in the context of "certifying" or "validating." The object of such was either impersonal or personal. In each instance, ample scriptural precedent existed. An

36. Donald Q. Cannon and Lyndon W. Cook, eds., *Far West Record: Minutes of the Church of Jesus Christ of Latter-day Saints, 1830-1841* (Salt Lake City: Deseret Book Co., 1983), 19-25, 25 Oct. 1831.

37. *Millennial Star* 1 (Apr. 1841): 298-99.

38. Joseph Smith to James Arlington Bennett, 13 Nov. 1843, in *Niles' National Register*, 3 Feb. 1844.

example of the former occurs in Isaiah, which describes the validation of the law by God's servants: "Bind up the testimony, seal the law among my disciples" (8:16). This passage was quoted without change in the Book of Mormon (2 Ne. 18:16) and was the basis of commandments to LDS missionaries whose labors effected the sealing of the law and testimony: "Therefore tarry ye, and labour diligently, that you may be perfected, in your ministry to go forth among the gentiles, for the last time, as many, as the mouth of the Lord shall name, to bind up the law, and seal up the testimony, and to prepare the saints, for the hour of judgments."[39]

More common than sealing a concept was validating or certifying an ordinance. For instance, the impetus for the endowment doctrine was the idea that authority and power were not necessarily connected, that the pronouncement of intent, even though performed by one having authority, did not guarantee effect. Similarly, it became common practice to seal or validate an ordinance to assure that it would be recognized by God, both in this life and, where applicable, in the life to come.

In some cases the sealing was part of the ordinance, while in others it was a separate ritual following the ordinance it validated. Although neither the Bible nor the Book of Mormon mentions the sealing of an ordinance, both make clear that the disciples of Jesus were given power whereby whatever they "bound" or "sealed" on earth would be recognized and sanctioned in heaven. In the biblical case Jesus said first to Peter and later to the other disciples, "Whatsoever thou shalt bind on earth shall be bound in heaven: and whatsoever thou shalt loose on earth shall be loosed in heaven" (Matt. 16:19, 18:18). The Book of Mormon contains a nearly identical injunction: "Whatsoever ye shall seal on earth shall be sealed in heaven" (Hel. 10:7).

The earliest known instance of sealing an ordinance occurred at a general conference in January 1832: "At this conference, the Prophet Joseph was acknowledged President of the High Priesthood, and hands were laid on him by Elder Sidney Rigdon, who sealed upon his head

---

39. Revelation dated 27 Dec. 1832, in "Kirtland Revelations Book," 41, LDS archives; also DC, 1835 VII:23. Note that this revelation reversed the order described in Isaiah, sealing the testimony, while Isaiah sealed the law. The dedicatory prayer of the Kirtland House of the Lord in 1836 reverted to Isaiah: "Enable thy servants to seal up the law, and bind up the testimony" (DC, LDS 109:46).

the blessings which he had formerly received."[40] Four types of ordinances were often sealed. It was optional for ordinations and blessings and was mandatory for anointings preceding the late Kirtland (i.e., 1836) and Nauvoo endowments and the "second anointing" which began in 1843.

A revelation in March 1832 first mentioned the use of seals for ordinations:

> Q. What are we to understand by sealing the one hundred and forty-four thousand, out of all the tribes of Israel—twelve thousand out of every tribe?
>
> A. We are to understand that those who are sealed are high priests, ordained unto the holy order of God, to administer the everlasting gospel; for they are they who are ordained out of every nation, kindred, tongue, and people, by the angels to whom is given power over the nations of the earth, to bring as many as will come to the church of the Firstborn (DC, 1921 77:11).

The following year Smith referred to himself as "him who is ordained and sealed unto this power."[41] In 1835 the Kirtland High Council, in blessing Elisha Groves, stated, "We seal the blessings of the High Priesthood upon the[e] which thou has already received."[42]

With the advent of patriarchal blessings, several men had their previous ordinations sealed, as in the case of Lyman Wight ("I seal upon thee thine ordination, which ordination is after the order of Melchezedek"[43]), and the unusual case of James Newberry who was both ordained and sealed: "You are bless'd with the holy priesthood which I confer upon you, and seal it with a sealing blessing upon your head, even that which is after the order of Melchizedek."[44] In spite of these examples, however, there is no evidence that the sealing of ordinations became a common practice.

More common was the sealing of blessings, usually pronounced as

40. Orson Pratt diary, 25 Jan. 1832, LDS archives.

41. Joseph Smith to "Mr. Editor," 4 Jan. 1833, in Dean C. Jessee, ed., *The Personal Writings of Joseph Smith* (Salt Lake City: Deseret Book Co., 1984), 272-73.

42. "Kirtland Council Minutes," 17 Aug. 1835.

43. Patriarchal blessing of Lyman Wight, given by Joseph Smith, Sr., 29 Dec. 1835, RLDS Library-Archives.

44. Patriarchal blessing of James Newberry, given by Hyrum Smith, 30 May 1841, RLDS Library-Archives.

part of the blessing. An early example is the 1833 blessing of George A. Smith by his father who concluded by saying "all these blessings shall be yours and I seal them upon your head in the name of Jesus Christ."[45] The most common form occurred with patriarchal blessings, where the majority contained a statement by the patriarch sealing the blessing(s) pronounced therein.[46]

While the sealing of ordinations and blessings was done informally and usually as part of the ordinance being sealed, anointings relating to endowment were sealed in a separate, formal ordinance. During the winter of 1835-36, as the House of the Lord neared completion, the elders prepared for the endowment by being washed and anointed. On 28 January 1836 Smith met with the Quorum of the Twelve and the Quorum of the Seventy to seal the anointings:

> I proceeded with the quorum of the presidency to instruct them [the twelve] & also the seven presidents of the seventy Elders to call upon God with uplifted hands to seal the blessings which had been promised to them by the holy anointing. As I organized this quorem with the presedincy in this room, Pres. Sylvester Smith saw a piller of fire rest down & abide upon the heads of the quorem as we stood in the midst of the Twelve.
>
> When the Twelve & the seven were through with their sealing prayers I called upon Pres. S. Rigdon to seal them with uplifted hands & when he had done this & cried hosannah that all [the] congregation should join him & shout hosannah to God & the Lamb & glory to God in the highest.[47]

Throughout the remainder of the winter church leaders met periodically with men who had been washed and anointed to seal the anointings. Multiple sealings were suggested by the patriarchal blessing of Jonathan Crosby, Jr., who was told, "I seal all former blessings, even the blessing of the holy anointing, which thou has received."[48] Al-

---

45. Blessing of 31 May 1833, from the "Record Book of Bathsheba W. Smith," 46-48, typescript, Special Collections, Harold B. Lee Library, Brigham Young University, Provo, Utah.

46. Of 131 patriarchal blessings given between 1835 and 1844, of which I have copies, 103 (79 percent) contain language which seals the blessings. It is likely that other forms of blessing were commonly sealed, but the fact that most were not transcribed makes it impossible to determine the incidence.

47. *Joseph Smith Diary*, 123-24, 28 Jan. 1836.

48. Patriarchal blessing of Jonathan Crosby, Jr., given by Joseph

though the purpose was primarily to assure the recipient of the validity of the ordinance, the elders remained open to further assurances, as indicated by Smith in the dedicatory prayer of the House of the Lord: "Let the anointing of thy ministers be sealed upon them with power from on high."[49]

After the Saints left Ohio and were expelled from Missouri, they settled in Illinois and began to build the temple in which they anticipated another endowment. Although the Nauvoo endowment was more developed and structured, it retained the same washings and anointings, including the sealing of the anointing. One of the nine original initiates, Heber C. Kimball, wrote, "I was aniciated into the ancient order[,] was washed and annointed[,] and Sealled."[50] Sealing the anointing continued as part of the endowment ritual through the remainder of Smith's life.

In 1843 another ordinance was added to those which would be practiced only in temples. Known as the "second anointing," it conferred a higher level of confidence to recipients of their ultimate exaltation. Although details of this ordinance were not commonly recorded, contemporary records confirm that the recipients received a sealing of their additional anointing.[51]

Whereas the above examples relate to the certification of ordinances, another form of sealing, unrelated to another ordinance, carried the assurance of eternal life (or, in some cases, eternal damnation). It was the earliest form of sealing in the Restoration that could be considered an ordinance. Biblical precedents came from the New Testament and deal with an assurance of salvation, as seen in the Epistle to the Ephesians: "And grieve not the holy Spirit of God, whereby ye are sealed unto the day of redemption" (4:30; see also 2 Cor. 1:21-22, Eph. 1:13, Rev. 7:2-4, 9:4). Similarly, the Book of Mormon speaks of assured salvation: "Therefore, I would that ye should be steadfast and immovable, always abounding in good works, that Christ, the Lord God Omnipotent, may seal you his, that you may be brought to

Smith, Sr., 21 Feb. 1836, in "Caroline Barnes Crosby Journal and Autobiography," Utah State Historical Society, Salt Lake City.

49. *Joseph Smith Diary,* 146-52, 27 Mar. 1836.

50. *Heber C. Kimball Diary,* 55, June 1842.

51. See entries of 27, 28, 30, and 31 Jan. and 2, 4, and 26 Feb. 1844, *Wilford Woodruff's Journal,* 2:343-52; also entries of 28, 30, and 31 Jan. 1844, "Brigham Young Manuscript History," LDS archives.

heaven, that ye may have everlasting salvation and eternal life" (BM, LDS, Mosiah 5:15). The essential difference between these scriptural precedents and the practice of the Latter-day Saints was that the actual sealing in the former instance was done by Jesus, the Holy Spirit, or angels, whereas in the latter case any elder holding the High Priesthood could "seal up the Saints unto eternal life."[52]

The week after the October 1831 conference, two revelations confirmed this power. Divine approval was required: "And of as many as the Father shall bear record, to you shall be given power to seal them up unto eternal life."[53] In addition, "To them [the elders] is power given, to seal both on earth and in heaven, the unbelieving and rebellious; yea, verily, to seal them up unto the day when the wrath of God shall be poured out upon the wicked" (BC I:2, 1 Nov. 1831). This new power was reminiscent of that spoken of in the Book of Mormon: "For behold, if ye have procrastinated the day of your repentance even unto death, behold, ye have become subjected to the spirit of the devil, and he doth seal you his" (Alma 34:35).[54]

Within days of the October 1831 general conference, elders holding the High Priesthood began to exercise their newly-conferred authority and sealed entire congregations to eternal life. During the month of November, for instance, Reynolds Cahoon recorded three such instances:

> tuesday came to shalersville held a meting in the Evning with the Br[ethren]. and after labaring with them some length of time Br. David seeled them up unto Eternal life. . . .
> Thurs. 17 Nov[.] held a meting . . . Broke bread with them[,] sealed up the Church unto Eternal life . . .
> Sateurday Evening held a Met with the Brth at Mr. Reevs & Blest the Children in the name of the lord & sealed the Church unto eternal life.[55]

Although Cahoon gave no details concerning how the sealing was to be done, Jared Carter described such a sealing in early 1832:

---

52. *Far West Record*, 19–25, 25 Oct. 1831.

53. Revelation of Nov. 1831, in *Evening and Morning Star*, Oct. 1832; also DC, 1835 XXII.

54. The following spring Orson Hyde, while on a missionary journey, "sealed up many to the day of wrath" (Orson Hyde diary, 19 Mar. 1832, LDS archives).

55. Reynolds Cahoon diary, LDS archives.

During my labors in Benson I witnessed many manifestations, both in spirit and miracles, a few of which I will mention. The first instance of god manifesting his power to the Church was on the last day I held meetings with them. While I, in the commencement of the meeting, was praying, I was directed to pray most earnestly that God would grant unto us sealing grace. After this I felt directed by the spirit to declare unto the brethren that that day was a sealing time with them, as I had prayed in faith, that they might be blessed. My communication to them caused some of the brethren to tremble, for this was something that they had never before experienced; but I exhorted them to call more earnestly on the Lord. We then began to pray, but the spirit, as I viewed it in my mind, was not yet poured out; therefore, I again arose and devoted a few minutes to call upon the Lord with one accord. Accordingly, all of us lifted our voices to God, and while we were praying, the Spirit rested down upon us. We then administered the Sacrament and it appeared to me that the Church of Christ in that locality was sealed up to the Lord, and it was likewise made plain to me that every one of us present should meet again in Zion. I then felt as though I could leave them without fear, for I had a testimony that God would keep them.[56]

Other instances of group sealings occurred in April 1832 (performed by Joseph Smith[57]) and in August and September 1833 (performed by Lyman Johnson).[58] By this time the practice of sealing individuals rather than groups had begun, and while no instances of group sealings have been found after 1833, individual sealings increased dramatically. The first known instance occurred in January 1833 at the opening of the School of the Prophets. Entry into the school required the ordinance of washing of feet, which, at least in this setting, constituted the sealing of the recipient to eternal life:

The President said after he had washed the feet of the Elders, as I have done[,] so do ye[,] wash ye therefore one anothers feet pronouncing at the same time that the Elders were all clean from the blood of this generation but that those among them who should sin wilfully after they were thus cleansed and sealed up unto eternal life should be given over unto the buffettings of Satan until the day of redemption.[59]

---

56. Jared Carter journal, LDS archives.

57. See Joseph Knight's "Early History of Mormonism," in *Brigham Young University Studies* 17 (Autumn 1976): 39.

58. Orson Pratt diary, 26 Aug. and 8 Sept. 1833.

59. "Kirtland Council Minutes," 23 Jan. 1833.

No further instances were recorded during the two years between September 1833 and September 1835, at which time Elizabeth Ann Whitney received a patriarchal blessing from Joseph Smith, Sr., declaring, "I seal thee up unto eternal life."[60] This statement soon became a commonplace part of patriarchal blessings, and half (66 of 131) of the available blessings given between 1835 and 1844 contain declarations of sealing to eternal life.[61]

While patriarchal blessings appear to have remained the most common vehicle for this type of sealing, Wilford Woodruff, as an exception, recorded his simultaneous ordination and sealing to eternal salvation in 1836: "Spent this 31st DAY of MAY at Br Fry [at] Eagle Creek and found it to be the most interesting, important & instructive day of my LIFE. For on this Glorious DAY I was ordained unto the High Priesthood and also as one of the Second Seventy & sealed up unto Eternal LIFE under the hands of my Beloved Brethren, VIZ Elder's David W Patten & Warren Parrish."[62] Another vehicle was an 1842 wedding ceremony in which Smith and his plural wife, Sarah Ann Whitney, were instructed, "let immortality and eternal life henceforth be sealed upon your heads forever and ever."[63]

While these examples have in common the assurance of eternal life, occasionally one was sealed against the effects of evil. Three patriarchal blessings, all given by Joseph Smith, Sr., express this sentiment. Phoebe W. Carter was told: "I lay my hands on thy head & place a seal on thy forehead and if thou art faithful and keep the commandments of God NO power shall take it off it shall be a seal against the destroyer."[64] To Benjamin C. Ellsworth, Father Smith said, "I place a seal on thee that the Enemy may not have power over

---

60. Newel K. Whitney papers, Lee Library. This is the first instance of such a sealing occurring in the patriarchal blessings I have been able to examine.

61. The patriarchal blessing of Sarah Mackley, given by Joseph Smith, Sr., on 14 May 1836 went one step further: "These blessings I seal on thy head and of thy children after thee and seal *them* up to eternal life" (emphasis added; typescript of blessing in RLDS Library-Archives).

62. *Wilford Woodruff's Journal,* 1:74, 31 May 1836.

63. Unpublished revelation, LDS archives.

64. Patriarchal blessing of Phoebe W. Carter, given by Joseph Smith, Sr., 10 Nov. 1836, in *Wilford Woodruff's Journal,* 1:144-45, 15 Apr. 1837.

thee."[65] And Marinda Nancy Hyde was told: "I seal thee against the Destroyer."[66] In all three cases, the recipient was also "sealed unto eternal life," so it is not clear if sealing against evil was considered an independent ordinance. Despite the diversity of forms and vehicles, with different vehicles predominating at various times, one sees a single intent in these sealings: the assurance that God accepted the recipient and guaranteed eternal life.[67]

The final form of sealing (and the one most prevalent in the Latter-day Saint church today) was the linking of one person to another such that a familial relationship was assured not only in this life but after the resurrection. Two forms of person-to-person sealing gradually developed. In the first, husband and wife were joined to each other. In the second, which was outlined by Smith but apparently not put into practice until after his death, child and parents were linked to each other. While there is no direct scriptural precedent, the latter practice developed from the promise that what was bound on earth would be bound in heaven.

Smith's innovations with respect to marriage began as early as 1831, allegedly involved relationships outside his marriage to Emma Smith as early as 1835, and culminated in formal plural marriages as early as 1841.[68] While the specific nature of the wedding ceremony prior to 1842 is not known, the exact wording of Smith's July 1842 marriage to Sarah Ann Whitney was given by revelation.[69] It is clear

---

65. Patriarchal blessing of Benjamin Clopson Ellsworth, given by Joseph Smith, Sr., 15 July 1837, RLDS Library-Archives. Note that in this and the preceding example "seal" is used as a noun, rather than a verb.

66. Patriarchal blessing of Marinda Nancy Hyde, given by Joseph Smith, Sr., 10 May 1838, in Howard H. Barron, *Orson Hyde: Missionary, Apostle, Colonizer* (Salt Lake City: Horizon Books, 1977), 315-16.

67. While this concept was appealing to Latter-day Saints in general, some considered it offensive, even blasphemous. William and Wilson Law, who had been prominent church leaders prior to their disaffection, wrote in 1844 of Joseph Smith: "He'll SEAL YOU UP, be damned you can't/ No matter what you do—/ If that you only stick to him,/ He swears he'll take you through" (*Warsaw Message*, 7 Feb. 1844).

68. For example, see Richard S. Van Wagoner, *Mormon Polygamy: A History* (Salt Lake City: Signature Books, 1986).

69. Unpublished revelation dated 27 July 1842, LDS archives.

that the purpose of the ceremony was to create a marriage which would survive death ("you both mutually agree . . . to be each others companion so long as you both shall live . . . and also through out all eternity"), though no use of the word "seal" was made with respect to the marriage ordinance itself. The ceremony concluded with the statement, "let immortality and eternal life henceforth be sealed upon your heads forever and ever," a statement consistent with the decade-old practice of sealing people to eternal life.[70]

Nearly a year later, in conversation with William Clayton and Benjamin F. Johnson, Smith discussed marriage for eternity and used the word "sealed," though in reference to Clayton's prior "sealing to eternal life" not to the marriage bond:

> Addressing Benjamin says he "nothing but the unpardonable sin can prevent him [Clayton] from inheriting eternal glory for he is sealed up by the power of the Priesthood unto eternal life having taken the step which is necessary for that purpose." He said that except a man and his wife enter into an everlasting covenant and be married for eternity while in this probation by the power and authority of the Holy Priesthood they will cease to increase when they died (ie. they will not have any children in the resurrection) but those who are married by the power & authority of the priesthood in this life & continue without committing the sin against the Holy Ghost will continue to increase & have children in the celestial glory.[71]

A careful reading of Clayton's diary entry shows that by entering eternal marriage, Clayton would be "sealed up unto eternal life." That is, rather than being sealed to his wife, Clayton would himself be sealed. While this explanation may seem like a distinction without a difference, it is an important one, for although this form of marriage eventually evolved into the sealing of one person to another, which had no direct scriptural precedent, the earlier form (in which the recipient was sealed to eternal life rather than to a person) was in obvious continuity with scriptural precedents and other Latter-day Saint usages of "sealing" already discussed in this section.

---

70. Although later reminiscences often applied the term "sealing" to such marriages, no contemporary document uses the term in such a connotation.

71. George D. Smith, ed., *An Intimate Chronicle: The Journals of William Clayton* (Salt Lake City: Signature Books in association with Smith Research Associates, 1991), 102, 16 May 1843.

On 12 July 1843 the revelation authorizing plural, as well as everlasting, marriage was committed to paper. Two passages in this revelation used the word "sealed" in relationship to marriage, and in both cases it is the ordinance of marriage which is sealed (or certified in heaven), not the people to each other. That is, the ordinance of marriage itself promised the eternal union of husband and wife, while the sealing served to validate that ordinance in the same manner in which the other heretofore mentioned ordinances were sealed:

> If a man marry a wife, and make a covenant with her for time and for all eternity, if that covenant is not by me or by my word, which is my law, and is not sealed by the Holy Spirit of promise, through him whom I have anointed and appointed unto this power, then it is not valid neither of force when they are out of the world . . .
>
> If a man marry a wife by my word, which is my law, and by the new and everlasting covenant, and it is sealed unto them by the Holy Spirit of promise, by him who is anointed . . . [it] shall be of full force when they are out of the world; and they shall pass by the angels, and the gods, which are set there, to their exaltation and glory in all things, as hath been sealed upon their heads (DC, LDS 132:18-19).

A later passage reaffirms that it is the ordinance, not the couple, which is sealed: "Whatsoever [not whosoever] you seal on earth shall be sealed in heaven" (v. 46). When Wilford and Phebe Woodruff were united eternally several months later, Wilford recorded that Hyrum Smith "sealed the marrige Covenant between me and my wife."[72]

This form of marriage was available not only to those church members who previously had been married only for "time," but was extended to the dead so that their marriage unions also would be in force in the afterlife. In referring to this, one church member wrote to his daughter that "many of the members of the Church have already availed themselves of this privilege, & have been married [not sealed] to their deceased partners."[73]

Later the same month Woodruff recorded what is apparently the first use of the term "seal" in direct reference to the binding together of husband and wife: "Br Joseph said now what will we do with Elder P. P. Pratt. He has no wife sealed to him for Eternity. He has one

---

72. *Wilford Woodruff's Journal,* 2:326-27, 11 Nov. 1843.

73. Jacob Scott to Mary Warnock, 5 Jan. 1844, RLDS Library-Archives.

living wife but she had a former Husband and did not wish to be sealed to Parly, for Eternity. now is it not right for Parley to have another wife that can."[74] Thereafter, this use of the term became standard, as in a patriarchal blessing the same month which promised Susanah Bigler that "if thou desirest thou shalt be sealed to thy companion for all Eternity."[75]

The final form of sealing during Smith's ministry involved the perpetuation of the parent-child relationship in post-mortal existence. As with sealing of spouses, this began to develop under different terminology, which gradually shifted towards the use of the term "seal." The development had its genesis in the prophecy of Malachi: "Behold, I will send you Elijah the prophet before the coming of the great and dreadful day of the Lord: And he shall turn the heart of the fathers to the children, and the heart of the children to the fathers, lest I come and smite the earth with a curse" (4:5-6).

Although an 1835 revelation (DC, 1835 XXIX:2) and the 1836 vision of Elijah (DC, LDS 110:16) repeated Malachi's prophecy, the theology of the relationship between parent and child did not begin to develop until 1839 when Smith indicated that that relationship extended to the dead.[76] The ordinance of baptism for the dead was initiated in 1840, implicitly turning the hearts of the children to their parents as they performed the ordinance in behalf of their deceased ancestors. Two years later Smith made explicit the connection, using the term "welding link" rather than "seal":

> It is sufficient to know in this case, that the earth will be smitten with a curse, unless there is a *welding link* of some kind or other, between the fathers and the children, upon some subject or other, and behold, what is that subject. It is the baptism for the dead. For we without them cannot be made perfect; neither can they without us be made perfect. Neither can they or us, be made perfect without those who have died in the gospel also; for it is necessary in the ushering in of the dispensation of the fulness of times; which dispensation is now beginning to usher in, that a whole, and complete, and perfect union,

---

74. *Wilford Woodruff's Journal*, 2:340-41, 21 Jan. 1844.

75. Patriarchal Blessing of Susanah Bigler, given by John Smith, Jan. 1844, George A. Smith papers, Marriott Library.

76. Andrew F. Ehat and Lyndon W. Cook, eds., *The Words of Joseph Smith* (Provo, UT: Religious Studies Center, Brigham Young University, 1980), 22.

and *welding together* of dispensations, and keys, and powers, and glories should take place, and be revealed, from the days of Adam even to the present time.[77]

In other words, as of 1842 the linkage of parent to child in fulfilment of the prophecy of Malachi was to occur through the ordinance of baptism for the dead. Neither the word "seal" nor any additional ordinance was yet part of Latter-day Saint theology.

The most important step in the development of parent-child theology occurred a year later. In the course of a funeral sermon Smith made the first known statement linking Elijah with the concept of sealing and moved closer to the concept of sealing child to parents by promising that the salvation of children could be assured if parents had a "seal" placed on them. The sermon began with an emotional description of the horrors Smith foresaw in an afterlife without familial relationships:

> There is a thought more dreadful than that of total annihilation. That is the thought that we shall never again meet with those we loved here on earth. Suppose I had some Idea of a resurection and glory beyond the grave which God and angels had secured and yet had not any knowledge [or] intelligence of any law[,] of any order by which it is to be obtained. Well you lose a friend [and] you come up in the resurection hoping to [meet] him again but find yourself separated from them to all eternity and become aware of the fact that through ignorance of the principles of the resurection and reunion you will never behold that dear friend nor ever enjoy his society. this thought I say of being disappointed in meeting my friend in the resurection is to be more dreadful than of ceasing to suffer by a cessation of being.[78]

Smith juxtaposed one Old Testament and one New Testament scripture to demonstrate how the generations might be guaranteed a bond which would connect them in the afterlife. First he quoted Malachi's prophecy about the turning of hearts, then moved to the Book of Revelation: "Hurt not the earth, neither the sea, nor the trees, till we have sealed the servants of our God in their foreheads" (7:3).

---

77. Joseph Smith "To the Church of Jesus Christ of Latter Day Saints," 6 Sept. 1842, in *Times and Seasons* 3 (1 Oct. 1842): 934-36, emphasis added; see also DC, LDS 128.

78. Joseph Smith sermon at the funeral of Elias Higbee, 13 Aug. 1843, in Ehat and Cook, 239.

He proceeded to explain the verse: "It means to seal the blessing on their heads[,] meaning the everlasting covenant[,] thereby making their calling & election sure. When a seal is put upon the father and mother it secures their posterity so that they cannot be lost but will be saved by virtue of the covenant of their father."[79]

For the first time, then, Smith indicated that the sealing of parents to eternal life would also save their children, or as one account of the sermon recorded, the "doctrine of Election[,] sealing the father & children together."[80] In other words, there was not yet an indication of a specific ordinance for the purpose of binding child to parent; rather, such binding came as a byproduct of sealing parents to eternal life. Furthermore, while the effect would endure past death, it did not yet extend to deceased progenitors, for it flowed only from parent to child, not vice versa.

The final development in this doctrine, which for the first time spoke of the direct sealing of children to parents and made the flow bidirectional to include deceased ancestors, occurred in a sermon the following year, three months prior to Smith's death:

> What is this office & work of Elijah, it is one of the greatest & most important subjects that God has revealed, He should send Elijah to seal the children to the fathers & fathers to the children. Now was this merely confined to the living to settle difficulties with families on earth, by no means, it was a far greater work. Elijah what would you do if you was here[?] [W]ould you confine your work to the living alone. No. I would refer you to the scriptures where the subject is manifest, i.e., without us they could not be made perfect, nor we without them, the fathers without the children nor the children without the fathers. I wish you to understand this subject for it is important & if you will receive it this is the spirit of Elijah that we redeem our dead & connect ourselves with our fathers which are in heaven & seal up our dead to come forth in the first resurrection & here we want the power of Elijah to seal those who dwell on earth to those which dwell in heaven[.] [T]his is the power of Elijah & the keys of the Kingdom of Jehovah.[81]

Perhaps because of the late date of this sermon, only weeks before

---

79. *William Clayton's Journal,* 115-16, 13 Aug. 1843.

80. Willard Richards account, in Ehat and Cook, 239.

81. *Wilford Woodruff's Journal,* 2:359-66, 10 Mar. 1844.

Smith's death, the sealing of children to parents did not begin until after his death.

The relationship of Elijah to sealing necessitates a postscript because of the generally accepted teaching among Latter-day Saints that Elijah restored the sealing power to Joseph Smith in 1836.[82] As has been shown, the power to seal was bestowed upon the elders in 1831, five years before the vision of Elijah, and while the forms embodied by the concept of sealing evolved throughout the rest of Smith's ministry, all later forms were in continuity with the earliest form, and there is no point along the continuum where one can detect the influence of angelic ministration. Furthermore, no contemporary account of the 1836 vision of Elijah used the term "seal" with reference to his mission. Indeed, Smith himself made no explicit connection between Elijah and sealing until 1843—seven years after the vision—and the connotation of sealing most commonly used today by Latter-day Saints did not develop until 1844. What, then, is one to make of the Latter-day Saint claim that Elijah restored the sealing power in 1836?

The answer appears to devolve from a model which recognizes Latter-day Saint revelation as primarily process rather than event. This means that doctrines and ordinances during Smith's ministry developed gradually. The two most dramatic examples were endowment and sealing, both of which showed continual development from 1831 to 1844. Yet though each showed continual development, punctuated by several key changes of greater magnitude, in no case was a key change attributable to angelic administration. Thus the theology of Elijah began as early as 1830 and showed accelerated development in the mid-1830s and again in the early 1840s. The theology of sealing began in 1831 and developed on a different trajectory, with the two intersecting no earlier than 1843. The developing theology eventually proclaimed that all ordinances and all priesthood came through the auspices of Elijah. The explicit linkage of Elijah and sealing in 1843 therefore formalized what was already implied and accepted. The prominence given Elijah and sealing during the final year of Smith's life overshadowed Elijah's role in other ordinances, and thus one may

---

82. For example, see two of the most influential works on Latter-day Saint doctrine: Joseph Fielding Smith, *Doctrines of Salvation* (Salt Lake City: Bookcraft, 1955), 2:111-12; and Bruce R. McConkie, *Mormon Doctrine* (Salt Lake City: Bookcraft, 1966), 683.

understand the special significance still accorded the relationship between Elijah and sealing in the Latter-day Saint church today.

Washing Feet

In the autumn of 1832, while several elders were on proselyting missions, Joseph Smith received a revelation requiring that the brethren return to Kirtland for further preparation "to go forth among the gentiles for the last time."[83] The additional preparation would occur in a School of the Prophets, enrollment in which would require a new ordinance not previously practiced or mentioned in the Restoration but drawing on the precedent established by Jesus. The revelation read:

> And ye shall not receive any among you, into this school save he is clean from the blood of this generation: and he shall be received by the ordinance of the washing of feet; for unto this end was the ordinance of the washing of feet instituted.
> And again, the ordinance of washing feet is to be administered by the president, or presiding elder of the church. It is to be commenced with prayer; and after partaking of bread and wine he is to gird himself, according to the pattern given in the thirteenth chapter of John's testimony concerning me (DC, 1835 VII:45-46).

The school opened on 23 January 1833, the minutes reading as follows:

> Conference opened with Prayer by the President [Smith] and after much speaking praying and singing, all done in Tongues[,] proceded to washing hands faces & feet in the name of the Lord as commanded of God[,] each one washing his own[,] after which the president girded himself with a towel and again washed the feet of all the Elders wiping them with the towel . . .[84]

As Smith washed the feet, he pronounced the elders clean from the sins of the world and sealed them to eternal life.

Subsequent entrants into the school went through the same process, as Orson Pratt recorded when he was admitted the following month.[85] The ordinance was otherwise not performed for over two years, at which time preparations were being finalized for dedication

---

83. "Kirtland Revelation Book," 41; also DC, 1835 VII:23.
84. "Kirtland Council Minutes," 23 Jan. 1833.
85. Orson Pratt diary, 18 Feb. 1833, in *Utah Genealogical and Historical Magazine* 27 (Oct. 1936): 166.

of the Kirtland House of the Lord. In October 1835 Smith met with the Quorum of Twelve Apostles to inform them of the preparatory ordinance necessary prior to the endowment. He wrote: "Also [told them to] attend this fall the Solemn Assembly of the first Elders for the organization of the School of the Prophets and to attend to the ordinence of the washing of feet and to prepare ther hearts in all humility for an endowment with power from on high."[86]

A month later Smith again met with the twelve and in giving further instructions regarding the endowment reemphasized the necessity of the preparatory ordinance: "The house of the Lord must be prepared, and the solemn assembly called and organized in it, according to the order of the house of God; and in it we must attend to the ordinance of washing of feet."[87]

The evening of the dedication, 27 March 1836, Smith met with church officers "and instructed the quorums respecting the ordinance of washing of feet which we were to attend to on wednesday following"[88] a solemn assembly. On the first day of the assembly church officers were instructed to "cleans our feet and partake of the sacrament that we might be made holy before Him, and thereby be qualified to officiate in our calling upon the morrow in washing the feet of the Elders."[89] The following morning the First Presidency began washing the feet of the several hundred men present. Erastus Snow recorded the scene:

> And it came to pass that all the Lords anointed assembled in the Lords house & recieved the ordinance of the washing of feet & they continued there meeting from morning untill evening & from evening untill morning & the angels of the Lord apeared unto them & cloven tongues like fire sat upon many of them & they prophecied and spake with other tongues as the spirit gave them uterence.[90]

As some elders were absent, the endowment was repeated several times over the following month, once in 1837 and once again in 1839.

---

86. *Joseph Smith Diary*, 36, 5 Oct. 1835.

87. Ibid., 12 Nov. 1835.

88. Ibid., 27 Mar. 1836.

89. Ibid., 29 Mar. 1836.

90. "E[rastus]. Snow Sketch Book No. 1," 9 Nov. 1818-5 Dec. 1837, Huntington Library.

In each instance the washing of feet was the final preparatory ordinance.[91]

Although Hyrum Smith suggested in a general conference talk in April 1842 that the Nauvoo endowment would be the same as its Kirtland predecessor,[92] the ceremony which Joseph Smith introduced the following month did not include the washing of feet. Indeed, there is no record of this ordinance being performed between 1839 and 1843, when the second anointing was introduced by Smith. Thereafter, the washing of feet was resumed as part of this new ordinance, although in a different format, as the wife washed the feet of her husband. Although few recipients left accounts of the procedure, Heber C. Kimball suggested in his diary account of 1 April 1844 that it drew on the precedent of Mary washing the feet of Jesus prior to his crucifixion: "I Heber C. Kimball recieved the washing of my feet. and was anointed by my wife Vilate fore my burial. that is my feet head Stomach. Evan as Mary did Jesus. that she mite have a claim on him in the Reserrection."[93]

Patriarchal Blessings

As he approached the end of his life, the Old Testament patriarch Jacob gathered his sons and grandsons and gave each a prophetic blessing (Gen. 49:1-28). Similarly, the final recorded act of Book of Mormon prophet Lehi was to bless his sons and daughters (BM, LDS, 2 Ne. 4:5-12). From these precedents came the Latter-day Saint ordinance of the patriarchal blessing, one of the most common and prominent yet personal of all ordinances.

The first predecessor appears to have occurred in January 1833 in connection with the opening of the School of the Prophets. In the course of washing the feet of the Elders, Joseph Smith asked a blessing of his father, "which he obtained by the laying on of his fathers hands;

---

91. Charles C. Rich diary, 12-16 Apr. 1836, LDS archives; Kirtland Elders' Quorum Record, 30 Apr. 1836; *Wilford Woodruff's Journal*, 1:131-36, 6 Apr. 1837; and Manuscript History of Brigham Young, 17 Nov. 1839.

92. *Times and Seasons* 3 (15 Apr. 1842): 763.

93. *Heber C. Kimball Diary*, 56, under entry entitled "Strange Events." Similarly, Wilford Woodruff wrote in his diary on 5 May 1844: *"Phebe washed my feet that I might be clean evry whit"* (*Wilford Woodruff's Journal*, 2:393).

pronouncing upon his head that he should continue in his Priests office untill Christ come."[94]

Four months later, John Smith, brother of Joseph Smith, Sr., conferred "a Fathers blessing" on his son, George A. Smith, the text of which has evidently been preserved in family records.[95] Although neither the office of patriarch nor the concept of a patriarchal blessing had yet been mentioned in the Restoration, the blessing pronounced by John Smith was typical of subsequent blessings in commenting on the recipient's pre-mortal existence ("God hath looked upon thee even before thou wast born"), the nature of his mortal mission ("thou shall be an instrument in the hands of the Lord in bringing thousands to the knowledge of the truth . . . you shall do mighty miracles in the name of the Lord"), and the reward awaiting him in the afterlife ("thy name is written in Heaven and sealed by the finger of God, never to be blotted out, and you shall have the blessings of the Celestial worlds").

On 18 December 1833, in a reversal of roles, Joseph Smith, Jr., gathered his family and gave blessings to his parents and siblings. In blessing his father he said he "shall be numbered among those who hold the right of patriarchal priesthood."[96] Then in blessing his older brother Hyrum, he established the tradition of primogeniture to be associated with the office of presiding patriarch: "He shall stand in the tracts of his father and be numbered among those who hold the right of patriarchal priesthood, even the evangelical priesthood and power shall be upon him, that in his old age his name may be magnified on the earth."[97]

The first patriarchal blessings given by an ordained patriarch[98]

---

94. "Kirtland Council Minutes," 23 Jan. 1833.

95. "Record Book of Bathsheba W. Smith," 46-48.

96. "Patriarchal Blessings Book," Vol. 1, beginning at the bottom of p. 8, LDS archives.

97. Ibid. Although Smith blessed his other brothers at the same time, he made no such promise to them. To his mother, he said, "She is a mother in Israel, and shall be a partaker with my father in all his patriarchal blessings."

98. On two occasions in 1834 fathers gave their sons blessings in the same manner that John Smith had the previous year. In February, following organization of the Kirtland High Council, Joseph Smith, Sr., blessed Joseph Jr. and John Johnson blessed Luke Johnson (Kirtland Council Minutes, 19 Feb. 1834). In July, following organization of the

POWER FROM ON HIGH

occurred within the Young family rather than the Smith family. In 1873, shortly after Brigham Young ordained twenty-six new patriarchs in one day,[99] he explained how he and his brother Joseph Young had consulted Smith in the summer of 1834 about the propriety of their father giving them blessings. Smith ordained Father Young a patriarch, who then gave father's blessings to his children.[100] Smith then authorized his father, previously ordained a patriarch, to give blessings to his family. Although there is no earlier record to verify Young's statement, the chronology he described is consistent with the historical record. The first known patriarchal blessings of Joseph Smith, Sr., were given to his children on 9 December 1834. At that time he said, "I desire, and for a long time have, to bless my children before I go hence."[101]

Within four months Joseph Smith, Sr., began giving blessings to church members outside the Smith family, and the ordinance, though never held to be essential, became popular. Thousands received blessings from Joseph Smith, Sr., and other patriarchs prior to Joseph Smith Jr.'s death in 1844.[102] While it appears that patriarchal blessings were originally intended to have been given by one's own father,[103] it

---

Missouri High Council, Peter Whitmer, Sr., blessed David, John, and Christian Whitmer and Joseph Knight blessed Newel Knight (*Far West Record*, 71-73, 7 July 1834).

99. Journal History, 7 May 1873.

100. Discourse of 30 June 1873, in *Deseret Weekly News*, 23 July 1873, 388.

101. Oliver Cowdery minutes of the Smith family Patriarchal Blessing meeting, 9 Dec. 1834, typescript, Irene Bates Collection, RLDS Library-Archives.

102. The earliest non-Smith blessing I have been able to identify is one pronounced by Orson Pratt on 29 April 1835. No exact count of the total number of blessings is available, due both to the archival policy of the LDS church restricting access to its early patriarchal blessings books and the fact that some early blessings were given to recipients in written form but no written copy was maintained by the church. For example, the William Smith patriarchal blessings book (RLDS Library-Archives) contains not only the blessings given by William in 1845 but also several given years earlier by Joseph Smith, Sr., then in the possession of the recipients.

103. Orson Pratt's blessing, for example, stated that it was "to secure unto thee the blessings which thou oughtest to claim at the hands of thy natural father, but inasmuch as his mind is not perfectly strong, in

176

soon became the practice of a patriarch to bless any church member who requested it.

An analysis of patriarchal blessings before mid-1844 yields valuable insights into the nature of the ordinance and into the organizational and doctrinal developments within the larger church community during this period.[104] One-hundred-thirty-one blessings (seventy-six to males, fifty-five to females), given between 1835 and 1844, have been analyzed. One-hundred-sixteen were given by presiding patriarchs (Joseph Smith, Sr., sixty-two; Hyrum Smith, thirty-eight; John Smith, thirteen; Joseph Smith, Jr., three), and fifteen by local patriarchs. Topics represented in the blessings included lineage, apocalyptic promises, promises of special powers and endowment, and the right to preach to the dead as well as occasional unique or unusual promises.

Pronouncement of the recipient's genealogical lineage through an Old Testament figure occurred infrequently until 1837 when this became a standard part of most blessings. Of sixty-one blessings in which lineage was stated, most were said to be of the Hebrew tribe of Ephraim or of his lineal ancestors (Abraham, Jacob or Joseph). Four were said to be of the tribe of Manasseh, four of Caleb, one each of Zebulon and Benjamin, and two of Melchizedek.

Two types of promises were given regarding the end of the world. The more common was the assurance that the recipient would not die before the second coming of Christ, although this occurred only in one blessing given by a patriarch other than Joseph Smith, Sr., who himself included it 37 percent of the time. Since all twenty-four recipients subsequently died, the nature of the promise is problematic.[105]

---

consequence of infirmities, and is also absent from this place, that thou mayest rejoice in the assurance of the blessings of the Lord, I therefore confer them upon thee" (29 Apr. 1835). Thirty percent of the available thirty-seven blessings given prior to November 1836 mention the recipient's status as an "orphan"—either literally or because a living father was unable to confer such a blessing, while none of 94 given between November 1836 and 1844 mentions such status.

104. Irene Bates Collection.

105. One explanation of the outcome might be that the blessing was conditional, and that the death of the recipient was *ipso facto* proof that he or she had failed to conform to the conditions attached to the blessing. Indeed, seven blessings did attach conditions to the promise. Even in these instances, however, one may wish to withhold judgment,

Five additional blessings mentioned that the prolonging of life was contingent on the recipient's desire to live until the Second Coming, making it possible, though improbable, that the recipients chose not to exercise the option. But half of the twenty-four blessings in question contained no qualifiers. Since the promise was unconditional, one is left to conclude that the patriarch, presumably with the best of intentions, promised things which simply were not to be. The fact that twenty-three of the promises of prolonged life were made by Joseph Smith, Sr., suggests that the personality of the patriarch influenced the content of the blessing. The possibility that a patriarch might promise too much was in fact acknowledged occasionally by church leaders. The most dramatic example of this came in the priesthood session of the October 1905 general conference when church president Joseph F. Smith warned: "Patriarchs are extravagant in their promises to the people. Keep within legitimate bounds and be careful that promises are dictated by the Lord."[106]

Another explanation for failed promises was the suggestion that all blessings, regardless of qualifying language, are conditioned upon righteousness. This issue was raised in 1835 by Edward Partridge, presiding bishop of the church, who wrote to his wife: "You inform me that you and the children were sick, I was somewhat disapointed at this inteligence as I had fondly anticipated that you would be blessed with health in my absence, from what was in my [patriarchal] blessing, but all blessings are conditional, and perhaps if none of you have been unfaithful I may have been."[107] While this explanation was more

---

inasmuch as one such blessing was given to Apostle Willard Richards who, it may be argued, led an exemplary life.

106. Anthony W. Ivins diary, 9 Oct. 1905, Utah State Historical Society, Salt Lake City. A poignant, and rare, acknowledgement by an officiator came from Abraham H. Cannon, a member of the First Council of Seventy, who wrote that a woman "told me that when I was here last in blessing her new born babe I had promised it should live to manhood. Several weeks thereafter it was taken sick with pneumonia and while in this condition the Elders who administered to it promised it continued life. Yet it died, and being their first and only son out of several children the blow was a severe one. I could not account for the failure of our promises that it should live except that sympathy instead of the Spirit of God prompted the utterances" (Abraham H. Cannon diary, 25 July 1891, LDS archives).

107. Edward Partridge to Lydia Partridge, 2 Nov. 1835, in

commonly applied than the alternative,[108] its underlying logic is at odds with such instances as blessing sick infants or the continual tendency, seen most vividly in the case of the second anointing, to provide recipients with promises of unconditional assurance.

The second type of apocalyptic promise, which extended only to men, pertained to the description in the Book of Revelation, Chapter 7, of 144,000 men who would participate in the "winding up" scene. Between 1835 and 1844, fourteen men (18 percent) were promised membership in this group. Lorenzo Barnes's 3 May 1835 blessing read: "Thou shalt stand when wickedness is swept off from the Earth even with thy brethren the hundred & forty & four thousand sealed out of the Twelve Tribes of Israel." Unlike the promise of prolonged life, which ceased with the death of Joseph Smith, Sr., in 1840, the promise of membership with the elect continued through 1844.

Three types of unusual power were promised to recipients of patriarchal blessings: healing, raising the dead, and self-translocation. Although it was the privilege of all priesthood bearers to administer to the sick, nine men (12 percent) were given special healing powers, notably Lorenzo Snow ("thy shadow shall restore the Sick; the diseased shall send to thee their aprons and handkershiefs and by thy touch their owners may be made whole"—15 December 1836) and Heber C. Kimball ("thou shalt have the gift of healing greater than thou has hitherto had, even to the anointing and opening of the eyes of the blind"—14 April 1840). In addition, five women (9 percent) were promised power to heal, although three of these recipients were also told that their power was to be used only in the absence of their husbands or "the Elders." Four men (Orson Pratt, Ethan Barrows, Lorenzo Snow, and Arnold Stephens) were promised power to raise the dead, all in blessings given by Joseph Smith, Sr.

The most unusual special power promised was the ability to transport oneself from one place to another by miraculous means. Because of the unusual nature of such promises, all six are listed below, in chronological order (note that all are men):

"History of Edward Partridge by his son, Edward Partridge (1833-1900)," 25, LDS archives.

108. For example, an 1851 editorial in the *Deseret Weekly News* stated: "All blessings promised by the Priesthood, which has come down from the heavens, are conditional, no matter whether expressed or implied" (27 Dec. 1851).

Jonathan Crosby, Jr. (21 February 1836): "Thou shalt go from land to land, and preach in large ships of the ocean, and have power over the winds and waves. Be wafted from place to place, by the power of God. Be caught up to the third heavens, and behold unspeakable things, whether in the body or not. . . . And when thy mission is full here, thou shalt visit other worlds, and remain a Priest in eternity."

Ethan Barrows (22 March 1836): "Thou shalt have power to translate thyself from land to land and from country to country, from one end of heaven to the other, and when thy work is done thou shalt translate from earth to heaven."

Oliver B. Huntington (7 December 1836): "Thou shalt have power with God even to translate thyself to Heaven, & preach to the inhabitants of the moon or planets, if it shall be expedient."

Lorenzo Snow (15 December 1836): "Thou shalt have power to translate thyself from one planet to another; and power to go to the moon if thou so desire."

William Jackson (6 February 1844): "Thou shalt waft thyself from place to place on the wings of the wind to accomplish thy mission speedily."

George Washington Johnson (13 August 1844): "Thou shalt have power to go from land to land and from sea. From island to island and from Planet to Planet."

At the same time patriarchal blessings were first being given, the Saints were preoccupied with completing the Kirtland House of the Lord so that the elders could receive their endowment. Only one Patriarchal Blessing prior to the 1836 endowment promised such to its recipient, Lorenzo Barnes: "Thou shalt be endowed with power from on high" (3 May 1835). The next blessing to contain a similar promise did not occur for another six years. The summer following announcement of the construction of a temple in Nauvoo, church leaders indicated that an endowment of the elders would occur in the new building.[109] Three months later Levi Gribble's patriarchal blessing stated "then shall you be a chosen vessel having received the anointing, and the enduements, in the Lord's House" (4 October 1841). Five additional blessings given between this time and May 1842 (when the Nauvoo endowment was first given) contained the same promise. All were given to men, and all noted that an anointing would accompany

---

109. *Times and Seasons* 2 (1 July 1841): 455-56.

the endowment—something not contained in Lorenzo Barnes's 1835 blessing. In September 1843 Emma Smith became the first female to receive an endowment. The following month the endowment was first promised to a woman, Ann Eliza DeLong, in the context of a patriarchal blessing (16 October 1843).

Until Smith's vision of the Celestial Kingdom in January 1836,[110] the Latter-day Saint theology of afterlife presumed that the fate of the dead was finalized at death. While baptism for the dead accommodated the new vision, the baptisms did not begin until 1840. In the interim the first theological shift to accord with the 1836 vision drew on 1 Peter 3:18-20 and 4:6, which described Jesus' preaching in the world of spirits following his crucifixion. The first known reference to this doctrinal shift came in a patriarchal blessing to Stephen Post on 26 March 1836, only two months after Smith's vision: "Thou shalt preach to people of other planets, and thou shalt preach to spirits in prison." The Patriarchal Blessing of Lorenzo Snow (15 December 1836) also promised that he would have "power to preach to the spirits in prison." The clearest delineation of the doctrine came three weeks later when Wilford Woodruff was ordained a seventy by Zebedee Coltrin and promised "that I should visit COLUB & Preach to the spirits in Prision & that I should bring all of my friends or relatives forth from the Terrestrial Kingdom (who had died) by the Power of the Gospel."[111]

Unusual features found in some patriarchal blessings included ordinations to the offices of elder[112] and high priest,[113] a promise that the plates of the Book of Mormon would "be brought into the bosom of the church" during the recipient's lifetime,[114] and promises of special leadership positions for the recipient or offspring.[115]

---

110. *Joseph Smith Diary,* 117-20, 21 Jan. 1836.

111. *Wilford Woodruff's Journal,* 1:118-19, 3 Jan. 1837.

112. Samuel Merrill and Philemon Merril, 2 Jan. 1841; James Twist, 17 Feb. 1842; Bates Collection.

113. Noah Hubbard, 3 June 1844, Bates Collection.

114. Howard Coray, 20 Oct. 1840, Bates Collection.

115. Wilford Woodruff (15 Apr. 1837) was promised he would be a "special witness." He was subsequently ordained an apostle (26 Apr. 1839). Bathsheba Bigler (7 Feb. 1839) was told she "shalt have a Son who shall be . . . a prophet and Seer." She later (1841) married George A. Smith, and their son, John Henry Smith, rose to the positions of apostle and counselor in the First Presidency, both of which include the

The patriarchal blessing is an ordinance unique to the Mormon Restoration. Ideally, the blessing is literally the word of God to the recipient. In some cases, such as promises of high leadership positions to Wilford Woodruff and Bathsheba Bigler on behalf of her future son, the predictions were accurate. In others, such as the promise of living until the Second Coming, the failure was obvious, leaving one to conclude that either God did not speak the truth, that the recipient was unworthy, or that the patriarch was excessive. In spite of failed blessings, the confidence of Latter-day Saints in patriarchal blessings remains high, with the blessings serving both to reassure and to provide a blueprint for one's future activities.

Marriage

Although traditional marriages were always encouraged in the Restoration, and an 1831 revelation (BC LII:16, Mar. 1831) even condemned those who forbade marriage, it appears that none were performed by Latter-day Saint officials for the first five years of the church's existence. A statement on marriage, dated 17 August 1835, in the collection of revelations published that year, first authorized the performance of marriages by church officials while still recognizing the validity of those performed by others:

> We believe, that all marriages in this Church of Christ of Latter Day Saints, should be solemnized in a public meeting, or feast, prepared for that purpose: and that the solemnization should be performed by a presiding high priest, high priest, bishop, elder, or priest, not even prohibiting those persons who are desirous to get married, of being married by other authority. We believe that it is not right to prohibit members of this church from marrying out of the church, if it be their determination so to do, but such persons will be considered weak in the faith of our Lord and Savior Jesus Christ (DC, 1835 CI).

In spite of the statement's tolerance of marriages performed by "other authority," Joseph Smith suggested the priority of Latter-day Saint vows when he performed his first marriage on 24 November 1835, stating "that it was necessary that it should be Solemnized by the authority of the everlasting priesthood."[116]

---

titles of "Prophet, Seer and Revelator."

116. *Joseph Smith Diary,* 67, 24 Nov. 1835.

Although plural marriages may have occurred as early as 1835, and certainly by 1841,[117] there is no record of the wording of the ceremonies, and hence no indication if the initiation of plural marriages brought changes in the theology of marriage other than plurality. However, the text of the 1842 marriage ceremony of Smith and Whitney, designated as a revelation, did signal a theological change in that it implied that marriage would survive death.[118]

The following year Smith added a dimension to eternal marriage by stating that it enabled post-mortal procreation:

> He said that except a man and his wife enter into an everlasting covenant and be married for eternity while in this probation by the power and authority of the Holy priesthood they will cease to increase when they die (ie. they will not have any children in the resurrection[)] but those who are married by the power & authority of the priesthood in this life & continue without committing the sin against the Holy Ghost will continue to increase & have children in the celestial glory.[119]

The same day, Smith told Benjamin F. Johnson and his wife that they must be "re-married" to qualify for the indicated blessings. Johnson later wrote: "I thought it was a joke, and said I should not marry my wife again, unless she courted *me*, for I did it all the first time. He chided my levity, told me he was in earnest, and so it proved, for we stood up and were sealed by the Holy Spirit of Promise."[120]

On 28 May 1843 Joseph and Emma Smith were sealed to each other.[121] Two months later a revelation which authorized plural marriage formalized this new type of marriage which underwent no further changes during Smith's lifetime:

> And again, verily I say unto you, if a man marry a wife by my word, which is my law, and by the new and everlasting covenant, and it is sealed unto them by the Holy Spirit of promise, by him who is anointed, unto whom I have appointed this power and the keys of this priesthood; and it shall be said unto them—Ye shall come forth in the first resurrection; and if it be after the first resurrection, in the next resurrection; and shall inherit thrones, kingdoms, principalities,

---

117. See Van Wagoner.

118. Unpublished revelation, 27 July 1842, LDS archives.

119. *William Clayton's Journal*, 102, 16 May 1843.

120. Benjamin F. Johnson, *My Life's Review* (n.p., n.d.), 96.

121. *Joseph Smith Diary*, 381, 28 May 1843.

and powers, dominions, all heights and depths—then shall it be written in the Lamb's Book of Life, that he shall commit no murder whereby to shed innocent blood, and if ye abide in my covenant, and commit no murder whereby to shed innocent blood, it shall be done unto them in all things whatsoever my servant hath put upon them, in time, and through all eternity; and shall be of full force when they are out of the world; and they shall pass by the angels, and the gods, which are set there, to their exaltation and glory in all things, as hath been sealed upon their heads, which glory shall be a fulness and a continuation of the seeds forever and ever.

Then shall they be gods, because they have no end; therefore shall they be from everlasting to everlasting, because they continue; then shall they be above all, because all things are subject unto them. Then shall they be gods, because they have all power, and the angels are subject unto them (DC, LDS 132:19-20).

Washing and Anointing

As finishing touches were applied to the Kirtland House of the Lord, Joseph Smith and other members of the First Presidency participated in the ordinance of washing and anointing, a hitherto unmentioned ordinance.[122] Smith described the event as follows:

> At about 3. oclock P.M [21 January 1836.] I dismissed the school and the presidency, retired to the loft of the printing office, where we attended to the ordinance of washing our bodies in pure water, we also perfumed our bodies and our heads, in the name of the Lord at early candlelight, I meet with the presidency, at the west school room in the Chapel to attend to the ordinance of annointing our heads with holy oil—also the councils of Kirtland and Zion, meet in the two adjoining rooms, who waited in prayer while we attended to the ordinance,—I took the oil in my left hand, father Smith being seated before me and the rest of the presidency encircled him round about.— we then streched our right hands to heaven and blessed the oil and concecrated it in the name of Jesus Christ—we then laid our hands on our aged fath[er] Smith, and invoked, the blessings of heaven,—I then annointed his head with the concecrated oil, and sealed many bless-

---

122. Although Smith made no reference to the origins of this ordinance, Oliver Cowdery wrote that they "were annointed with the same kind of oil and in the man[ner] that were Moses and Aaron" ("Oliver Cowdery's Kirtland, Ohio 'Sketch Book,'" *Brigham Young University Studies* 12 [1972]: 416, entry for 21 Jan. 1836), thus establishing an Old Testament precedent.

ings upon him, the presidency then in turn, laid their hands upon his head, beginning at the eldest, untill they had all laid their hands on him, and pronounced such blessings, upon his head as the Lord put into their hearts—all blessing him to be our patraark [Patriarch], and to annoint our heads, and attend to all duties that pertain to that office.—I then took the seat, and father annoint[ed] my head, and sealed upon me the blessings, of Moses, to lead Israel in the latter days, even as moses led him in days of old,—also the blessings of Abraham Isaac and Jacob.—all of the presidency laid their hands upon me and pronounced upon my head many prophesies, and blessings, many of which I shall not notice at this time, but as Paul said, so say I, let us come to vissions and revelations,—The heavens were opened upon us and I beheld the celestial Kingdom of God, and the glory thereof, whether in the body or out I cannot tell,—I saw the transcendant beauty of the gate through which the heirs of that Kingdom will enter, which was like unto circling flames of fire, also the blasing throne of God, whereon was seated the Father and the Son,—I saw the beautiful streets of that Kingdom, which had the appearance of being paved with gold—I saw father Adam, and Abraham and Michael and my father and mother, my brother Alvin that has long since slept [123]
. . .

Although none of the accounts of this event describe the new ordinance as essential for the endowment, such a link was made three days later when the First Presidency "conversed upon the time of, and preparation and sanctification for the endowment."[124] The following evening the quorums of the priesthood met with the First Presidency "to receive instructions relative to washing and annointing."[125]

On 28 January the quorums met in the upper floor of the House of the Lord and began to wash and perfume their bodies and anoint them with oil in preparation for the endowment, with several participants reporting visions in association with the event.[126] Washings and anointings continued in the House of the Lord throughout the remainder of the winter, up to the day prior to the solemn assembly when the endowment occurred. Thereafter the ordinance was performed sporadically, and only in preparation for the endowment of those who had not participated in the earlier assembly.

---

123. *Joseph Smith Diary*, 117-20, 21 Jan. 1836.
124. Cowdery, 24 Jan. 1836.
125. Ibid., 25 Jan. 1836.
126. *Joseph Smith Diary*, 123-24, 28 Jan. 1836.

A revelation in January 1841 which detailed the proposed Nauvoo temple raised again the subject of initiatory rites and mandated that they be performed only in the temple (DC, LDS 124:37-39). On 4 May 1842 the Nauvoo endowment was first given, preceded the same day by the purification of washings and anointings.[127] Whereas these ordinances had occurred throughout the winter in Kirtland in anticipation of an endowment, those given in Nauvoo throughout the remainder of Smith's life would occur on the same day as the endowment ceremony for a person receiving it. In both cases, the function was the same: preparation of the recipient for the endowment.

---

127. Brigham Young Manuscript History, 4 May 1842; HC, 5:2; L. John Nuttall diary, 7 Feb. 1877.

Chapter Six

Ordinances:
The Second Anointing

When the elders at the Kirtland solemn assembly were washed and anointed in March 1836, Joseph Smith stated that the church organization was complete and that the elders "had passed through all the necessary ceremonies."[1] In spite of this assurance, the vision of Elijah four days later signalled further developments in Latter-day Saint doctrine and ordinances. Elijah delivered "the keys of this dispensation,"[2] the importance of which was not fully clarified for another four years when Smith explained that there would yet be other ordinances introduced into the church through the auspices of Elijah, including animal sacrifice.[3] Although animals were never incorporated into church rituals, other ordinances were introduced. Three months later a revelation concerning the Nauvoo temple used for the first time a term which became synonymous with the ordinance of "second anointing," namely the "fulness of the priesthood":

> There is not place found on earth that he may come and restore

---

1. Scott H. Faulring, ed., *An American Prophet's Record: The Diaries and Journals of Joseph Smith* (Salt Lake City: Signature Books in association with Smith Research Associates, 1987), 153-55, 30 Mar. 1836.

2. *Joseph Smith Diary,* 157-58, 3 Apr. 1836; see also Doctrine and Covenants (Salt Lake City: Church of Jesus Christ of Latter-day Saints, 1981), sec. 110 (hereafter cited in the text as DC, LDS).

3. Joseph Smith discourse, 5 Oct. 1840, in Andrew F. Ehat and Lyndon W. Cook, eds., *The Words of Joseph Smith* (Provo, UT: Religious Studies Center, Brigham Young University, 1980), 43.

again that which was lost unto you, or, which he hath taken away, even the fulness of the priesthood . . .

And verily I say unto you, let this house be built unto my name, that I may reveal mine ordinances therein unto my people; for I design to reveal unto my church, things which have been kept hid from before the foundation of the world.[4]

This concept was soon in the public consciousness, as indicated by a letter written the same year and published in the church newspaper: "In the Temple built by divine command, I am informed we are to have made known to us the fulness of the priesthood."[5]

Patriarchal blessings given during the following weeks confirmed this expectation. The blessing of James Twist (11 February 1842) promised him "the Priesthood after the Order of Melchesidec with all its glory and fullness." His wife's blessings contained no such promise. Similarly, the blessing of Heber C. Kimball (9 March 1842) promised him the priesthood "with a fulness," but that of his wife, given the same day, said nothing about such a promise. The fact that the ordinance when given a year and a half later involved both men and women suggests that the form continued to develop in Smith's mind prior to its initiation. An article later the same year emphasized the importance of the fulness of the priesthood but added no details: "Now brethren, if so great and glorious have been the blessings realized in so early a stage of the work[,] what may we expect when the building is completed, and a house prepared where the Most High can come and restore that which has been taken away in consequence of transgression; even the FULNESS of the priesthood."[6]

On 16 July 1843 Smith indicated a link between the marriage relationship and fulness of the priesthood: "[Smith] showed that a man must enter into an everlasting covenant with his wife in this world or he will have no claim on her in the next. He said that he could not reveal the fulness of these things untill the Temple is completed &c."[7]

---

4. Revelation of 19 Jan. 1841, in *Times and Seasons* 2 (1 June 1841): 425-27; see also DC, LDS, 124.

5. Joseph Fielding to Br. Robinson, 28 Dec. 1841, *Times and Seasons* 3 (1 Jan. 1842): 648-49.

6. "The Temple of God in Nauvoo," 28 Oct. 1842, in *Times and Seasons* 4 (15 Nov. 1842): 10-11.

7. George D. Smith, ed., *An Intimate Chronicle: The Journals of William Clayton* (Salt Lake City: Signature Books in association with

The following week Smith gave for the first time details of the ordinance: "Here we learn in a priesthood after the order of Melchisedeck—Prophet priest & king. & I will advance from prophet to priest & then to King[,] not to the kingdoms of this earth but of the most high god."[8]

Two weeks later, in an apparent reference to this statement, Brigham Young clarified the relationship between fulness of the priesthood and the titles of king and priest, with the latter serving to enable the former:

> For any person to have the fulness of [the Melchizedek] Priesthood [he] must be a king & a Priest. A person may have a portion of that Priesthood the same as Governors or Judges of England have power from the King to transact business but yet he is not the king of England. A person may be anointed king & priest before they receives their kingdom.[9]

While fulness of the priesthood up to this time had been portrayed as a special order in the Melchizedek Priesthood, a discourse by Smith later in August took a different thrust by stating that there were three priesthoods, not two, and that what had previously been called Melchizedek Priesthood was now Patriarchal Priesthood. The fulness of priesthood—which, he indicated, had not yet been experienced in the church—was now called Melchizedek Priesthood.[10]

One month later, shortly after Emma Smith became the first female to be given the endowment, Joseph and Emma became the first recipients of the fulness of the priesthood, or second anointing. The account in Smith's diary is cryptic: "Baurak Ale [Joseph Smith] was by common consent, & unanimous voice chosen president of the quorum. & anointed & ord[ained] to the highest and holiest order of the priesthood (& companion)."[11] That this anointing included the title of

---

Smith Research Associates, 1991), 110-11, 16 July 1843.

8. *Joseph Smith Diary,* 398-400, 23 July 1843.

9. Brigham Young Manuscript History, 6 Aug. 1843; see also Scott G. Kenney, ed., *Wilford Woodruff's Journal* (Midvale, UT: Signature Books, 1983), 2:271-72, 6 Aug. 1843.

10. Discourse of 27 Aug. 1843. Five accounts of this discourse were published in Ehat and Cook.

11. *Joseph Smith Diary,* 416, 28 Sept. 1843.

"king" was confirmed by William Clayton.[12] A later account, written by Wilford Woodruff, clarified the diary entry: "Joseph Smith led in prayer he prayed that his days might be lengthened & ha[ve] dominion over his Enemies, and all their Households be blessed . . . Then by common consent Joseph Smith the Prophet Received his second Anointing of the Highest & Holiest order."[13] Second anointings were conferred throughout the autumn and winter,[14] usually involved ranking church officers, and, with a single known exception,[15] were given to husband and wife simultaneously.

On 10 March 1844 Smith delivered a discourse on the subject of Elijah in which he gave his most complete explanation of the second anointing. He said, "The spirit, power, and calling of Elijah is, that ye have power to hold the keys of the revelations, ordinances, oricles, powers and endowments of the fulness of the Melchizedek Priest-hood."[16] The function of the ordinance was to assure salvation: "The

---

12. *William Clayton Journal,* 122, 19 Oct. 1843.

13. "Historian's Private Journal," 1858, typescript, 24, archives, Historical Department, Church of Jesus Christ of Latter-day Saints, Salt Lake City, Utah (hereafter LDS archives).

14. Second anointings during this period were recorded in the diaries of Joseph Smith, William Clayton, Wilford Woodruff, and Heber C. Kimball.

15. The exception was Apostle Parley P. Pratt. Wilford Woodruff wrote in his diary for 21 January 1844: "P. P. P. received his 2d Anointing. Joseph [Smith] said Concerning Parley P. Pratt that He had no wife sealed to him for Eternity as He would want a wife in the Resurrection or els his glory would be Cliped. Many arguments He used upon this subject which ware rational & consistant. ~~Br. Joseph said now what will we do with Elder P. P. Pratt. He has no wife sealed to him for Eternity. He has one living wife but she had a former Husband and did not wish to be s[e]aled to Parly, for Eternity~~" (*Wilford Woodruff's Journal,* 2:340). Although an exception was made in the case of Pratt, perhaps because of his membership in the Quorum of Twelve Apostles, the implication was that the exception was temporary. Indeed, Woodruff's biographer Matthias F. Cowley explained that Pratt "had been instructed by the Prophet that it was his duty to have his wife sealed to him for eternity in order that his glory might be full" (Matthias F. Cowley, *Wilford Woodruff—History of His Life and Labors* [Salt Lake City: Deseret News, 1909], 197-98).

16. *Wilford Woodruff's Journal,* 2:359-66, 10 Mar. 1844.

power of Elijah is sufficient to make our Calling & Election sure, & the same doctrin whare we are exhorted to go on to perfection."[17] Another account of the discourse employed the term "sealed up unto eternal life,"[18] which had been used in similar contexts since 1831. Other ordinances considered essential for exaltation[19] were generally held to be conditional—that is, the ordinance enabled exaltation, but the subsequent righteousness of the recipient secured it. By contrast, the second anointing guaranteed one's exaltation, and thus may be viewed as the crowning ordinance of Smith's ministry.[20]

---

17. Ibid.

18. James Burgess account, in Ehat and Cook, 333-34.

19. The term "exaltation" generally refers to the post-mortal attainment of the highest possible level of immortal existence, defined as the highest degree in the Celestial Kingdom.

20. Two uncommon sins, the shedding of innocent blood and "sin against the Holy Ghost," could negate the second anointing (see the Burgess account of the discourse, in Ehat and Cook).

Chapter Seven

Judicial Systems

A judicial system which relies on the judgment of God would be inherently fair, since an omniscient judge would not condemn falsely. The Book of Mormon endorsed the idea: "Now it is better that a man should be judged of God than of man, for the judgments of God are always just, but the judgments of man are not always just."[1]

The earliest instance of punitive action in the Restoration derived from Martin Harris's loss of the original Book of Mormon manuscript. Because Joseph Smith had defied divine counsel in lending the manuscript to Harris, it was he who was the subject of censure, delivered via revelation:

> Behold thou art Joseph, and thou was chosen to do the work of the Lord, but because of transgression, if thou art not aware thou wilt fall, but remember God is merciful: Therefore, repent of that which thou hast done, and he will only cause thee to be afflicted for a season
>
> . . .
>
> And this is the reason that thou hast lost thy privileges for a season.[2]

The disadvantage of relying on God or God's prophet for judicial verdicts is it appears to function best in small groups. Both the Book of Mormon and early documents of the Restoration describe the transition to a human-based judicial system as the movements grew.

---

1. Mosiah 29:12, in The Book of Mormon (Salt Lake City: Church of Jesus Christ of Latter-day Saints, 1981) (hereafter cited as BM, LDS).

2. *A Book of Commandments, for the Government of the Church of Christ, Organized According to Law, on the 6th of April, 1830* (Independence, MO: W. W. Phelps & Co., 1833), III:4-5 (July 1828); hereafter cited in the text as BC.

For example, the same passage which extolled the virtues of God's judgment went on to describe the appointment of "judges to rule over them, or to judge them according to the law" (BM, LDS, Mosiah 29:41). A later passage in the Book of Mormon described the details of the judicial system which served as a model for the earliest tribunal in the Restoration:

> And they were strict to observe that there should be no iniquity among them; and whoso was found to commit iniquity, and three witnesses of the church did condemn them before the elders, and if they repented not, and confessed not, their names were blotted out, and they were not numbered among the people of Christ. But as oft as they repented and sought forgiveness, with real intent, they were forgiven (BM, LDS, Moro. 6:7-8).

Shortly after the church was organized, a conference was held at which the "Articles and Covenants" was read. Although a preventive role was assigned to teachers,[3] and expulsion of sinners from the church was mentioned, no details of judicial tribunals were given aside from an admonition that transgressors "shall be dealth with according as the scriptures direct."[4] A revelation in February 1831 outlined a more concrete judicial system. Tribunals were to consist of "two elders of the church or more,"[5] similar to the injunction of the Book of Mormon. However, the newly-created office of bishop was also attached to the tribunal. Its role was not specified, and the wording of this part of the revelation is awkward: "And if it can be, it is necessary that the bishop is present also."

The sin of murder was separated from those of adultery, robbing, stealing, and lying. The former could be tried only by a civil court, whereas the latter fell under the jurisdiction of a church tribunal. At least two witnesses, "of the church, and not of the world," were required. For settling disputes among members, a separate set of rules applied. Two steps were required prior to submitting the matter to the elders. First, "thou shalt take him between him and thee alone; and if he confess, thou shalt be reconciled." That failing, "thou shalt take

---

3. *Painesville Telegraph*, 19 Apr. 1831.

4. Ibid.

5. "Items of Law for the Government of the Church of Christ," 23 Feb. 1831. This was published the following year in *Evening and Morning Star* 1 (Oct. 1832): 34, and later in BC XLIV.

another with thee." If the dispute could not then be resolved through arbitration, "thou shalt deliver him up unto the church, not to the members but to the elders."

A revelation two weeks later reversed the order of elders and bishops and signalled a trend towards bishops becoming the primary judicial officers in the church: "And unto the bishop of the church, and unto such as God shall appoint and ordain to watch over the church, and to be elders unto the church, are to have it given unto them to discern all those gifts, lest there shall be any among you professing and yet be not of God" (BC XLIX:23, 8 Mar. 1831).

The priority of bishop in the judicial system was confirmed by a revelation in August 1831: "And whoso standeth in this mission [bishop], is appointed to be a judge in Israel, like as it was in ancient days, to divide the lands of the heritage of God unto his children; and to judge his people by the testimony of the just" (BC LIX:21, 1 Aug. 1831).

The shift away from a Book of Mormon model, in which elders served as judges, was concurrent with the addition of the first offices deriving from a biblical, rather than Book of Mormon precedent. The judicial role of bishop represented a curious chimera of Old Testament and New Testament interpretation, for the office of bishop is confined to the New Testament, while the role of "judge in Israel" comes from the Old Testament.

Another passage in this revelation emphasized the principle underlying most proceedings during Smith's ministry, namely that the attitude of the sinner was more important than the nature of the sin. Referring to an unspecified sin of Ziba Peterson, the revelation stated: "Let that which has been bestowed upon Ziba, be taken from him: And let him stand as a member in the church, and labor with his own hands, with the brethren, until he is sufficiently chastened for all his sins, for he confesseth them not, and he thinketh to hide them" (BC LIX:74-75). In other words, it was Peterson's intractability, not the sin itself, which brought condemnation. Three days later, in a special conference, Peterson finally confessed, "which was satisfactory to the Church as approved by unanimous vote."[6]

---

6. Donald Q. Cannon and Lyndon W. Cook, eds., *Far West Record: Minutes of the Church of Jesus Christ of Latter-day Saints, 1830-1841* (Salt Lake City: Deseret Book Co., 1983), 9-10, 4 Aug. 1831.

Although all church members were subject to discipline, leaders gradually gained a favored status. For example, charges were brought against Smith in October 1831, alleging mismanagement of a church farm. After a conference of elders decided that he be reproved for "the unwise course" he had taken,[7] a revelation the following month, "regulating the Presidency of the Church," changed the rules: "Inasmuch as the President of the high priesthood [i.e., Joseph Smith] shall transgress he shall be had in remembrance before the common court of the church who shall be assisted by twelve councellors of the high priesthood."[8]

Another revelation, given simultaneously, provided similar insulation to the office of bishop: "No bishop or judge, which shall be set apart for this ministry, shall be tried or condemned for any crime, save it be before a conference of high priests; and in as much as he is found guilty before a conference of high priests, by testimony that cannot be impeached, he shall be condemned or forgiven, according to the laws of the church."[9]

The introduction of the office of high priest in the autumn of 1831, and the revelation specifying a council of "high priests even twelve," set the stage for the most important judiciary of the church: the high council. Although the first high council was not formally organized until 1834, the number and nature of its constituents and its jurisdiction were determined by the 1831 revelation. Bishops were to judge simple cases, but complex issues and appeals were to go to the council of twelve high priests:

> And again verily I say unto you the most important business of

---

7. Ibid., 10 Oct. 1831.

8. "Revelation given November 1831 Cuyahoga Co. Ohio regulating the Presidency of the Church," in "Kirtland Revelation Book," 84-86, archives, Historical Department, Church of Jesus Christ of Latter-day Saints, Salt Lake City, Utah (hereafter LDS archives). This revelation was combined with another from 1835 to *Doctrine and Covenants of The Church of the Latter Day Saints: Carefully Selected from the Revelations of God* (Kirtland, OH: F. G. Williams & Co., 1835), III; hereafter cited in the text as DC, 1835.

9. *Evening and Morning Star* 1 (Oct. 1832): 35; also DC, 1835 XXII:3. A further layer of insulation was added in the 1835 revision of this revelation, which required that bishops be tried before the First Presidency.

the church and the most difficult cases of the church inasmuch as there is not satisfaction [upon the] decision of the judges [i.e., bishops] it shall be handed over and carried up unto the court of the church before the President of the high Priesthood and the President of the court of the high priesthood shall have power to call other high priests even twelve to assist as councellors and thus the president of the high priesthood and his councellors shall have power to decide upon testimony according to the laws of the church and after the decision it shall be had in remembrance no more before the Lord for this is the highest court of the church of God and a final decision upon controversies.[10]

Courts of high priests functioned periodically between 1831 and 1834, always composed of men called to serve on an *ad hoc* basis. On 17 February 1834 the first high council was organized in Kirtland, its composition and function dictated by revelation.[11] It was to consist of twelve high priests permanently called to serve on the council. In the event one or more members were absent, members *pro tem* could be chosen by the permanent members, a minimum of seven of whom were required to be present for the council to function. Either two, four, or six members of the council would speak on each case, the number being determined by the complexity of the case. Half the designated members would speak in behalf of the defendant, the remainder in behalf of the plaintiff. After hearing all testimony, the president of the council, who was not one of the twelve members, would render a decision. Upon hearing his decision, council members who had not previously spoken on the case could "throw any farther light upon the subject, so as to correct the decission of the president," after which the council would by majority vote confirm or overturn the decision. In difficult cases "respecting doctrine, or principle, if there is not a sufficiency written to make the case clear to the mind of the council, the president may inquire and obtain the mind of the Lord by revelation."

Two types of formal judicial bodies remained intact following the formation of high councils: the bishop's council and the "council of high priests abroad." The former was a standing body to act in routine

---

10. "Revelation . . . regulating the Presidency."

11. "Kirtland Revelation Book," 111-15; also DC, 1835 V. No analogous rules were indicated, during Smith's lifetime, for the functioning of bishops' courts.

cases, while the latter was "only to be called on [for] the most difficult cases of church matters; and no common or ordinary case is to be sufficient to call such councils." Cases from either venue could be appealed to the high council.

One additional, informal mechanism existed for judicial action under unusual circumstances. "When there is no Bishop," wrote Smith in 1833, "they are to be tried by the voice of the Church."[12] The following year Smith explained that such a tribunal did not necessarily require ordained officers: "even if there is not another ordained member in the church, let the church appoint some brother to preside and let them do as one church did in ancient days [and] try them who say they are apostles and are not, but are liars," then let them demand their license, raise their hands against them and thus they are expelled from the communion of the church."[13]

With a single exception, the judicial system of the church underwent no significant changes from 1834 when the Kirtland high council was organized through Smith's death in 1844. That exception, occurring in 1838, involved Smith and other members of the presidency of the church.

The collapse of the Kirtland Bank, which had been chartered under Smith's direction, happened in late 1837 and precipitated a crisis. Many apostatized, while others sought vengeance of Smith, whom they blamed for the disaster. On the night of his covert departure from Kirtland, Smith received a revelation which complicated the procedure for removing a member of the First Presidency. The 1831 revelation "regulating the Presidency of the Church" had allowed for removal of the president upon the consent of a court "assisted by twelve councellors of the high priesthood"[14]—a body which later became the high council. Despite the growth of the church, and the formation of other stakes and high councils, the 1831 revelation could still be interpreted to mean that Smith could be removed by action of a single high council. Indeed, the text of the revelation was preceded by the query, "Whether the descision of Such an Council of one Stake shall

---

12. Joseph Smith to Brother Carter, 13 Apr. 1833; B. H. Roberts, ed., *History of the Church of Jesus Christ of Latter-day Saints, Century I* (Salt Lake City: Deseret Book Co., 1971), 1:338-39.

13. Joseph Smith to J. G. Fosdick, 3 Feb. 1834, Oliver Cowdery letterbook, 23-24, Huntington Library, San Marino, California.

14. "Kirtland Revelation Book," 84-86.

be conclusive for Zion and all her Stakes."[15] The new revelation, favorable to Smith's continuing tenure, indicated that a decision by a single high council would not be binding on the entire church, and that "except a majority is had by the voice of the Church of Zion and a majority of all her Stakes, the charges will be considered not Sustained."

---

15. "Revelation Given at the French Farm in Kirtland, Geauga Co., Ohio. In the presence of J. Smith Jr., S. Rigdon V. Knight & Geo. Robinson January 12th 1838." This revelation, not published during Smith's lifetime, was recorded in "The Scriptory Book of Joseph Smith," 51-53, and is published in Lyndon W. Cook, *The Revelations of the Prophet Joseph Smith* (Provo, UT: Seventy's Mission Bookstore, 1981), 328-29.

Chapter Eight

Women and Priesthood

The changing relationship between women and organized religion is one of the most hotly debated and potentially divisive religious issues of our time. Among Christian traditions some, such as Anglican and United Methodist, have extended to women full participation, including priesthood ordination, while others, notably Roman Catholic, have continued to limit women's ecclesiastical role and specifically exclude them from ordination to priesthood.

Recent works have served to highlight the intensity of the debate within the Latter-day Saint tradition.[1] Unlike other Christian traditions, whose debates encircle questions of biblical interpretation, the LDS discussion has relied almost exclusively on Restoration sources, which include the LDS canon and non-canonical historical materials. Because of the unique role of Joseph Smith in producing virtually all of the LDS canon and in shaping early doctrinal and procedural matters, an understanding of the roles of women during his life is an essential part of contemporary debate.

Smith never explicitly confirmed or denied the possibility of women assuming a role equal to that of men at all levels of church ministry and administration. However, in the course of his ministry women gradually began to do things which today are generally associated with priesthood.

For the first five years following organization of the church in 1830, there is no record of women exercising priesthood-like functions.[2] In 1835, when patriarchal blessings were first given to general

---

1. For example, see Maxine Hanks, ed., *Women and Authority: Re-emerging Mormon Feminism* (Salt Lake City: Signature Books, 1992).

2. On the eve of the opening of the School of the Prophets in

church members, Elizabeth Ann Whitney, wife of Kirtland Bishop Newel K. Whitney, was promised, "When thy husband is far from thee and thy little ones are afflicted thou shalt have power to prevail and they shall be healed."[3] Similar promises were made to other women, including Sarah Mackley in 1836,[4] Flora Jacobs in 1837,[5] and Susan Johnson[6] and Louisa C. Jackson[7] in 1844. Of 131 blessings surveyed between 1835 and 1844, 9 percent of those given to women contained specific promises of power to heal the sick, compared to 12 percent of those given to men.

Authorization to heal also came in other ways. At about the time of the dedication of the Kirtland House of the Lord, Louisa Leavitt lay ill. Not having resources to pay a physician, her mother "prayed earnestly to the Lord to let us know what we should do. There was an angel stood by my bed to answer my prayer. He told me to call Louisa up and lay my hands upon her head and in the name of Jesus Christ, administer to her and she should recover."[8]

Two years later, in the aftermath of the Haun's Mill Massacre,

---

January 1833, members of both sexes exercised the gift of speaking in tongues. See Joseph Smith, "History," *Times and Seasons* 5 (1 Dec. 1844): 723.

3. Patriarchal blessing to Elizabeth Ann Whitney by Joseph Smith, Sr., 14 Sept. 1835, Irene Bates Collection, Library-Archives, Reorganized Church of Jesus Christ of Latter Day Saints, Independence, Missouri.

4. "When [thy husband] is gone to fill his mission thou shall have faith to rebuke illnesses in thy family." Patriarchal blessing to Sarah Mackley by Joseph Smith, Sr., 14 May 1836, Bates Collection.

5. "Thou shall have authority to lay thy hands on thy children when the Elders cannot be had and they shall recover[;] diseases shall stand rebuked." Patriarchal blessing to Flora Jacobs by Joseph Smith, Sr., 13 June 1837, Bates Collection.

6. "Thou shalt have that portion of the Priesthood in thy companion that he holds, and power to drive the destroyer from thy house when thy companion is not present to assist thee." Patriarchal blessing to Susan Johnson by John Smith, 18 Jan. 1844, Bates Collection.

7. "Thou shalt have power to heal the sick in their own houses." Patriarchal blessing to Louisa C. Jackson by John Smith, 6 Feb. 1844, Bates Collection.

8. Sarah Sturdevant Leavitt, "Autobiographical Sketch," in Kate B. Carter, ed., *Our Pioneer Heritage* (Salt Lake City: Daughters of Utah Pioneers, 1964), 7:244.

Polly Wood took the initiative to heal a wounded survivor, apparently in the absence of specific authorization:

> A little after sunset I saw Sister Polly Wood. I motioned for her to come to me. I could not call her neither could I stand up. She came and tried to lead me back, but I was too weak. She then kneeled down and placed her hands on my wounds and prayed the Lord to strengthen and heal me. I never heard a more powerful prayer. The Lord answered her prayer and I received strength and walked back to Haun's house by resting three or four times. I had bled so much that my blood would hardly stain a white handkerchief.[9]

Following organization of the Nauvoo Female Relief Society in March 1842, members of the society took the initiative in administering to women. In the fifth meeting,

> Mrs. Durfee bore testimony to the great blessings she received when administered to after the close of the last meeting, by Prest. E[mma]. Smith & Councillors [Sarah] Cleveland and [Elizabeth Ann] Whitney. she said she never realized more benefit thro' any administration—that she was heal'd, and thought the sisters had more faith than the brethren.[10]

Durfee's enthusiasm was not universally shared, and in the next meeting of the society Joseph Smith, responding to those who claimed "that some persons were not going right in laying hands on the sick," explicitly endorsed their actions, stating, "If the sisters should have faith to heal the sick, let all hold their tongues, and let every thing roll on."[11]

Another area in which women seemed to function in a priesthood capacity came about 1843 when women were first included in the endowment.[12] Since 1836 the elders had been washed and anointed to prepare for the endowment. Once women were included in the

---

9. Nathan K. Knight account, in Journal History, 30 Oct. 1838, archives, Historical Department, Church of Jesus Christ of Latter-day Saints, Salt Lake City, Utah (hereafter LDS archives).

10. "Nauvoo Female Relief Society Minutes," 19 Apr. 1842, LDS archives.

11. Ibid., 28 Apr. 1842.

12. It should be noted that while Smith's mother, Lucy Mack Smith, occasionally gave blessings other than for healing (see Caroline Barnes Crosby Journal and Autobiography, 1807-82, Utah State Historical Society, Salt Lake City), a more general exercise of this activity by women was not demonstrated.

endowment, they too required this preparatory ordinance. Because the washing was literal rather than merely symbolic and involved being bathed in a bathtub,[13] women were called on to administer this ordinance to other women. For example, Heber C. Kimball wrote, "my wife Vilate and menny feemales was recieved in to the Holy Order, and was washed and inointed by Emma [Smith]."[14]

While it is instructive to examine the areas in which women came to function in a manner analogous to male priesthood officers, it is also essential to emphasize that most activities associated with priesthood were never extended to women during Smith's lifetime. For example, there is no evidence that during that period they performed ordinations. Even though Emma Smith was "ordained" president of the Female Relief Society,[15] as were her two counselors, men performed the ordinations. Although women administered to the sick by laying on hands, they never performed the ordinance of baptism for healing. Not only did women not serve as missionaries, but an 1835 meeting of the Kirtland high council ruled that "it is not advisable for any Elder to take wife with him on a mission to preach."[16] Nor did women baptize, confer the Holy Ghost, administer the sacrament, bless babies, curse, cast out devils, endow, seal, or marry.

Thus, if one examines the historical record it becomes apparent that from a functional point of view, there was a gradual trend towards inclusion of women in activities associated with priesthood which had previously been denied to them. Yet this trend never included more than a small minority of priesthood activities. What about a theoretical point of view? Does the historical record provide useful clues as to the direction Smith may have been heading regarding women and priesthood?

There is no record that Smith ever stated or implied that women would eventually be ordained to the same priesthood as men. Neither, however, did he indicate that such ordination was not possible. There is abundant evidence, both from Smith and from other contemporary

---

13. Stanley B. Kimball, ed., *On the Potter's Wheel: The Diaries of Heber C. Kimball* (Salt Lake City: Signature Books in association with Smith Research Associates, 1987), 165-66, 8 Dec. 1845.

14. Ibid., "Strange Events," 56, 20 Jan. 1844.

15. "Nauvoo Female Relief Society Minutes," 17 Mar. 1842.

16. "Kirtland Council Minutes," 19 Aug. 1835.

church leaders, that a trend of gradual ecclesiastical empowerment of women was anticipated, though perhaps not to full parity with men. Most statements suggesting increased female empowerment carried caveats.

The earliest indication of a changing role for women was the patriarchal blessing. The promise of healing power for women occurred as early as September 1835, and similar promises occurred in blessings given throughout the remainder of Smith's life.[17] Although no such blessings are known to have been given by Smith himself, they were given by his father and his uncle, both in the capacity of presiding patriarch. Smith's 1842 endorsement of female healings indicates that he was aware of such promises and was sympathetic.

The most dramatic change occurred with the organization of the Nauvoo Female Relief Society in 1842. Although women had acted independently to propose formation of a society, Smith reacted to their proposal by initiating one of his own design. Since there is no record of his having considered such an organization prior to the women's suggestion, it appears that his plans for it came together quickly and that they were patterned after the society he knew best, namely the priesthood. In the opening meeting he described the presiding body the society would choose and instructed them to function in a manner parallel to that of their priesthood counterpart, to "preside just as the [First] Presidency, preside over the church."[18] Carrying the priesthood analogy further, he stated, "If any Officers are wanted to carry out the designs of the Institution, let them be appointed and set apart, as Deacons, Teachers &c. are among us."[19] Although a case could be made that this sounds like a priesthood organization for women, such a claim is not supported by subsequent records. Neither Smith nor the members of the society gave any indication that it was part of, or a replica of, the male priesthood. Smith's suggestion that the society have

---

17. There is no record indicating the circumstances surrounding such promises. While it is possible that Patriarchs giving the blessings were influenced directly by Smith's theological development, the absence of pre-1840s sources linking Smith with female healings suggests that the promises came through patriarchs in the course of giving the blessings rather than through environmental influence. Within the LDS tradition, such a process is termed "inspiration."

18. "Nauvoo Female Relief Society Minutes," 17 Mar. 1842.

19. Ibid.

deacons and teachers, "if any Officers are wanted," was never acted upon. Had the society been meant to be a priesthood of women, then a parallel structure would probably have been assumed. Even Smith's statement in a society meeting two weeks later that "he was going to make of this Society a kingdom of Priests as in Enoch's day"[20] appears figurative, inasmuch as it was not succeeded by a structure similar to the Holy Order of Melchizedek.

What is clear from the society minutes is that Smith intended women to exercise more fully the gifts of the spirit and to use the society to gain knowledge and intelligence. For instance, his endorsement of female healings on 28 April 1842 was preceded by Sarah Cleveland's statement that "the Prophet had given us liberty to improve the gifts of the gospel in our meetings."[21] He then admonished "this Society to get instruction thro' the order which God has established."[22]

To expedite the acquisition of knowledge, Smith gave the members of the society "keys":

> He spoke of delivering the keys to this Society and to the Church . . . that the keys of the kingdom are about to be given to them, *that they may be able to detect every thing false*—as well as to the Elders. . . .
> I now turn the key to you in the name of God and this Society shall rejoice and *knowledge* and *intelligence* shall flow down from this time.[23]

While one might interpret this passage as signalling the emergence of a female priesthood, a careful reading indicates that the keys were to "unlock" barriers to knowledge and intelligence. In the absence of evidence demonstrating subsequent movement towards a parallel priesthood, one cannot be sure of the intent.

Certainly Nauvoo's other male leaders did not envision a separate female priesthood. In a society meeting in May 1842 Bishop Newel K. Whitney told the women:

> In the beginning God created man male and female and bestow'd

---

20. Ibid., 30 Mar. 1842.

21. Ibid., 19 Apr. 1842. The gift of speaking in tongues was "improved" during this meeting. Nine days later Smith reacted to an apparent overzealousness on the part of the women, telling them not to "indulge too much in the gift of tongues" (ibid., 28 Apr. 1842).

22. Ibid., 28 Apr. 1842.

23. Ibid., emphasis added.

upon man certain blessings peculiar to a man of God, of which
woman partook, so that without the female all things cannot be
restor'd to the earth—it takes all to restore the Priesthood. It is the intent of the Society, by humility and faithfulness, [to do so] in connex-
ion with those husbands that are found worthy.[24]

A notion of "shared priesthood" gained momentum after the
endowment was extended to women the following year,[25] particularly
in patriarchal blessings to women. Four such blessings, one given by
Hyrum Smith and the others by John Smith, went well beyond any
previous blessings in linking women and priesthood, yet all carried the
caveat that such empowerment was necessarily linked to the priesthood
of the husband:

16 October 1843: "You shall be endowed with power, as far as ministrations and priesthood was ordained to be given unto man, and unto
their help mate."[26]

18 January 1844: "Thou shalt have that portion of the Priesthood in
thy companion that he holds."[27]

January 1844: "Thou art a Daughter of Abraham, through the loins of

24. Ibid., 27 May 1842.

25. D. Michael Quinn has recently argued that women were given
Melchizedek Priesthood as part of the endowment (Quinn, "Mormon
Women Have Had the Priesthood Since 1843," in Hanks, 365-409).
While it is clear that the concept and structure of priesthood continued
to develop throughout Smith's ministry, and that gradual inclusion of
women in some aspects of priesthood function occurred, Quinn's conclusion that "every endowed Mormon woman has received the Melchizedek priesthood" (375) is an overstatement. For example, Quinn is
confident that the "keys" given to women of the Female Relief Society
in 1842 were "priesthood 'keys'" (374) despite the ambiguity of Smith's
statement. Quinn does not reconcile the discrepancy between women
holding Melchizedek Priesthood while not performing most of the
functions requiring priesthood authority. He claims that "ordained *offices*
are not the priesthood but only appendages to the priesthood" (375),
citing DC, 1921 84:29-30, when, in fact, at the time this revelation was
given the concept of priesthood did not exist independent of offices.

26. Patriarchal blessing to Ann Eliza DeLong by Hyrum Smith,
Bates Collection.

27. Patriarchal blessing to Susan Johnson by John Smith, Bates
Collection.

Manassah and a lawful heir to the Priesthood in common with thy companion."[28]

6 February 1844: "Thou art of the blood of Abraham through the Loins of Manasseh and a lawful heir to the Priesthood & shall possess it in common with thy companion."[29]

As intriguing as these blessings are, there is no record of Smith's concurrence, and his death only a few months later, coupled with the resulting confusion, hindered further development of the subject by his successors.

One must consider the possibility that the absence of any proscription against ordaining women stemmed not from tacit approval of the possibility of a female priesthood but from near-universal acceptance of the status quo. For instance, Apostle Parley P. Pratt wrote to a non-Mormon publication to respond to an erroneous report as follows: "The piece further states that 'a woman preacher appointed a meeting at New Salem, Ohio, and in the meeting read and repeated copious extracts from the Book of Mormon.' Now it is a fact well known, that we have not had a female preacher in our connection, for we do not believe in a female priesthood."[30]

In summary, no definitive evidence exists indicating that Smith intended to ordain women to the same priesthood as men. Nor did he proscribe such a possibility. Some data exist to bolster claims that women should be ordained, yet other data support an opposite claim. One is reminded of Joseph Smith's description of his early quest to discern which church he should join: "The teachers of religion of the different sects understood the same passage of scripture so differently as to destroy all confidence in settling the question by an appeal to the Bible" (JS-H 2:12, in PGP).

This is not to say that current dialogue concerning the ecclesiastical status of women is either unimportant or insoluble. To the contrary, it appears to be one of the crucial issues facing the contemporary church. Its ultimate resolution, however, will likely occur through a

---

28. Patriarchal blessing to Susannah Bigler by John Smith, Bates Collection.

29. Patriarchal blessing to Louisa C. Jackson by John Smith, Bates Collection.

30. Parley P. Pratt to Editor of the *New Era*, in *Times and Seasons* 1 (Jan. 1840): 46.

combination of sensitivity to the historical record both during and after Smith's ministry, consideration of the world in which we now live, and deference to the decisive role available to the sitting president of the church to draw upon sources beyond himself for understanding.

Index

A

Aaron, linked to authority to baptize, 10; literal descendants could be bishops without being high priests, 66

Aaronic priesthood — *see priesthood, Aaronic*

Alma, baptized self and Helam simultaneously, 4; mode of baptism described in Book of Mormon, 83

angel, account of restoration of authority by, 9

anointing, second — *see second anointing*

apostle, title applied to Oliver Cowdery in 1830, 7; Joseph Smith and Oliver Cowdery called "apostles and elders," 8; Quorum of Twelve received their ordination from those authorized by an angel, 9; first publication naming Peter, James and John as restorers of the apostleship, 10; use of term replaced that of "disciple," 12; early relationship of term to "elder," 13; probable selection of twelve apostles in 1830, 13; no mention of earlier apostles when Quorum of Twelve organized in 1835, 15; vision establishing formation of Quorum of Twelve Apostles in 1835, 25; primary function of Quorum of Twelve was to take gospel to all nations, 25; Quorum of Twelve functioned as traveling high council, 25; primacy of Quorum of Twelve over other councils, 25; distinction between apostleship and Melchizedek priesthood, 30; existed by 1830, 56; primary mission was to declare the gospel to all nations, 56; model for early function was Book of Mormon, 56; substituted for "disciple" by 1830, 56; early relationship to "elder," 56; twelve apostles described in 1830, 57; no record of new apostles being chosen between December 1830 and February 1835, 57; requirement to "have seen both the Father and the Son," 58; Kirtland House of the Lord would serve to prepare apostles, 58; role of Zion's Camp in formation of 1835 Quorum of Twelve Apostles, 58; role in opening foreign nations to the gospel, 58; formation of Quorum of Twelve Apostles in 1835, 58; special

B

INDEX

Book of Mormon, 84; about 80 people baptized prior to formal organization of church, 85; exclusivist claims of LDS baptism, 85; 1831 revelation specified eight years as the minimum age for baptism, 85; clarification of requirement for total immersion, 85; as a punitive measure, 86; accidental drownings, 86; 1832 revelation reserved the highest level of heaven (Celestial Kingdom) for those receiving LDS baptism while living, 86; 1832 revelation assigned to Terrestrial Kingdom or lower those who did not receive LDS baptism while living, 87; 1836 vision removed prior restriction on entry into Celestial Kingdom, 87; Nauvoo temple font used for rebaptism for remission of sins, baptism for the dead, and baptism for the restoration of health, 91

baptism for dead, announced during 1840 funeral sermon, 37; specifically linked to Elijah, 39; not linked to 1836 vision in which Alvin Smith, who died without an LDS baptism, was nonetheless seen in the Celestial Kingdom, 87; salvation of the dead linked to acceptance of gospel in afterlife, but not to baptism, 87; thief on the cross was saved without baptism, 87; 1840 sermon marked first mention in LDS setting, 88; early LDS practice allowed proxies of either sex, 88; early LDS practice only allowed for those who "would have embraced the gospel," 88; performed in Mississippi River, Ohio and Iowa prior to construction of font in Nauvoo temple, 89; from 1840-

44 no other proxy ordinance was required for salvation of the dead, 89; introduction in 1840, 144

baptism for remission of sins, Joseph Smith and Sidney Rigdon initiated practice in 1841, 89; rebaptism considered a privilege, not a cause for remorse, 90; nearly all church members had been rebaptized by 1843, 90

baptism for restoration of health, Old and New Testament precedents, 90; improvement in health following 1832 baptism of John Smith, 91; improvement in health following 1839 baptism of John Rigdon, 91; 1841 epistle by Quorum of Twelve Apostles foresaw Nauvoo temple font as a place for healing through rebaptism, 91; occasionally practiced outside of temple font, 92

Bennett, John C., rise and fall of his prominence within the Restoration, 133

bishop, 1832 revelation described it as an appendage to the office of high priest, 28; 1835 revelation placed it within the Aaronic priesthood, 29; origin of office and possible role of Sidney Rigdon, 63; called "the divinely established order" by Alexander Campbell, 63; 1831 revelation authorizing calling of first LDS bishop, 64; early role defined by revelation, 64; primary function was redistribution of personal wealth, 64; secondary function was to sit in judgment of transgressors, 64; tertiary function was to preside over lesser priesthood, 64; revelation calling for a second

213

Holy Ghost without the laying on of hands, 93; President Joseph F. Smith commented on receiving the Holy Ghost without the laying on of hands, 93; form of ordinance in early LDS practice, 94; examples in association with all four types of baptism, 94

Cowdery, Oliver, began work as Joseph Smith's scribe in 1829, 3; 1829 revelation to Cowdery described mode of baptism, 5; called an apostle in 1829, 7; "conversed with angels," 7; absence from church from 1838-48 may explain silence on Elijah theology, 44; ordination to authority to baptize did not include designation of an office, 81; received the Holy Ghost without the laying on of hands, 93; failure to heal caused public criticism by Sidney Rigdon, 101; failure to work miracles elicited criticism from Sidney Rigdon and led to initiation of LDS endowment theology, 116

cursing, LDS ordinance, 107; biblical, but not Book of Mormon precedents, 108; cleansing of feet as a curse on those not accepting the gospel, 108; mentioned in eight published LDS revelations, 108; practice of cursing by LDS missionaries began by 1831, 109; 1835 directive suggested that cursing was practiced too frequently, 110; outpouring of cursing directed against Missourians during 1836 Kirtland endowment, 110; literal fulfillment expected, 110; curses against individuals, 111

D

deacon, not present within Restoration until 1831, 26; 1832 revelation described it as an appendage to the office of priest, 28; primary function was to assist teachers, 50; possible role of Sidney Rigdon in introducing office, 69; not mentioned in Book of Mormon, 69; retroactive insertion into the text of DC, LDS 20, 69; office never had unique functions, 69; only one known instance of presiding over a congregation, 70; no record of responsibility to pass bread and wine of sacrament, 70; prohibited from administering the sacrament, 96

dead, all ordinances required for the living also necessary for the dead, 41; greatest responsibility of living is to seek after dead, 42; salvation of the dead required proxy endowment, 142; summary of development of LDS theology of salvation of the dead, 142; 1840 marked first time proxy ordinances were required for salvation of the dead, 144; all ordinances required for the salvation of the living were also essential for the dead, 145; proxy endowments for the dead not practiced until 1877, 146; extension of "sealing" theology to the dead occurred in 1844, 170; patriarchal blessing promised recipient would preach to the dead, 181

dead, raising of, attempt to raise dead occurred at 1831 endowment, 19; biblical and Book of Mormon precedents, 149; not among gifts promised to LDS elders until 1831, 149; description of unsuccessful attempt to raise a dead child, 150; persistence of belief in power to raise the dead, 150; unsuccessful attempt by elders to "resurrect" Joseph Brackenbury, 150; power to raise the dead promised to the Quorum of Twelve Apostles in 1835, 151; patriarchal blessings promised power to raise the dead, 151; patriarchal blessings promised some individuals that they would not die, 152; rumors of Joseph Smith's resurrection, 153; power to raise the dead promised in patriarchal blessings, 179

Detroit, cursed by missionaries, 109

disciple, equated with elder in the Book of Mormon, 6; identified by the Book of Mormon as having apostolic authority to confer the Holy Ghost, 12; use of term replaced by "apostle," 12; used in Book of Mormon and early Restoration as synonym for apostle, 56

Doctrine and Covenants, revisions of previous revelations prior to 1835 publication, 10

E

elder, one of first three offices of Restoration, 2; equated with disciple in the Book of Mormon, 6; Joseph Smith, Oliver Cowdery and David Whitmer ordained to this office in June 1829, 6; Joseph Smith and Oliver Cowdery called "apostles and elders," 8; identified by the Book of Mormon as having apostolic authority to confer the Holy Ghost, 12; early relationship of term to "apostle," 13; Joseph Smith referred to as "first elder," 21; Oliver Cowdery referred to as "second elder," 21; 1832 revelation described it as an appendage to the office of high priest, 28; duties described, 54; able to confer gift of the Holy Ghost, 54; highest office during first year of Restoration, 55; diminution of importance upon creation of higher offices, 55; judicial role, 55; generic use of title, 55; "first elder" as designation of those to receive 1836 endowment, 55; early relationship to "apostle," 57; judicial role in early Restoration, 194

Elijah, Old Testament prophet whose appearance to Joseph Smith in 1836 marked the beginning of a major thrust in priesthood theology, 2; 1830 revelation mentioning his eventual coming, 15; vision of Elijah in Kirtland House of the Lord, 35; second only to Jesus Christ in LDS theology by 1844, 35; 1838 account of Moroni retroactively inserted Elijah as custodian of priesthood, 35; expectation of imminent return began by 1830, 35; 1835 revised revelation further refined role within Restoration, 36; 1836 vision committed his keys to Joseph Smith and Oliver Cowdery, 36; "sealing" not linked to Elijah by 1836 vision, 36; 1838 history linked Elijah with priesthood restoration, 37; 1839 discourse described his role in the relationship of living and dead, 37; 1840 sermon said he held keys of all priesthood ordinances, 38; emphasis on his role in priesthood coincided with de-emphasis of roles of John the

Baptist, and Peter, James and John, 38; specifically linked to baptism for the dead, 39; first use of term "sealing" with respect to Elijah, 39; linked to "fullness of priesthood," 41; mission described, 41; paramount figure in priesthood theology, 41; mission of Elijah includes seeking after our dead, 42; possible explanation for involution of Elijah theology following death of Joseph Smith, 44; not linked to the theology of "sealing" until 1843, 169; discussion of relationship between Elijah and "sealing" theology, 171

endowment, continual association of term with missionary empowerment, 20; St. Luke described the resurrected Christ directing his disciples to remain in Jerusalem until they were endowed with "power from on high," 115; endowment of "power from on high" necessary to supplement authority, 115; summary of LDS practice and theology of endowment, 115; despite continual development of endowment theology, primary function remained empowerment of missionaries, 116; promised in patriarchal blessings, 180

endowment, 1831, revelation promised endowment upon movement of Church to Ohio, 15; receipt contingent upon personal preparation, 16; to occur during June general conference, 16; to include ordination, 16; to include power to raise the dead, 17; description, 17; ordination to a new "order" was chief element, 17; misunderstanding concerning nature of, 17; list of accounts written by participants, 18; comparison to Day of Pentecost, 18; consisted in part of ordination to "Order of Melchizedek" or "high priesthood," 19; placed LDS elders on a par with ancient apostles, 19; associated with healing power, 19; included unsuccessful attempt to raise a dead child, 19; improper association with the term "Melchizedek priesthood," 19; national publicity following, 20; required ordination to the "high priesthood," also known as "order of Melchizedek," 71; endowment of elders with "power from on high" contingent upon removal of church to Ohio, 117; missionary work in "all nations" dependent upon receipt of endowment in Ohio, 117; similarity between 1831 Ohio endowment and Lucan account of Jerusalem endowment, 117; personal preparation required before endowment, 118; 1831 endowment to be pentecostal, 118; Joseph Smith redaction of Genesis 14 shed light on development of endowment theology, 118; combined Old Testament concept of Order of Melchizedek with New Testament concept of Pentecost, 119; would include ordination, 119; multiple accounts of 1831 endowment, 119; equation of 1831 endowment with power to work miracles, 120; failed expectations in aftermath of 1831 endowment, 120; later development included power to "seal Saints unto eternal life," 120; shift in emphasis from here-and-

now to other-worldly power,
121; beginning of development
independent of high priesthood,
121

endowment, 1833, association with
School of the Prophets, 31; continuation of development of endowment theology begun in
1831, 121

endowment, 1836, "greater endowment" would accompany
completion of Kirtland House
of the Lord, 32; pentecostal nature, 32; role in preparing elders
for foreign missions, 32; contingent upon completion of Kirtland House of the Lord, 122;
comparison of 1836 endowment
with its predecessors, 122; 1836
endowment would empower
elders to redeem Missouri, 123;
1836 endowment would be a
"greater endowment" than its
predecessors, 123; Twelve Apostles admonished not to go on
missions until receiving this endowment, 125; to confer power
over tangible things, 125; preparatory ordinances necessary,
126; included "sealing" of
anointing, 126; anticipation of
miraculous powers, 127; occurred during Solemn Assembly
following dedication of the
House of the Lord, 127; pentecostal in nature, 127; miraculous
events in association with 1836
endowment, 128; denials of miraculous events by William
McLellin and David Whitmer,
128; comparison of 1836 endowment with Day of Pentecost, 129; empowerment of
missionaries accomplished by
1836 endowment, 129; repeti-
tion of 1836 endowment for

those not present originally,
130; cessation of further endowments following departure of
church leaders from Kirtland,
131; washing of feet was final ordinance preparatory to the 1836
endowment, 173; washing and
anointing were ordinances preparatory to 1836 endowment,
184

endowment, Nauvoo, resumption
of development of endowment
theology in Nauvoo, 131; endowment in connection with
Nauvoo temple not anticipated
in its earliest design, 132; provi-
sions for 1845 Nauvoo endowment not incorporated into
original temple plans, 132; Kirtland and Nauvoo endowments
initially thought to be identical,
132; Nauvoo endowment em-
phasized empowerment of missionaries, 133; late shift in form
of Nauvoo endowment, 133;
first linkage by Joseph Smith
with Freemasonry, 136; inclusion of special knowledge as a
new part of endowment theology, 136; all nine recipients
were Masons, 136; continuity
between Kirtland and Nauvoo
endowments, 137; Joseph
Smith's description of Nauvoo
endowment, 137; no official
written form existed until 1877,
137; similarities and differences
between Kirtland and Nauvoo
endowments, 138; advanced
form of Nauvoo endowment ne-
cessitated re-endowment of
those men who participated in
earlier forms, 138; Nauvoo endowment added Old Testament
elements to the New Testament
antecedents of the Kirtland endowments, 138; incorporation

ual bore less resemblance to LDS endowment, 148

G

Genesis, Joseph Smith's revision of Genesis 14 described an order which would be associated with the 1831 endowment, 16; role of Genesis 14 in development of office of high priest, 71; Joseph Smith redaction of Genesis 14 shed light on developing endowment theology, 118

H

Harris, Martin, conversion to divinity of Book of Mormon, 3; submitted "the Articles and Covenants of the Church of Christ" to the *Painesville Telegraph* in 1831, 8

healing, warning against miracle seeking excluded healing, 98; attempts to heal yielded mixed results, 99; reports in non-Mormon newspapers of attempts to heal, 99; reports of successful attempts, 99; failure of 1830 missionaries to heal, 100; 1830 revelation stated necessity of acting "in faith" to effect healing, 101; not effective in those "appointed unto death," 101; some given a gift of healing, 101; role of recipient's faith in healing, 102; miraculous healings of malaria victims in Nauvoo, 102; elders chastised by Joseph Smith for failure to heal while administering "the form without the power," 102; healings prior to 1835 did not involve anointing with oil, 102; use of oil as part of the healing ordinance, 103; hands of healer

usually laid on head, but sometimes on afflicted body part, 104; healing by verbal command with no bodily contact, 104; healing of self, 105; healing by the use of artifacts, 106; gift of healing possessed by some, 107; special healing powers promised in patriarchal blessings, 107; women promised healing power in patriarchal blessings, 107; promise of special healing power given to men and women in patriarchal blessings, 179

healing by baptism — *see baptism for restoration of health*

Helam, baptized by Alma, 4

high council, account of angelic restoration of authority given to, 9; organization in 1834, 24; judiciary function, 24; Quorum of Twelve to act as a special traveling high council, 60; authority relative to Quorum of Twelve Apostles, 61; judicial decisions subject to appeal, 61; emergence as primary judicial body, 196; judiciary function described by revelation, 197

high priest, office was not originally associated with "high priesthood," 19; formal designation of office in late 1831, 20; later requirement that a bishop also be a high priest, 64; only Book of Mormon office not incorporated into initial Restoration organization, 70; likely role of Sidney Rigdon in introducing office of high priest, 70; gradual shift from "elders holding the high priesthood," to "high priests," 72; priority over other offices was established by an 1831 revelation, 72; role of

Q

T

Nauvoo Female Relief Society, 83

teacher, one of first three offices of Restoration, 2; identified by the Book of Mormon as possessing lesser authority to baptize, 12; 1831 "Articles and Covenants" removed from teachers authority to baptize, 12; only office to establish effective group function before 1836, 27; 1832 revelation described it as an appendage to the office of priest, 28; duties described, 50; Book of Mormon model showed teachers and priests sharing duties, 50; no ordinances described during Joseph Smith's lifetime, 51; visiting homes of members became primary responsibility, 51; acted as standing ministers, 51; role in mediating disputes, 51; had exclusive right to preside over congregations, 52; ordination prayer specified in Book of Mormon, 81; prohibited from administering the sacrament, 96; role in judicial system, 194

temple, Kirtland — see House of the Lord

temple, Nauvoo — see Nauvoo temple

Terrestrial Kingdom — see Kingdom, Terrestrial

tithing, replaced earlier forms of wealth redistribution in 1838, 67

translocation, power to translocate oneself promised in patriarchal blessings, 179

Twelve Apostles — see apostle

W

washing and anointing, ordinances

preparatory to 1836 endowment, 126; given prior to 1836 endowment, 184; description of these ordinances prior to 1836 endowment, 184; in preparation for Nauvoo endowment, 186; women authorized to perform, 203

washing of feet — see feet, washing of

Whitmer, David, remarks concerning restoration of authority to confer Holy Ghost, 6; denied angelic restoration of authority, 11; denied miraculous events in connection with 1836 endowment, 14

Whitmer, John, called "an apostle of this church," 14

Whitney, Elizabeth Ann, ordained as counselor in the Nauvoo Female Relief Society by Apostle John Taylor, 83

Whitney, Newel K., suggested sharing of husband's priesthood by wife, but did not endorse separate female priesthood, 206

Wight, Lyman, taught, unsuccessfully, that all disease "is of the Devil," 113

wine, encouraged as part of sacrament in spite of ban on "strong drinks," 96; use of coconut milk in place of wine for sacrament, 96

women, promised healing power in patriarchal blessings, 107; included in 1843 endowment, 140; LDS debate relies primarily upon Restoration documents, 201; Joseph Smith never explicitly confirmed or denied possibility of ordination of women, 201; gradual trend towards fuller participation, 201; role of patriarchal blessings in authorizing